I0801802

ENDURING FAITH®
Confirmation Curriculum

LEADER GUIDE

30-LESSON BIBLE OVERVIEW

CONCORDIA PUBLISHING HOUSE • SAINT LOUIS

Copyright © 2019 Concordia Publishing House
3558 S. Jefferson Ave., St. Louis, MO 63118-3968
1-800-325-3040 • cph.org

Edited by Pete Jurchen and Mary Laesch

Series Editors: Pete Jurchen and Lisa A. Krenz

Manufactured in India/061664/418877.

4 5 6 7 8 9 10 11 12 33 32 31 30 29 28 27 26

Contents

Unit 1: Bible Basics

Essential Questions

What is the Bible?

How did we get the Bible?

Why does it matter?

Focus Statements

1. The learner will be able to explain what the Bible is and how it is organized.
2. The learner will be able to summarize how we got the Bible and why we can trust the Bible is true.
3. The learner will be able to identify the key components of the narrative of salvation and how the different books of the Bible fit into that overall narrative.

Assessment Options

1. Preassessment Options

Before you begin, have each learner spend a few minutes writing down answers to these questions.

- Write down the books of the Bible that you know, in order if you can.
- How did we get the Bible?
- What is the overarching narrative or story of what happens in the Bible? Summarize it in a few sentences.

After they have written these down, either collect the answers to read and leave feedback or quickly go over them together as a class. You'll get a good idea of where each learner is coming from as you begin.

2. Formative Assessment Options

Formative assessments are ways to monitor student learning. Checking for understanding and giving feedback improves student learning as well as teacher instruction. Choose one or more of the following:

a. Checks for Understanding: Check how well your learners understand the content, using one of the activities in "Checks for Understanding" at the end of each lesson.

b. Weekly Memory: If your learners are not yet familiar with the books of the Bible in order, have them practice or review these each week. If your learners need extra help, consider looking online for song videos or memory helps.

c. Learning Log: Look in the back of the student book for the Learning Log. After each class, the students can write in their Learning Log one important thing they learned in class.

d. Reflection Tools: These may include sermon notes and self-reflections. As you move through the unit and your learners do these formative assessments, consider asking questions like these: What have you learned about sermons from taking sermon notes? How have you grown as a learner through the first three lessons?

3. Summative Assessment Options

Summative assessments evaluate student learning at the end of an instructional unit. Choose from the following assessment methods:

a. Learning Portfolio: Have students complete a variety of formative assessments over the course of this unit. At the end of the unit, learners will compile at least one of each type of formative assessment, along with completed lesson notes and other samples you require. If they've completed these tasks to your satisfaction over the course of the unit, this can serve as a great summative assessment. *Note:* At the beginning of the unit, make a list of samples you will collect so there are no surprises at the end.

b. Written Responses: Check for understanding by asking learners to write a short-answer paper with three to ten questions. This could be done inside or outside of class, and the length of the answers will vary. Here are some sample questions based on this unit:

- What are the books of the Bible?
- What are the different genres of the Bible?
- What are the two main divisions of the Bible?
- What are Law and Gospel?
- How did we get the Bible?
- What does it mean that the Bible is authoritative?
- What are the main divisions of the narrative of the Bible?
- Who is the main character of the Bible narrative? Why does that matter?

Teaching Tips

1. This unit may seem overwhelming at first. After all, there's a lot of content to be covered in a short amount of time. Do some preassessing with your learners before beginning this course, and adjust accordingly with your class time.
    - If your learners are really new at the basic mechanics of the Bible, consider cutting out certain sections of Lesson 2, which deals with the canon of Scripture. Lesson 2 is important, but make that content less of a priority if your learners don't understand the basic structure of the Bible.
    - If your learners already have a decent grasp of the books of the Bible and how to navigate Scripture, consider using Lesson 1 more as a quick review and taking more time with Lesson 2.
    - Lesson 3 outlines the overarching narrative of Scripture that we'll be using for the rest of the course. It serves as a kind of advance organizer for helping the learners wrap their heads around the flow of the narrative. If you need to cut certain sections because of focusing on the basics, use the middle section of Lesson 3 as a simple guide for the overall structure of the narrative of salvation rather than a full lesson.
2. After unit 1, for the remainder of the lessons in this course, the learners will be spending a lot of time in their Bibles, reflecting on the words of Scripture. For this unit, most of the primary text is in the student book. Consider your group as you use one or more of these teaching techniques.
    - As the facilitator, read through the longer sections while your learners follow along. When you get to a question, have each learner reflect independently in his or her student book before answering to the entire class.
    - Occasionally, divide your class into small groups to cover sections. As they work through sections, walk around and take a look at what they're doing. Then convene as a class.
    - These lessons were not written to be done as independent work in class. Instead, either go through the material with your learners or have them work in pairs or small groups. Your learners will have questions, so use this time to build community through asking and answering questions together.
3. Different learners will be at different reading levels coming into this course. Be mindful not to put the learners on the spot if they are having difficulty finding or reading a passage. Though we recommend that your learners bring and use their own print Bibles to class, some may benefit from audio Bible apps to help them navigate, read, or listen to the text. If so, help them learn how to use these.
4. Consider how you will arrange and decorate your space. Starting in unit 2, we suggest you put a visual timeline on the wall of your space to keep track of the events in the narrative of salvation. It may also be useful to put up a chart with the books of the Bible, in order and in their genres, for reference.

Color Key for Teacher Notes

Tan = Specific additional assessments

Blue = Extra activities or questions

Green = Educational tips and directions for specific activities

Gold = Explanations of theological concepts or background for the teacher

Overview of the Bible

Timeless Truth

God's Word is living and active in my life.

Lesson Focus

The learner will be able to explain what the Bible is and how it is organized.

This first unit is dense with words and information. Some learners may already know the books of the Bible by heart, and much of this unit may seem like review. To others, however, this information may be brand new. Before you begin, take a good look at the lessons in this unit and all the information and try to customize what you need to best match your students and your schedule.

1 Overview of the Bible

Consider This

Take a moment to write down your answer to this question:
What is your favorite book? Why?

Maybe you like books and reading, maybe you don't. Whatever you think of books, you can't escape the fact that books matter. They contain all sorts of thoughts and ideas and information.

There is no doubt that the book called the Holy Bible is the most important book in history—by far! It has been read, studied, debated, and bought more than any other book in history by a mile. What is in the Holy Bible has changed the course of human history, and things that were written down more than 3,500 years ago are still talked about today.

In other words, the Holy Bible is REALLY IMPORTANT! Over the course of these lessons, we'll learn about this book, but more important, we'll see how it points us to Jesus, how it is God's Word, and how God's Word is living and active in our lives.

The Holy Bible

Before we get ahead of ourselves, however, let's get into what the Holy Bible is.

The word *Bible* literally means "book," which is not surprising. It is a big book, but it's so much more. (We'll get to that on the next page.)

What about the word *holy*? What does that word mean? Take a moment to look it up. Write down a few key words to define *holy*.

So, what makes the Bible so special? It's not special because it's an important book. It's so special because it's all about Jesus. It points us to Jesus, and it shows us who He is and what He has done for us. More than that, in the Scriptures, we have God's Word, and God uses the words and message of this book to work faith and life in us. This is all because of Jesus. Read or listen to the two passages below. Circle one word or phrase that sticks out to you. Why is that?

[Jesus said,] "You search the Scriptures because you think that in them you have eternal life; and it is they that bear witness about Me." *John 5:39*

And beginning with Moses and all the Prophets, [Jesus] interpreted to them in all the Scriptures the things concerning Himself. *Luke 24:27*

I can explain what the Bible is and how it is organized.

5

Unit 1: Bible Basics

God's Word is living and active in my life.

Consider making this an icebreaker activity, especially if your learners don't know one another very well. After they write down their favorite books, encourage them to get up, walk around, and share their answers with at least a few other learners before sitting back down.

When something is "holy," it is special, set apart for religious uses, or sacred. This may be a difficult concept for some, but it's important to emphasize that the Bible is not just a book or even a special book; it is a sacred book, the Word of God, set apart by God for His purposes.

The spaces for writing on this page aren't very large. Some students may struggle to think of answers and fit them into small spaces accurately. Allow students to tell you answers or dictate answers for someone else to write.

Different contracts that we experience in our daily lives include things like cell phone plans and home mortgage contracts. These are not the same as the Testaments, but by talking about them you'll give the learners some idea of what a testament is.

Option: Encourage your learners to open up the Bible to a random spot and start reading. Then, instead of writing down their answers, they can tell you or one another what they read and what it was like. Likely, some of your learners will have trouble either reading or understanding, which is okay; the point of this activity is to help them see how important understanding the organization of the Bible really is.

If you have time and you're in a location that has a library of sorts (like a church resource library or a school library), get up and make a trip to see the books of the library. Help your learners see in person the importance of organizing books by genre.

Digging Deeper

What's in the Bible?

The Bible is all about the forgiveness and life we receive in Jesus, but what's in it? How do we look at it? How do we use it? Though we call the Bible a book, it's actually a collection of sixty-six books. These were written over a period of 1,500 years by many different authors.

The Bible has two divisions: the Old Testament and the New Testament. We don't use the word *testament* too much today. It's related to words like *covenant* and *contract*. What are different contracts or covenants you can think of? Brainstorm them now.

The **Old Testament** includes the first **thirty-nine books** of the Bible. These are the books that happened before Jesus was born. They all point us to Jesus. The name *Old* Testament is a little misleading because sometimes we think of old things as not important or out of style. Instead, these books can be thought of as the *first* covenant or promise that God made to His people to send the Savior, Jesus. Across the circle to the left of the cross, write the words *Old Testament*, the number *39*, and an arrow next to it pointing to the cross.

The **New Testament** includes, you guessed it, the last **twenty-seven books** of the Bible, which either record Jesus' life and mission or the life of Jesus' early followers in the Church. These point us back to Jesus and how He has fulfilled all of God's promises made for us in the Old Testament. Again, these are all about Jesus. Across the circle to the right of the cross, write the words *New Testament*, the number *27*, and an arrow next to it pointing to the cross. It all points to Jesus!

How Is the Bible Organized?

Have you ever just opened the Bible and flipped to a page and started reading? What was that like? Discuss with someone.

The books of the Bible are organized in a certain way that may seem confusing at first, but it makes sense when you know the system.

Have you ever been to a library? How are the books in a library organized? Write down or sketch your thoughts below, and then share with a partner.

In libraries, books are usually organized by their type. Fiction is in one section, nonfiction is in another; magazines are in one spot, and children's books in another. You get it. The same goes for the Bible. Instead of everything being ordered by the date they were written or their authors all in a row, the books of the Bible are put in categories, or ***genres***; then the books are generally organized by the dates they were written in that genre. The opposite page shows all the books, in their genres, in order. These are the sixty-six books of the Bible.

6

Navigating the Library

The first five books of the Old Testament—Genesis, Exodus, Leviticus, Numbers, and Deuteronomy—are what we call the ***Books of Moses***, or the Torah, meaning "Law of God." Write *Books of Moses* next to the Law books on the right. They were written down by Moses.

The next books in the Old Testament are called the ***Books of History***. These tell the history of God's people from the time of Moses up to the time of Jesus. Count the books of history at right and write their number next to the books. Also write *History* next to these books on the shelf.

Next are the ***Books of Wisdom and Poetry***. Count their number on the shelf and write that there too. These are books of poetry and wisdom written at different times during the Old Testament history, mostly by kings David and Solomon. Write *Wisdom/Poetry* next to these books.

The last group of Old Testament books are the ***Books of Prophecy***. Count the prophetic books on the shelf and write the numbers there. Also write the word *Prophets* next to them. These books record God's special messages to His Old Testament people, mostly during the second half of their history.

The New Testament has five different genres of books. The first four books—Matthew, Mark, Luke, and John—are called the ***Gospels***. Draw a heart around the Gospels at right. Each Gospel tells of the life and mission of Jesus, from four different writers and perspectives. These make up the heart of the Bible. Write *Gospels* next to these books on the shelf.

Next is the Book of the Acts of the Apostles, or just ***Acts***. It is the one book of history in the New Testament. It is about the life of the first Christians after Jesus ascended into heaven. Write the word *History* next to this book.

The next books are called the ***Pauline Epistles***. Count the number of Paul's Letters and write this down next to the books on the right. *Epistle* means "letter." These are letters that the apostle Paul wrote to the early Christians. Write *Paul's Epistles* somewhere next to these books.

Near the end are the ***General Epistles***. Count the General Letters and write the number next to the books on the shelf above. These are letters that other people besides Paul wrote to the early Christians. Write *General Epistles* next to these books.

The final book of the Bible is the only book of ***Prophecy*** in the New Testament, the Book of Revelation. This shows the visions God gave to the apostle John about life in the end times, or the time between Christ's first coming and second coming. Finally, write the word *Prophecy* next to the book Revelation on the shelf above.

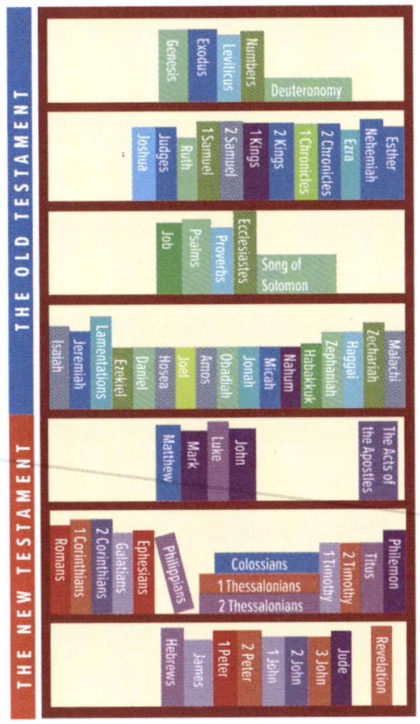

7

Quiz your learners to see how well they already know the books of the Bible in order. This can be either through verbal or written means. Be aware, though, to not embarrass your learners, as some may be self-conscious about their knowledge or lack thereof of the books of the Bible.

This section, admittedly, is a rather dense fill-in-the-blank activity. This curriculum series has been carefully written to avoid fill-in-the-blank as much as possible, but sometimes it is necessary for later recall of the facts. The learners will likely have to return to unit 1 throughout their Bible Overview study, so getting some accurate information now will be helpful. It may be best to just read the sections out loud while your learners follow along and write in their notes. This section was not intended for independent reading or learning by students. They will have extra space to process what they're writing down on the next page.

Instead of writing next to these books, students could also draw a line from the genre to that section. If your classroom has space for a large poster or a bulletin board, making this "Bible Bookcase" would be a good project for students to complete to decorate the classroom.

After the heavy reading and writing, take time to process. Encourage your learners to each write responses to these questions—individually first, but then sharing with either a partner or the group. Take a look at what patterns emerge, and consider highlighting those.

Practice with a Bible to learn how to identify chapters and verses. Have learners identify the book index at the front of the Bible to find where the books are located. Then walk them through how to find specific chapters and verses, modeling for them what the different numbers mean. Some learners may be embarrassed if they don't have the background knowledge, so doing everything together at the same time, even if some learners are already familiar with this, may be best for the class. It may be good to practice looking up different passages together and independently, just to get familiar with how this works, always being sensitive to students for whom reading is a challenge.

For specifics, refer to *Luther's Small Catechism with Explanation* (2017 edition), Questions 10–11.

CONNECTIONS

OKAY, TAKE A DEEP BREATH

So, that was a whole lot of information, but don't panic. We'll spend more time going over these details in the future. For now, let's reflect.

What is one interesting thing you've learned so far about the Bible? Take a moment to write it down.

What is something interesting that you've learned so far about the Old Testament? Briefly write it here.

What is something interesting that you've learned so far about the New Testament? Take a moment to write it down.

One Last Thing

Ever open up a Bible to a book and see a whole lot of numbers next to the titles of the books or scattered throughout the pages? Did you know that those numbers all over the place were not originally written there?

As people used the Bible more and more and made copies, later scholars eventually put in these numbers to help people quickly find sections or passages. We call these Bible references.

Understanding Bible References

The following diagram illustrates how a common Bible reference to John 3:16 breaks down.

Book Title	Chapter Number	Verse Number
John	**3:**	**16**

Using the Bible's table of contents, look up the book John, then chapter 3, and finally verse 16.

THE TWO GREAT TEACHINGS OF THE BIBLE

Throughout this Bible Overview, you will read a lot about the Law and the Gospel. These are the two central doctrines (or teachings) of the Bible. As you receive the Word of God, the Holy Spirit works both Law and Gospel in you. It's not just about knowing what's Law and what's Gospel. It's about understanding how God uses both to create faith and eternal life in you!

One way to remember how Law and Gospel work is the memory device *SOS*.

The Law **Shows Our Sin** (SOS)

The Gospel **Shows Our Savior** (SOS)

Brainstorm different ways the words of the Bible show us our sin and then show us our Savior, Jesus. Write these words or thoughts in the space above. Then, draw a cross in the space between as a reminder that the Bible, the Old and New Testament, is all about Jesus—what He has done and continues to do for us!

8

CHECKS FOR UNDERSTANDING

Before your learners leave, consider ways you can give them feedback for next week.

- **Mini Quiz:** Quiz your learners on a scratch piece of paper, including questions like these from the lesson: What do the words "Holy Bible" mean? What are the two big divisions of the Bible? How many books are in the Bible? What are some of the different genres of the Bible? What are the two main teachings of the Bible?
- **Memory Challenge:** Challenge your learners to memorize the books of the Bible in order. They can look up songs online to help with learning and retention.

How We Got the Bible

Timeless Truth

God's Word is living and active in my life.

Lesson Focus

The learner will be able to summarize how we got the Bible and why we can trust the Bible is true.

2 How We Got the Bible

Consider This

Okay, so the Bible is a library of sixty-six books, written over a period of some 1,500 years by dozens of people. Have you ever asked yourself, Self, how did we get all these books together? And how do we know they're God's Word? Take a moment now to brainstorm how you think all these different books ended up in our Bibles today. Write your ideas in the space below.

The Canon of Scripture

Before digging into why we have the books we do in our Bible, we first need to understand the idea of the canon of Scripture. We are not talking about a kind of gun (that's spelled *cannon*). Instead, we are talking about *canon*, an old word that roughly means "a measuring rod," like a ruler.

Now, think about what a ruler or a tape measure is used for. What would happen if you wanted to build a house and didn't have any rulers or measuring tools? What would the house look like? Write down some thoughts below.

When we talk about the different books of the Bible, one important thing to keep in mind is that God's people, throughout God's entire plan of salvation, have considered these books the "measuring rod" of God's Word. ***They are God's Word, and we can measure any claim about the truth, who God is, who we are, and anything else against what these sixty-six books of the Bible say.*** For the rest of this lesson, we'll look at what we believe about the Bible: how it's **inspired**, **inerrant**, and **authoritative**; how it was **collected**; and how it all points us to **Jesus**.

I can summarize how we got the Bible and why we can trust that the Bible is true.

9

God's Word is living and active in my life.

Unit 1: Bible Basics

There are a lot of conflicting reports in the world today about how we got the Bible. In fact, it's likely that your learners have already heard from a variety of sources that the Bible is a man-made book and that people over the years have manipulated it to suit their own desires. The point of this icebreaker is to get your learners to start writing this stuff down, and for you to be able to take a look at what they've heard, read, or seen and what they believe about the Bible. Use this as a preassessment for the lesson, and make sure to highlight answers from today's lesson that may speak to their particular questions.

This lesson could begin any number of ways, but we've chosen to start by talking about canonicity because it is useful in understanding how we use the Bible. We do not worship a book. Scripture is God's Word, but God's Word is also living and active in proclamation and the Sacraments. If we didn't have a Bible, we would still have God's Word among us. By thinking about the canon of Scripture as a measuring tool, we can think about how we compare claims about God's Word to Scripture, and we can also use the Bible to validate truth claims against what God has revealed to us in Scripture.

Don't let writing be a road block to thinking and sharing. Be sensitive to students who have great thoughts and ideas, but for whom putting them down on paper is an overwhelming task. Give students the option to share ideas verbally with you or a partner, especially in these opening activities.

Be sensitive to learners who are new to reading the Bible or have trouble reading. Either help these learners find the Bible passages (extra practice after the last lesson) or listen to the Bible on an app.

Textual variants are an important thing to talk about, especially when your learners will be confronted with so many lies throughout their lives. Take the time to look up several footnotes that show textual variants. Use this as an opportunity to talk, not about the unreliable nature of Scripture (which it isn't), but about the reliable nature of Scripture. Talk about how all this attention to detail, even over small fragments, shows just how open, honest, and transparent Bible scholars are when looking at the history of the text. Again, emphasize that the doctrine of God's Word hasn't changed even with small variations over the millennia due to slight copy errors.

For specifics and more on this, refer to *Luther's Small Catechism with Explanation* (2017 edition), Question 8.

Digging Deeper

God's Word Is Inspired

We believe the Bible is inspired by God. What does that mean? Read **2 Timothy 3:16** and **2 Peter 1:21**. What does the Bible say about who wrote it? Write your thoughts below.

It may be hard to understand, but the Bible teaches that God breathed through His prophets in the Old Testament and through the apostles in the New Testament. These people wrote down God's Word on scrolls. Every word they wrote flowed from God. At the same time, God used the human skills and personalities of the writers to record His Word. In the end, the Bible is truly from God, but through it we also get to know the human writers who recorded it.

God's Word Is Inerrant

In addition to being inspired, we believe that the Bible is inerrant. The word *inerrant* means "without error." This means that it contains no mistakes and is always reliable as God's Word. We trust what it says and know that it will never lead us astray.

Why do we need the truth so much today? What lies do Satan, the world, and our sinful flesh throw at us every day? Write your thoughts here.

A Word about Variations

Over the centuries, as scribes made copies of scrolls or books, occasionally they made variations to the text, usually leaving out a word or misspelling a word. *Thousands* of scholars have collected thousands upon thousands of fragments of these copies, and by the grace of God and the care of the scribes, there are very few of these textual variations. God's Word is inerrant, but sometimes scribes made mistakes. The central teachings of God's Word don't change, haven't changed, and never will change.

Find a footnote (a little line under the main text) in a Bible that records one of these variations. Does the variation affect the meaning of the text? Why or why not?

God's Word Has Authority

We believe the Bible is authoritative. What does that mean? Read **Isaiah 55:10–11**. What does the Bible say about what God's Word does?

Because God's Word has power and God uses it to do His work, we can have full confidence that it does what God says it does. The most important thing that it does is to show us our sin (the Law) and show us our Savior (the Gospel). Trust God's Word; it works!

Think About It . . .

Imagine you're talking to someone in your school or family about the Bible, and the person says the Bible is just a book. In your own words, summarize or paraphrase what you've learned about the Bible's inspiration, inerrancy, and authority, and why that matters.

10

How Did God Pass on the Canon?

We've looked at some things about what God's Word is and does, but we still haven't looked at the history of how we got the sixty-six different books of the Old Testament and New Testament canons. Let's step back in history and trace how God gave His gift of the Bible to us.

Roughly 1500 BC

While God's people are wandering in the wilderness after the exodus, Moses writes down the first five books of the Bible, called the Torah (the Law). These are written in the Hebrew language. Through Moses, God not only records for the first time the first history of God's people (Genesis) but also spends a lot of time talking to Moses, who then relays to the people what God says. God's people take the Torah with them into the Promised Land.

Roughly 1500–500 BC

While God's people are in the Promised Land, God continues to speak to them through prophets and poets, who record God's Word to them on scrolls. These are mostly written in Hebrew, though some pieces are recorded in Aramaic. These writings, the ones God's people consider God's Word, are likely kept and preserved in the temple. These make up the rest of the Old Testament. By the time of Jesus, these have been transferred into a book and translated into Greek.

Roughly 400–100 BC

During the Time between the Testaments, some other books are written. We call some of these the Apocrypha, or "writings." Jews in Jesus' day did not consider these books to be part of the canon. Roman Catholics have some of these books in their Bibles, but because Jews at the time of Jesus and the early Christians did not consider these books part of their canon, we Lutherans do not include them in our Bibles.

Roughly AD 51–90

After Jesus' resurrection, the Gospel message spreads. The apostle Paul writes letters to the early churches, and thirteen of them were collected. Matthew, Mark, Luke, and John were each also inspired by the Holy Spirit to write down accounts of the life of Jesus. Other witnesses or near-witnesses to Jesus' ministry write letters (including Revelation), and these are widely read. These are written in the Greek language. Within the first two centuries of the Church, Christians agree that these books are God's Word to them. Though there are some other books (called Gnostic gospels) out there, the Church as a whole does not agree to them or adopt them.

Each of the books in the New Testament had to meet certain important guidelines:

The author had to be a witness of Jesus or have been close to someone who was.

The Early Church had to use the book and consider it authoritative.

What's one interesting or new thing that you've learned from reading this page? Why is that?

11

Consider bringing a copy of the Apocrypha (Concordia Publishing House has a fine edition) for your learners to look at. Remind them that it is not considered part of the canon by Lutherans because the Jews in Jesus' day (and today) do not consider it authoritative. In fact, you can point out that the Roman Catholics did not officially consider it part of their canon until 1546, after the Protestant Reformation.

Option: Look up and bring pictures of the Dead Sea Scrolls, a fantastic find of the twentieth century. There was not enough space to include them in this lesson, but if you have time, look at some images of these scrolls and talk about how the scribes centuries or even millennia ago took such good care to transcribe the text of the Bible, and how there are only a few variations between then and now, even after centuries of transcription.

This lesson has a lot of concentrated listening and reading, so consider making this reflection more active. Have learners write their answers on sticky notes. Then have the group work together to categorize and compare responses.

When it comes to English translations, there's a lot that we just can't cover in this lesson. The focus is that translators must make choices about what they write. We must be open to acknowledge this. Consider looking up a list of English Bible translations online with your learners. Have them guess which ones are more literal and which are more paraphrased (paraphrases often have a lower reading level and literal translations a higher reading level).

Emphasize that as the text has been transmitted and copied over the centuries, God has always been at work preserving His Word and His people. We need to know all this so we are able to give an answer when the world questions us about the Bible. In the end, though, we trust that God's Word does what it says and that the Holy Spirit is constantly at work through the living and active Word to point us to Christ and offer us forgiveness, life, and salvation.

CONNECTIONS

WHAT ABOUT THE ENGLISH BIBLE?

So, how do we get from scrolls and early books written in Greek and Hebrew (and a little Aramaic) all the way to Bibles in English today? We translate! Translating from one language to another can be tricky, and over the centuries different people have translated the Bible into different versions of English to reflect changes in the language and peoples' reading habits.

One thing to keep in mind when looking at English translations is the two different ways we translate. Think of this as a sliding scale. On one end is literal translation, which means literally trying to translate what each individual word says without thinking about readability. On the other end is paraphrase translation, when you are less worried about translating what each word says than about paraphrasing or summarizing what the text means in easy-to-read language.

Note: In our church body, the LCMS, we often use the English Standard Version (ESV) in our life together. The ESV is somewhere between literal and paraphrase, slightly more on the literal side. Put an *X* on the line below where that would be and write *ESV*.

LITERAL ———————————————— **PARAPHRASE**

What do you think are some of the benefits of using a more literal translation? Why is that?

What do you think are some of the benefits of using a paraphrased translation? Why is that?

WHY DO I NEED TO KNOW ALL THIS?

There's a lot here, but it is super important to know. The world is filled with people who say all sorts of bad or wrong things about God's Word. The reality is that if we cannot trust God's Word, then the Christian faith is in trouble. But we can always trust God's Word because it is true and always points us to Jesus—what He has done for us and what He continues to do for us. Look over everything from this lesson one more time. Then, in your own words, write down a couple of sentences explaining why knowing how we got the Bible is so very important.

12

CHECKS FOR UNDERSTANDING

Before your learners leave, consider ways you can give them feedback for next week.

- **Exit Ticket:** Have each learner summarize on a scratch piece of paper, in his or her own words, how we got the Bible and why we believe the Bible is true. Have them leave this summary with you so you can review it for next time and see what they learned.
- **Learning Log:** Have each learner write down a key point he or she learned in this lesson about the nature of the Bible or how the Bible is God's Word.

Overview of the Bible Narrative

Timeless Truth

God's Word is living and active in my life.

Lesson Focus

The learner will be able to identify the key components of the narrative of salvation and how the different books of the Bible fit into that overall narrative.

Preassessment Option: To get a good feel for what your learners already know about the flow of events in the Bible, have them make a quick timeline, beginning with creation and ending with Jesus' second coming. Then give them just a few minutes to try to fill in as many Bible characters and events on that timeline as they can. When they're done, have them each compare with a partner. Look around at what they wrote down to get a feel for their background knowledge.

For some learners, making the timeline might seem overwhelming, whether they know a lot or don't know much at all. If this is the case, you might find out just as much or more by listening to students work in pairs or small groups on this rather than having them work independently.

3 Overview of the Bible Narrative

Consider This

The Value of a Good Story

Think about your favorite stories. They could be from books, movies, television shows, or somewhere else. Regardless of where they are from, think about what makes them great.

Think of things like who the hero is, what the story is about, what the characters learn, or any combination of these. Identify two. Then, in the spaces below, take thirty seconds to jot down the name of one of your favorite stories and write or draw some details that stick out to you about what makes that story great. Go!

When you're done, switch books with a partner and do the same thing in his or her book with a different story. Then, pass books back and compare what you found.

Stories and God's Word

The amazing thing is that the Bible tells the greatest story of all time. It is all about good and evil, wars and struggle, romance and journeys. At the heart of this story is Jesus, the one whom God promised at the beginning of the story of salvation; who came to conquer sin, death, and hell for us; and who has promised to come again. And it's all true!

From here on out, we'll be using the word ***narrative*** when we talk about the events of the Bible. A *narrative* is a written account of something that happened. Sometimes when people hear the word *story*, they think of something make-believe. To avoid that confusion, we'll use the word *narrative* instead.

This timeline is, admittedly, simplistic and generalized. Our intention is not to trivialize the precision of Scripture or its historical accuracy. Instead, by giving general dates and landmark names, the intent is to provide a simple reference for understanding how the different main characters of the narrative of Scripture relate to one another in the Bible. The hope is that after learning the general times and people, the learners will continue digging into Scripture and learning the nuance of the narratives. Feel free to supplement this timeline with more precise dates, like those found in a resource like *The Lutheran Study Bible*.

To help learners write on their timelines, write a "master" timeline on the board for all the class to see. Fill in the different sections on the board so learners can copy the information on their timelines and stay together at the same pace.

Digging Deeper

The Timeline of God's Narrative of Salvation

The narrative of the Bible is big, long, and epic. It's a narrative of God creating, man falling into sin, God promising restoration, and God fulfilling His promises, among many other things. In this lesson, we'll begin to think through the timeline of events in this big narrative. Let's look at the timeline in the middle of this page. The earliest narratives in the Bible happened, well, at the beginning of everything.

- Next to the 1 in the red arrow, write the words **The Beginning**.
- The next major narratives of salvation, where we get lots of characters and historical references, really begin around 2000 BC. Next to the 2, write **2000 BC**.
- Now fill in the rest, thinking in chunks of about 500 years. Next to 3, write **1500 BC**.
- Next to 4, write **1000 BC**.
- Next to 5, write **500 BC**.
- Above the next spot on the timeline, AD 1, **draw a star**. This is the point in the timeline when God fulfilled His promise and sent Jesus to us!
- At the next point on the timeline, 6, write **AD 33**. Then **draw a cross**. This is when Jesus finished His earthly ministry.
- In the right arrow, by the 7, write **The Church**. This is the Time of the Church, and though we don't have any more Bible being written, Christ's Church goes on with us!

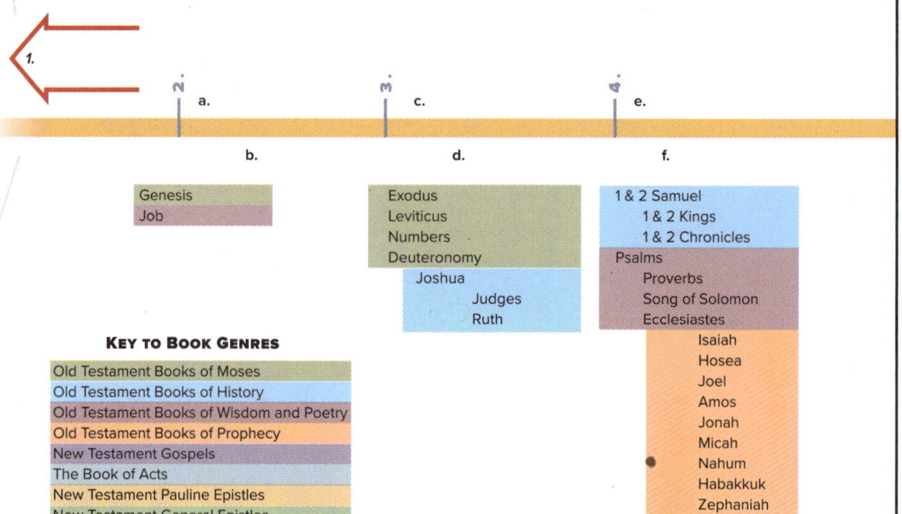

Key to Book Genres

- Old Testament Books of Moses
- Old Testament Books of History
- Old Testament Books of Wisdom and Poetry
- Old Testament Books of Prophecy
- New Testament Gospels
- The Book of Acts
- New Testament Pauline Epistles
- New Testament General Epistles
- The Book of Revelation

14

Filling in the People in God's Narrative of Salvation

There's tons here, right? Let's keep filling in this narrative of salvation by adding some really important names of a bunch of vital people above these landmark dates. This should help us remember the order of the big narratives of salvation and when the people involved in them lived.

- Above the arrow on the left, The Beginning, write down the names **Adam and Eve** and **Noah.**
- Above 2000 BC, write the name **Abraham** (or **Abe** for short).
- Above 1500 BC, write the name **Moses** (or **Mo**).
- Above 1000 BC, write the name **David** (or **Dave**).
- Above 500 BC, write the name **Daniel** (or **Dan**).

  (These people lived roughly in these time periods; it's not exact, but it's a start for showing when these people lived.)
- You already have a star above AD 1 to remember about the time when Jesus was born.
- Above AD 33, write **Jesus' death and resurrection** (or draw a **cross** and **open tomb**). This is key to everything.
- Above the arrow on the right, The Church, write down the names **Peter** and **Paul**. These were two of the central apostles in the Early Church.

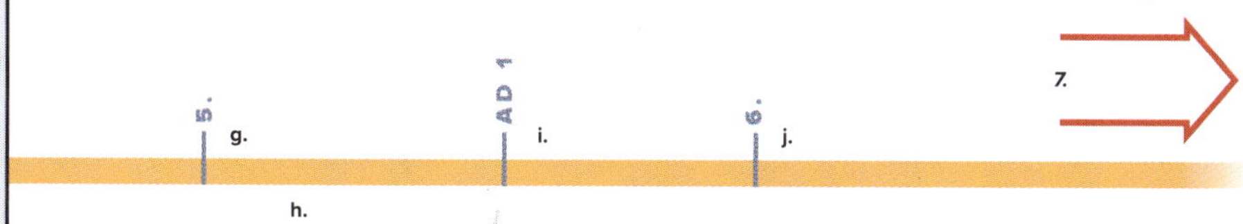

Ezra
Esther
Nehemiah
Jeremiah
Lamentations
Ezekiel
Obadiah
Daniel
Haggai
Zechariah
Malachi

Matthew
Mark
Luke
John

Acts
Romans
1 & 2 Corinthians
Galatians
Ephesians
Philippians
Colossians
1 & 2 Thessalonians
1 & 2 Timothy
Titus
Philemon
Hebrews
James
1 & 2 Peter
1, 2 & 3 John
Jude
Revelation

Think About It . . .

Look at the different books of the Bible and where they fit in the timeline. (They're color coded by genre.) What is one thing that sticks out to you? Why is that? Share with a friend.

15

Quiz your learners as you work together on the timeline. After they've filled in the dates and the critical people in their books, see if they can remember those facts on their own. Have them close their books, and you cover the timeline on the board. Then ask about people and dates and see what they can recall. Committing this to memory, as best as possible, will help them as they continue through this Bible Overview curriculum. We will be using this basic narrative framework a lot throughout the upcoming lessons.

For the sake of time and energy, we've provided the names of the books of the Bible instead of having the learners write them down. As an optional activity, have your learners open their Bibles to the list of books and identify which book of the Bible falls where on the timeline. If your learners are confused about the order, refer back to Lesson 1, which talks about the different genres and that Bible ordering is not necessarily in chronological order.

Option: Have students put these timeline items on index cards (or you could make them prior to class). They can use the cards to make a giant timeline on the wall of your classroom. This will give students an opportunity to get up and move around, and it will take out the fine-motor requirements. If possible, you could leave the timeline up to use as a reference as you work through this curriculum.

Warn your learners to talk only about PG- or G-rated book series or shows. In addition, be careful to mention that the Bible is not fiction but is mostly written as a historical narrative and that it is God's Word. Using shows and series in activities like this helps illustrate one way to organize the events of the narratives in our minds; it is not an example of how we are to think of the Bible as fiction. The Bible is truth, God's Word is truth, and the narrative of salvation is true history.

CONNECTIONS

FILLING IN THE CHAPTERS IN GOD'S NARRATIVE OF SALVATION

The last piece of the puzzle is putting in the different chapters, or big chunks, of the narrative of salvation. Think of your favorite television or book series, one that has the same characters throughout the series. Write down the title below. Then, in your own words, write or sketch the plot (what happens) from one of the seasons or books. Then, write or sketch about the setting of that book and how it adds to the overall story of the series.

ONE SEASON / BOOK → **WHOLE SERIES**

Your show or book series may be made up of different seasons or books. Each season or book has its own big story to tell, but the seasons or books together make up one big story. The Bible narrative also tells one story of God's plan to send Jesus to restore creation, but it's made up of different chapters or seasons. Turn back and write these names in the different blanks on the timeline on the previous page.

a. **The Patriarchs**
b. **Slavery in Egypt**
c. **The Exodus**
d. **The Judges**
e. **The Kings**
f. **The Divided Kingdom**
g. **The Exile and Return**
h. **The Time between the Testaments**
i. **Jesus' Ministry**
j. **Jesus' Passion and Glorification**

THE BIG, EPIC PLOT OF THE BIBLE IS ALL ABOUT JESUS

The Bible tells one great big narrative, filled with so much that tells us about who we are, who God is, and what God has done for us. Even though there are so many different subplots going on, there is one central plot. It ties all the different narratives together. Read or listen to the passages below.

Read **Romans 3:10–11**. What does it tell you about humanity's relationship with God?

In the left-hand side of the picture, below the man, write ***sinful people***. On the right-hand side, write ***holy God***.

Now read **Galatians 4:4–5**. What does it tell you about what God chose to do for you?

In the picture, between the two sides, draw a cross as a bridge. This is the grand plot of the narrative of the Bible: God's big plan to restore you to Himself through Jesus!

16

Make sure not to skip over this final thought. It's easy to get so wrapped up in the historical events and people that make up the narrative of salvation that we miss the key concept: that the central message is all about Christ. Emphasize that we are saved by grace through faith, and it is God who saves us from our sins, not our own reason or strength. Consider reading the explanation of the Third Article of the Creed to your learners to show how God saves us and how He draws us into His great plan of salvation.

CHECKS FOR UNDERSTANDING

Before your learners leave, consider ways you can give them feedback for next week.

- **Exit Ticket:** Have learners each write down from memory, to the best of their abilities, the basic components of the Bible narrative timeline (without the books of the Bible) on a piece of paper and leave it with you before they go.
- **Unit Quiz:** See if your learners can recall, either on paper or from memory, the books of the Bible in order and/or summarize how we got the Bible. This doesn't have to be a big test, but it is an opportunity for you to see what they remember from the previous two lessons.

Unit 2: The Beginning

Essential Questions

Why am I here?

How does God interact with me?

How does Scripture reveal God's plan of salvation for me in Jesus Christ?

Focus Statements

4. The learner will be able to describe how the world came into being and express that he or she is God's special creation.
5. The learner will be able to describe how sin entered the world and share God's plan of salvation in Jesus Christ.
6. The learner will be able to explain why God sent the flood, and express how God was faithful to Noah and to His promise of a Savior for all humankind.
7. The learner will be able to make connections between the narratives of Abraham, Isaac, and Jacob, and will share how God worked in them to carry out His promise to send a Savior.
8. The learner will be able to describe how God guided Jacob, Joseph, and their families through difficult times. The learner will share that God is also with him or her in difficult times and gives hope in Jesus.

Assessment Options

1. **Preassessment Options**

   Before you begin, have each learner spend a few minutes writing down (or telling you) answers to these questions.

   - Describe how God created the world.
   - How did sin enter the world?
   - What is God's plan of salvation, and whom did He work through to fulfill it?

   After they have written these down, either collect the answers to read and leave feedback or quickly go over them together as a class. You'll get a good idea of where each learner is coming from as you begin.

2. **Formative Assessment Options**

   Formative assessments are ways to monitor student learning. Choose from the following:

   a. Checks for Understanding: These lessons cover a lot of information. Check how well your learners understand the content using one or both of the activities in "Checks for Understanding" at the end of each lesson.

   b. Weekly Summaries: Learners can write a two- to three-sentence summary of the events of the lesson. It may be a good habit to get your learners used to writing these summaries and reviewing them as you go through the different narratives.

   c. Learning Log: This is located at the back of the student book. Ask learners to write down one important thing or question from the lesson in their Learning Log. There is also a place for you to give feedback.

   d. Reflection Tools: These may include sermon notes, memory work, and self-reflections. As you move through the unit and your learners do these formative assessments, consider asking questions like these: How is memorizing Bible passages helping you? What connections are you making between sermons and the lessons as you take sermon notes? How is your understanding of the Bible and God's plan of salvation growing?

3. **Summative Assessment Options**

   Summative assessments evaluate student learning at the end of an instructional unit. Choose from the following:

   a. Learning Portfolio: Have students complete a variety of formative assessments over the course of this unit. At the end of the unit, learners will compile at least one of each type of formative assessment, along with completed lesson notes and other samples you require. If they've completed these tasks to your satisfaction over the course of the unit, this can serve as a great summative assessment. *Note:* At the beginning of the unit, make a list of samples you will collect so there are no surprises at the end.

b. Written Responses: You can check for understanding by asking your learners to write short answers to several questions. This could be done inside or outside of class, and length of the answers can vary. However, this is not a good option for students who struggle academically. Remember, your goal is to identify what students have learned, not how well they can write, so allow modifications as needed. For example, some students could dictate answers to questions to an adult or into a recording device.

   You may write your own questions or use the following questions based on the unit:

   - What do the accounts of creation, the fall, and God's promise after the fall tell you about our God?
   - Give an example of how God worked in the life of Abraham, Isaac, Jacob, or Joseph.
   - Choose one of the narratives from this unit. How does the truth of that narrative strengthen your faith?

Teacher Tips

1. This unit covers a lot of ground. If you feel that you will not be able to cover all the material, choose beforehand which narratives you want to focus on in each lesson.
2. You may want to use additional visual supplements for these lessons. Consider using a Bible story book with pictures or graphics for additional visuals to use with these lessons.
3. Because all of these units cover large sections of Scripture, there is a lot of reading and discussing. But your time together doesn't have to be dry or uninteresting! Your attitude will set the tone for the class. Show your interest and enthusiasm for God's Word. Encourage learners to ask questions and add to discussions. Allow your learners to move around your space, pair up with a partner to reflect, or work in small groups as you read and discuss. Be creative in your examination of the text together.
4. Keep in mind that your learners will vary in their knowledge and understanding of the Bible. You may be teaching this course to learners who have heard many of these Bible narratives before. Others may have a general idea of the narratives and message of the Bible. And for others, these Bible accounts may be completely new. You can help all learners feel more comfortable by asking for volunteers to read, marking Bible passages with a bookmark ahead of time, and grouping those who are familiar with the Bible with those who are less familiar with it.

Color Key for Teacher Notes

Tan = Specific additional assessments

Blue = Extra activities or questions

Green = Educational tips and directions for specific activities

Gold = Explanations of theological concepts or background for the teacher

Creation

Timeless Truth

God has created me to be His own.

Lesson Focus

The learner will be able to describe how the world came into being and express that he or she is God's special creation.

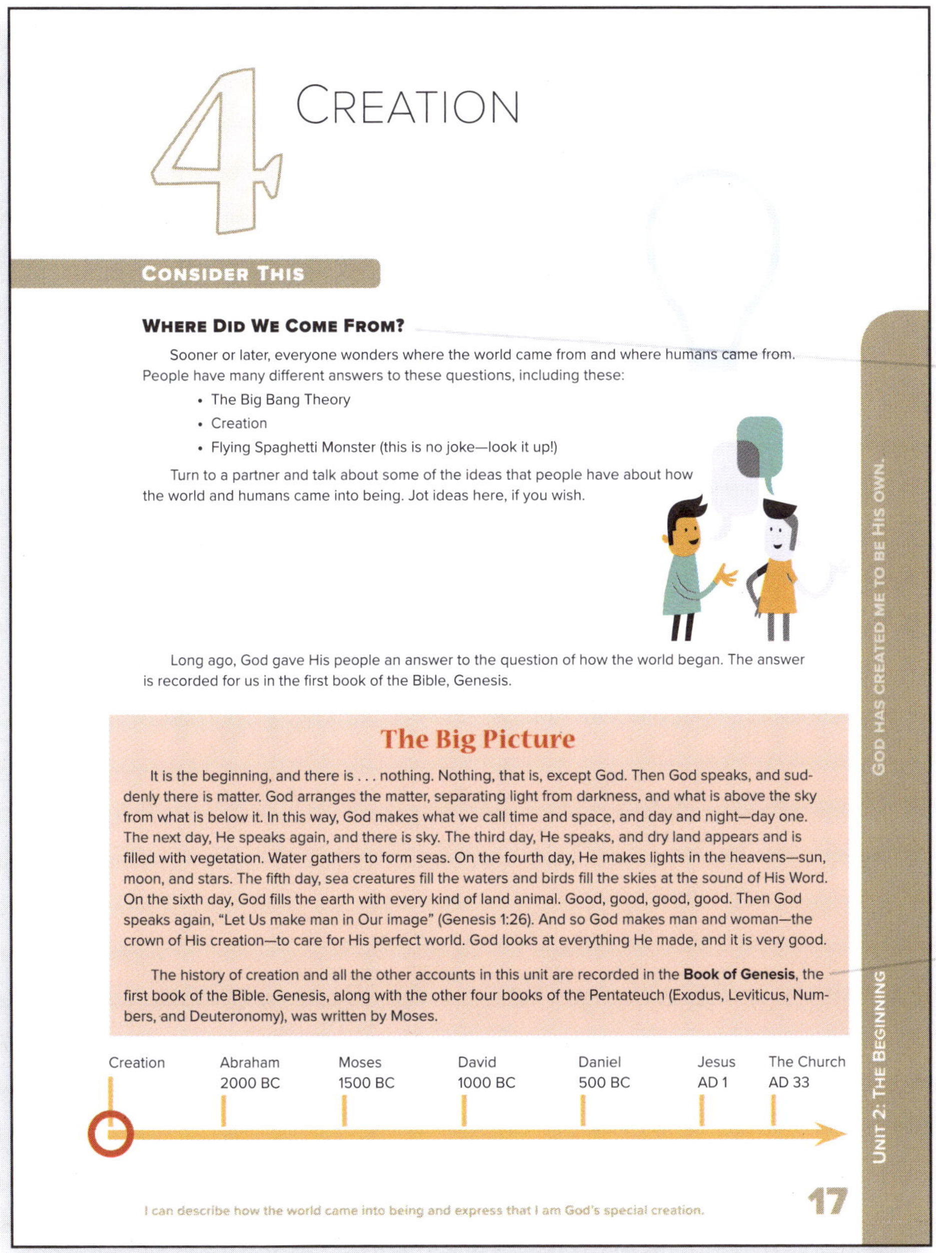

4 Creation

Consider This

Where Did We Come From?

Sooner or later, everyone wonders where the world came from and where humans came from. People have many different answers to these questions, including these:

- The Big Bang Theory
- Creation
- Flying Spaghetti Monster (this is no joke—look it up!)

Turn to a partner and talk about some of the ideas that people have about how the world and humans came into being. Jot ideas here, if you wish.

Long ago, God gave His people an answer to the question of how the world began. The answer is recorded for us in the first book of the Bible, Genesis.

The Big Picture

It is the beginning, and there is . . . nothing. Nothing, that is, except God. Then God speaks, and suddenly there is matter. God arranges the matter, separating light from darkness, and what is above the sky from what is below it. In this way, God makes what we call time and space, and day and night—day one. The next day, He speaks again, and there is sky. The third day, He speaks, and dry land appears and is filled with vegetation. Water gathers to form seas. On the fourth day, He makes lights in the heavens—sun, moon, and stars. The fifth day, sea creatures fill the waters and birds fill the skies at the sound of His Word. On the sixth day, God fills the earth with every kind of land animal. Good, good, good, good. Then God speaks again, "Let Us make man in Our image" (Genesis 1:26). And so God makes man and woman—the crown of His creation—to care for His perfect world. God looks at everything He made, and it is very good.

The history of creation and all the other accounts in this unit are recorded in the **Book of Genesis**, the first book of the Bible. Genesis, along with the other four books of the Pentateuch (Exodus, Leviticus, Numbers, and Deuteronomy), was written by Moses.

Creation | Abraham 2000 BC | Moses 1500 BC | David 1000 BC | Daniel 500 BC | Jesus AD 1 | The Church AD 33

Unit 2: The Beginning — God has created me to be His own.

I can describe how the world came into being and express that I am God's special creation.

17

Each lesson in the Bible Overview curriculum covers a broad section of Scripture. One way to help your students learn more about the details of the Bible narratives is to encourage families to read a Bible story book for devotions during the week.

This lesson doesn't deal with creation versus evolution, but it will be helpful to know what your students have heard and what they believe about how the world came into existence.

The events in Genesis happened before Moses' time, so Moses' knowledge of them may have come from oral traditions, written records, direct revelation from God, or a combination of the three. The date of writing is around 1446–1406 BC, during the time of the Israelites' wandering in the wilderness. We do not have a date for creation or other events before the time of Abraham.

As you walk through the days of creation with your students, help them to see the marvelous, organized way in which God created the universe and how different this is from the chaos and disorder that characterizes creation stories from other religions and evolution theory.

Listen to the account of creation from a Bible app, stopping after each day. Or have students follow along as various volunteers read the Bible text for each day, or read together as a group.

The days are set up so that students can see how God created matter and then filled it:

Day 1: God created light; the heavens were empty.

Day 2: God created the sky.

Day 3: God created land and plants and gathered waters into seas.

Day 4: God created the sun, moon, and stars to fill the heavens.

Day 5: God created birds to fill the skies and creatures to fill the seas.

Day 6: God created animals and people to fill the land.

DIGGING DEEPER

GENESIS 1–2

THINK ABOUT IT . . .

Who was there at the beginning? Take a close look at Genesis 1:1–2, 26. Then read John 1:1–3, 14.

GOD OF ORDER

Our God is a God of order. Take a look at how He created the universe. First, He created the raw materials (heavens and earth, light, time, and space); then He assembled them, like a builder constructing a house; then He filled them. Take a look at what God created on days 1–3; then see how He completed His creation on days 4–6.

Read **Genesis 1:1–5**.
Day 1. God created . . .

On day 4, God filled them.

Read **Genesis 1:6–8**.
Day 2. God created . . .

On day 5, God filled them.

Did You Know?

The Hebrew title for the first book of the Bible (the language in which the Old Testament was written) means "in the beginning."

Genesis is a Greek word meaning "origin." The Book of Genesis tells us about the origin of the universe, the human race, sin, God's great plan of salvation, and the origin of God's people.

Read **Genesis 1:14–19**.
Day 4. God created . . .

Read **Genesis 1:20–23**.
Day 5. God created . . .

18

Depending on the background knowledge and experience of your students, some may already know this creation account very well and others may not be at all familiar with it. This will affect how much time you need to spend on these sections.

Q. *Did God have a beginning?*

A. No. God has existed from all eternity. He *created* time, space, and all things. See **Psalm 90:2** and **Revelation 1:8**. That's hard for us to wrap our heads around, since we have birthdays and death days, beginnings and endings. But God is, was, and always will be.

Read **Genesis 1:9–13**.
Day 3. God created . . .

On day 6, God filled them.

Read **Genesis 1:24–31**.
Day 6. God created . . .

You Are Special

Actually, all of humankind is special. Humans are the crown of God's creation. But how do we really know that we're not just animals with the biggest brains?

1. Look at how God created humans—read **Genesis 2:7, 20–22**. Jot down below the special way that God made Adam and Eve.

2. God gave Adam and Eve a job, a purpose. What was it? See **Genesis 1:28**.

3. **Genesis 1:27** says, "So God created man in His own image, in the image of God He created him; male and female He created them."

Some people say that we evolved from apes, that we're just animals that can speak. Talk about how God created humans and how that makes us so different from animals.

Read **Genesis 2:1–3**.
Day 7. God . . .

Remember the Sabbath day, to keep it holy. Six days you shall labor, and do all your work, but the seventh day is a Sabbath to the Lord your God. . . . For in six days the Lord made heaven and earth, the sea, and all that is in them, and rested on the seventh day. Therefore the Lord blessed the Sabbath day and made it holy.

(Exodus 20:8–10, 11)

Think about It . . .

How long was each day of creation? Some people claim that each day could have been thousands of years instead of a twenty-four-hour period. Let's look at what the Bible says: Read Genesis 1:5, 8, 13, 19, 23, 31. Then look at Exodus 20:8–11 (above). What clues do you see that show each day of creation was twenty-four hours?

19

What does it mean to be made "in the image of God"?

It means that God made humans with an intellect that makes us separate from, and superior to, the animals. Humans are to be God's representatives on earth. Humankind was also created with perfect knowledge of God and His holy will. We lost that in the fall, but it is being restored through faith in Christ.

The Hebrew word for "day" is *yom* and means a twenty-four-hour period, especially when you read the context of "evening and morning" for each of the six days of creation.

Other sections of Scripture, such as Exodus 20:9–11, refer to a six-day creation.

For students who struggle with writing, write the necessary words on the board or on index cards for students to copy into the correct circle. For some students, it may be best not to require writing at all.

Option: Divide the larger group into three smaller groups and ask each group to discuss and answer one of the questions. After a set time, come together and ask each small group to share their reflections.

When you put students in groups, try to mix them up so that each group has people with different abilities. Some students will need some specific task direction. When you first start doing small groups, assign different students different tasks so they know exactly what to do. As they get better at working in small groups, you can give them less specific direction.

Remember that "Checks for Understanding" are tools you can use to help you and your students assess what they are learning. In addition, they provide you with an opportunity to give your students valuable feedback. These Checks can also help you adjust your teaching as needed as you see what students are grasping and where they might need more help.

Choose one activity from "Check for Understanding" to use at the end of each lesson.

Connections

Big Questions

The history of creation, recorded in Genesis 1–2, answers three big questions that many people have about life. As you consider each question, make notes on this page. Read **Genesis 1:26–31** and look back on the lesson to help you as you think.

Who am I?

Where did I come from?

Why am I here?

Timeless Truth Connection

God has created me to be His own. We see this timeless truth so clearly in the account of creation. God placed His special creation—you and me!—into the marvelous world that He created. God made us to be in relationship with Him. He formed man out of the dust of the ground, and He breathed into him the breath of life. He planted a beautiful garden for man that had all he needed for life. God still gives us everything we need to support this body and life.

Christ Connection

Where was Christ at the beginning? John 1 tells us that Christ was with God in the beginning—in fact, Christ, as part of the Trinity, created all things. "In the beginning was the Word, and the Word was with God, and the Word was God. He was in the beginning with God. All things were made through Him, and without Him was not any thing made that was made" (John 1:1–3).

20

Checks for Understanding

Before your learners leave, consider ways you can give them feedback for next week.

- **Exit Ticket:** Have students each write down on a piece of paper one question they still have after this lesson and leave the paper with you. Read through questions during the week so you can address them the next time you meet.
- **Learning Log:** Have learners reflect on the statement "God has created me to be His own" and write their thoughts in their Learning Log. Respond to their reflections with a quick note.

THE FALL TO CAIN AND ABEL

TIMELESS TRUTH

God has redeemed me to be His own.

LESSON FOCUS

The learner will be able to describe how sin entered the world and share God's plan of salvation in Jesus Christ.

5 THE FALL TO CAIN AND ABEL

CONSIDER THIS

WHY IS THERE EVIL IN THE WORLD?

In one minute, list three evil people or characters (real or fictional) and what makes these people so evil. Go!

1.
EVIL TRAITS:

2.
EVIL TRAITS:

3.
EVIL TRAITS:

God made a perfect, sinless world. Then Satan stepped in.

The Big Picture

God creates a beautiful world and two people: Adam and Eve. He tells them they can have *anything* except the fruit of one tree. Satan uses that forbidden fruit to tempt Eve, and it works. Eve is led to doubt God's word and even His love for them. She listens to Satan and takes a bite, then gives it to Adam. He takes a bite, and they know more than they ever wanted to know—they know sin and its consequences. Their sin leads to shame and fear and separation from God. God seeks them out and pronounces His judgment on them: pain and trouble in life, and then death. But God also pronounces mercy—a plan of salvation. He will not destroy or abandon His special creation. Instead, He will send a Savior, who will come from the offspring of Eve and crush Satan.

Adam and Eve have to leave the garden, but God continues to be with them. Eve bears a son, Cain, and another son, Abel, and many other sons and daughters. Abel trusts God, but Cain lets sin rule over him. In anger, Cain kills Abel, then goes "away from the presence of the LORD" (Genesis 4:16). Cain's descendants will follow in his evil ways. But God gives Adam and Eve another son, Seth. His family will carry on the promise of a Savior.

This section is found in the **Book of Genesis**, chapters 3–4. These events happened sometime after creation and before the time of Abraham.

Creation	Abraham 2000 BC	Moses 1500 BC	David 1000 BC	Daniel 500 BC	Jesus AD 1	The Church AD 33

I can describe how sin entered the world and share God's plan of salvation in Jesus Christ.

21

UNIT 2: THE BEGINNING — GOD HAS REDEEMED ME TO BE HIS OWN.

The point of this activity is to help students think about and identify the evil in this world.

Option: Instead of writing in their books individually, discuss as a group and have one or two students be scribes and write responses on the board or a large sheet of paper.

Read "The Big Picture" to the group, or ask for volunteers to read as the others follow along. Reading through this together will give you a chance to discuss it and see if there are any questions or comments before you continue with the rest of the lesson.

When asking students to read in class, never require students to read. Let students volunteer. If a student who isn't a good reader volunteers, divide the reading into smaller chunks and take turns. Or if you know a student really wants to read in class but struggles, give him or her the reading the week before to practice it a few times before he or she reads in class.

Genesis 3:4—"You will not surely die." An outright lie. Satan still persuades people to believe that there is no hell and that when people die they just cease to exist. Or he makes them think they'll get another chance.

Genesis 3:5—"God knows . . ." Satan's lie is that God is not good. He's holding back on you. He's keeping you from the privileges that you are entitled to, like deciding for yourself what is right and wrong. The temptation is still strong for humans to be godlike, or to be their own god.

Adam and Eve were hiding from God. Sin had made them fear God.

Adam blamed Eve for giving him the fruit. He also blamed God for giving Eve to him!

Eve blamed the serpent for deceiving her.

Genesis 3:16—Eve will have pain in childbearing; still today, there is pain in pregnancy and childbirth.

Genesis 3:17—Adam will suffer in his work. Work brings many hardships for us today.

Genesis 3:19—All humans will face temporal death.

DIGGING DEEPER

GENESIS 3–4

THE FALL INTO SIN

Read **Genesis 3:1–7**.

Satan, the father of lies, got Eve's attention with a seemingly innocent question: "Did God actually say . . .?" (v. 1). But it wasn't innocent. The devil was planting doubt in Eve's mind—doubt about what God had said and how good and fair He was. After reading this section, list the other ways that Satan tempted and deceived Eve.

v. 4

v. 5

Eve fell for Satan's lies. She wanted to be wise, "like God." So she ate the fruit and gave some to Adam. Immediately, they were both filled with shame. Now they knew sin and evil. Their sin also broke their relationship with God and each other.

Read **Genesis 3:8–13**.
What were Adam and Eve doing? Why?

How did Adam respond to God when God asked if he had eaten of the forbidden tree?

How did Eve respond when God asked her what she had done?

CAIN KILLS ABEL

God blessed Adam and Eve with many children, including their sons Cain and Abel. Cain was a farmer; Abel was a shepherd. Both brought offerings to God. Abel gave in true faith, but Cain did not (see **Hebrews 11:4**), so God was not pleased with Cain's offering. Cain became angry. God warned him to control his anger, but Cain didn't listen: he gave in to his anger and killed Abel. When God confronted Cain, he wasn't sorry—not until God punished him. Even then, Cain wasn't sorry for killing Abel; instead, he felt sorry for himself!

What happened to Cain? Read **Genesis 4:16** and see "Cain's Terrible Legacy" on the next page.

THINK ABOUT IT . . .

God punished Adam and Eve for their sin. Read Genesis 3:16–19. Then talk about how we feel the effects of God's punishment for sin today.

22

There is no rule that says that all students have to write the answers in their student book. For some students, it is just too much to come up with the correct spelling and then try to write it small enough to fit in the box. Some students get more out of discussing than writing. Others need to write to process information. Know your students and how they learn best. It's okay to do this activity as a large group and allow some students to write in their student books and others to discuss only.

God's Great Plan of Salvation

GENESIS 3:15 → JOHN 3:16

When Adam and Eve sinned, they ruined their relationship with God and with each other, as well as the perfect world that God had created. You might think that God would announce their destruction and start over. Instead, He announced His plan of salvation that He would fulfill through one of their descendants. Eve's offspring would one day crush the head of Satan, mortally wounding him. God's plan of salvation was His promise to send His Son, our Savior, Jesus Christ, to die in our place to pay for our sins. Why did He do this for Adam and Eve? Why did He do this for us? Love.

Q. Where did evil come from?

A. God created a perfect world, free from sin and evil. Satan, a fallen angel who rebelled against God (Jude 6), brought evil into God's creation when he tempted Adam and Eve to sin. Sin and evil have corrupted all of God's creation, including humankind. Every person is born into sin and is unable to fear, love, trust, and obey God. Our sinful human nature has corrupted the earth and has created a world full of suffering and sin; a world in need of a Savior.

For God so loved the world, that He gave His only Son, that whoever believes in Him should not perish but have eternal life.

John 3:16

CAIN'S TERRIBLE LEGACY

Cain's children followed his evil path. One of Cain's descendants, Lamech, even boasted about his sins. See **Genesis 4:19, 23–24**. What two sins do you see in these verses?

Discuss the ways that people today boast about their sinful behavior and how that affects others.

THE PROMISE CONTINUES

Sometime after Cain killed his brother, God blessed Adam and Eve with another son, and they named him Seth. *Seth* means "appointed." The name fit him, because Seth was the one appointed to carry on the promise of the Savior to future generations.

Discuss how Seth's descendants were different from Cain's. See **Genesis 4:26**.

23

Activity Option: Give each student an unlined note card and colored pencils. Have them write "God's Promise of a Savior" and the words of Genesis 3:15 on one side and "God's Promise for Everyone" and the words of John 3:16 on the other side. They can decorate it however they like and use it as a bookmark or keep it in their backpack as a reminder of God's love for them.

For students who will struggle to write all of the above on a note card in the allotted time and in the allotted space, have some cards that already have the words written on them and allow those students to decorate their card in their own way.

Genesis 4:26 says, "At that time people began to call upon the name of the LORD." Surely Adam's and Seth's family called on the Lord before, but they may have begun to worship God in an organized, public way at this time.

Option: Write the headings "The Problem of Sin" and "God's Plan of Salvation" on the board or a large sheet of paper. Ask two volunteers to act as scribes as you discuss as a group. Or split the group in two and let each group work together to respond to the prompt.

CONNECTIONS

The Problem of Sin

Write, draw, or doodle below the problems that you see in this world because of sin.

God's Plan of Salvation

Write, draw, or doodle below the hope that you have because of God's plan of salvation in Jesus Christ.

TIMELESS TRUTH CONNECTION

God has redeemed me to be His own. When Adam and Eve ate the fruit from the forbidden tree, they brought sin into the world. Their sin broke their relationship with God and with each other. Every person born from Adam and Eve (that's all of us!) are born into sin, and our sin separates us from God. But God sent His Son, Jesus, to redeem us through His death and resurrection. Jesus has brought us back into a loving relationship with God, our Creator.

CHRIST CONNECTION

When Adam and Eve listened to the devil and sinned, God did not give up on them. Instead, God gave Adam and Eve the promise of a Savior. This first promise, God's plan for the salvation of the world, is recorded in Genesis 3:15. One of Eve's offspring would be "bruised" by Satan, but He would crush Satan's head. This happened when Jesus willingly went to the cross to suffer and die for the sins of all humankind. Jesus Christ destroyed the power of Satan over us.

24

Summary Option: Give students several options of lesson summaries that read like newspaper headlines. Make some that are silly and don't apply at all and some that show part of the nuance of the lesson. Check for understanding by asking students to choose which is the best summary and why.

CHECKS FOR UNDERSTANDING

Before your learners leave, consider ways you can give them feedback for next week.

- **Summary:** See who can come up with the shortest summary of this lesson. Ask students to share their summaries with the group.
- **Learning Log:** Ask students to write one or two sentences that explain God's plan of salvation.

The Flood to Babel

Timeless Truth

God has redeemed me to be His own.

Lesson Focus

The learner will be able to explain why God sent the flood, and express how God was faithful to Noah and to His promise of a Savior for all humankind.

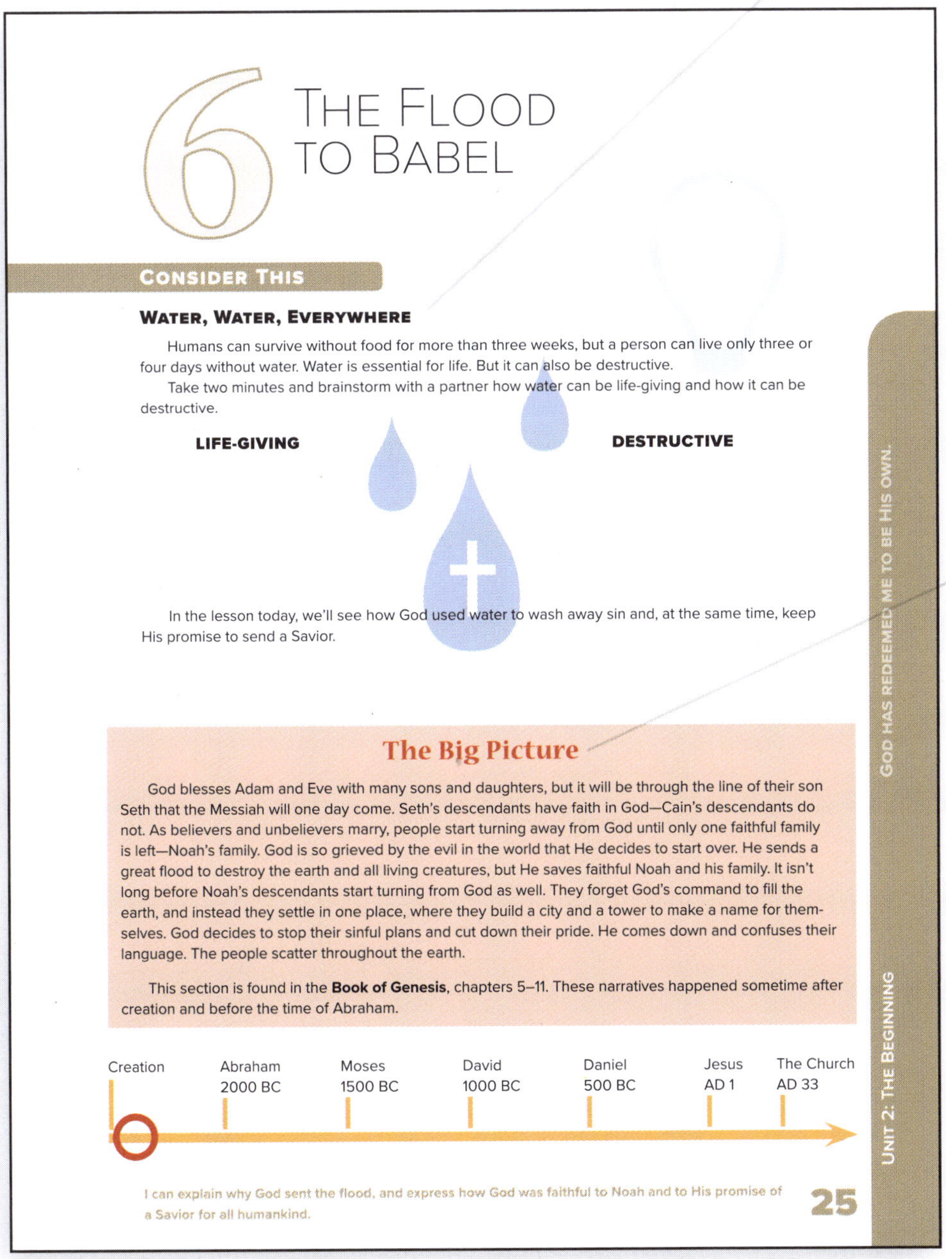

6 The Flood to Babel

Consider This

Water, Water, Everywhere

Humans can survive without food for more than three weeks, but a person can live only three or four days without water. Water is essential for life. But it can also be destructive.

Take two minutes and brainstorm with a partner how water can be life-giving and how it can be destructive.

LIFE-GIVING **DESTRUCTIVE**

In the lesson today, we'll see how God used water to wash away sin and, at the same time, keep His promise to send a Savior.

The Big Picture

God blesses Adam and Eve with many sons and daughters, but it will be through the line of their son Seth that the Messiah will one day come. Seth's descendants have faith in God—Cain's descendants do not. As believers and unbelievers marry, people start turning away from God until only one faithful family is left—Noah's family. God is so grieved by the evil in the world that He decides to start over. He sends a great flood to destroy the earth and all living creatures, but He saves faithful Noah and his family. It isn't long before Noah's descendants start turning from God as well. They forget God's command to fill the earth, and instead they settle in one place, where they build a city and a tower to make a name for themselves. God decides to stop their sinful plans and cut down their pride. He comes down and confuses their language. The people scatter throughout the earth.

This section is found in the **Book of Genesis**, chapters 5–11. These narratives happened sometime after creation and before the time of Abraham.

I can explain why God sent the flood, and express how God was faithful to Noah and to His promise of a Savior for all humankind.

25

Unit 2: The Beginning

God has redeemed me to be His own.

Referencing current events in the introduction helps students make connections between the Bible narrative and the world today. Has there been a flood or hurricane recently somewhere in the world? Is there a drought or problem with a contaminated water source?

Sadly, you may have students who have lived through such a catastrophic event. Be sensitive in your discussion, reminding students of God's care for us during such times.

Option: In addition to reading "The Big Picture" section, try illustrating as you go with stick figures on the board or on a piece of poster paper. Or if you have students who are particularly good at this type of thing, let them illustrate the events as you read or review them.

The genealogies listed in **Genesis 5**, **10**, and **11** are most likely not complete. Instead, they serve to move the narrative quickly from one major event to the next by summarizing the generations in between. While we can't establish the age of the earth by adding up these lists, they do point to a relatively young earth that is thousands instead of millions or billions of years old.

Digging Deeper

Genesis 5–11

Adam *930*
Seth *912*
Enosh *905*
Kenan *910*
Mahalalel *895*
Jared *962*
Enoch *365*
Methuselah *969*
Lamech *777*
Noah *600* at time of flood (died at *950*)

Generations of Promise

There are three lists of generations in this section: one in chapter 5, one in chapter 10, and one in chapter 11. Adam had many sons and daughters, but the lists in chapters 5 and 11 trace his descendants through Seth, because the Messiah would come through Seth's family. Skim **Genesis 5:1–32**. Now look at **verses 21–24** and **27** and write what you find out about Enoch and Methuselah in the ovals above.

Did you figure out what the number behind each name stands for?

Think About It . . .

Read Genesis 6:1–2. The sons of God began to marry the daughters of men. The "sons of God" were descendants of Seth, believers. The "daughters of man" were descendants of Cain, unbelievers. When believers started marrying unbelievers, they ended up turning away from God.

Why do you think they turned away from God?

The Account of Noah (The Flood)

Read **Genesis 6:5–7**. Write down one word that describes what the earth was like at Noah's time:

Now listen to or read **Genesis 6:8–22** and talk about it:

What did God plan to do?
What did He tell Noah to do?
What did Noah do?

Why did God save Noah and his family? See **Genesis 6:9** and **Hebrews 11:7**.

Flood Facts

Read or skim **Genesis 6–8**. Write down or draw facts about the ark, Noah's family, the flood, and what happened after the flood.

26

God saved Noah in order to continue His plan to send a Savior through Eve's offspring as He had promised. Noah and his family "walked with God" (Genesis 6:9). They were the only ones left on earth who had faith in God.

Options for "Flood Facts": Listen to the account of the flood from a Bible app.

Let students work together in groups at the board or on large sheets of paper. Ask them to draw pictures and add descriptions that help tell the account of Noah and the flood.

The ark was like a barge: 450 feet long (football field and then some), 75 feet wide, and as tall as a four-story building, with three levels.

Noah and his wife, and Noah's three sons and their wives, were saved on the ark. Noah took two of every living creature and food for humans and animals. God told Noah to bring seven pairs of clean animals also.

God shut them in the ark. It rained forty days and nights. Water burst from the earth and the sky. Mountains were covered. Everything on earth died.

God made the winds dry the earth. On the 150th day, the ark came to rest on Mount Ararat. Noah came out a year and eleven days after the flood began.

God's Covenant Promise

After one year and eleven days in the ark, God told Noah and his family to come out. God had delivered Noah and his family from destruction.

Noah made a burnt offering to God in thanksgiving. Then God made a covenant with Noah and all his descendants. Read about it in **Genesis 9:8–17**. What did God promise?

Did You Know?

Genesis 10 is known as the Table of Nations. This list fills in the gap between Noah and Abraham and shows how the people scattered into nations after God confused their language at the tower of Babel. This important list is the only one of its kind in existence. It demonstrates how all human beings descended from Noah after the flood.

Tower of Babel

After Noah and his family came out the ark, God gave them a command. Look up **Genesis 9:1**. What were they to do?

Ham, Shem, and Japheth's descendants did move around for a while, but then they decided to settle down in one place. Genesis 11:1 tells us that all people spoke the same language at that time.

Read **Genesis 11:1–4**. How did the people disobey God?

Now read **Genesis 11:5–9**. What did God do? What was the result?

Shem *600*
Arpachshad *438*
Shelah *433*
Eber *464*
Peleg *239*
Reu *239*
Serug *230*
Nahor *148*
Terah *205*
Abram *175*

What happened during the time of Peleg? See **Genesis 10:25**. Write it in the oval.

Did You Know?

Noah's son Ham, whom Noah cursed for his sinful behavior against him, became the father of Canaan. The Canaanites lived in the land that God's chosen people would conquer and possess. The Canaanites were known for their immoral lifestyle and idolatry.

27

Noah was a sinner, just as we are. Noah also had great faith in God and His promises. Noah's obedience to God is impressive. He did all that God asked him to do, putting full trust in God and His word.

God promised Noah and his family and all creation that He would never destroy the world again with a flood. The rainbow reminds us of God's promise to us.

Option: Have a discussion with your group about what it means to be proud. What or whom are you putting your trust in when you're prideful? How does that affect others?

God saw that the people of Babel no longer trusted in Him. They trusted in themselves. God pointed them back to Him. He's the only one who can save us.

The names in this section are tricky for modern readers. Help students by reading the names aloud for them and even practicing saying them together. If students are intrigued by biblical names, do some research on meanings or have students come up with modern versions.

Some of these Bible passages are long and can be difficult to the point of frustration for students who struggle with reading. Teach students to use Bible apps to find passages and listen to them or make them in larger print on their devices. Watch for negative behaviors that might indicate that students are overwhelmed by reading.

The floodwaters that covered the earth washed away all of sinful mankind.

Baptism is the "washing of regeneration and renewal of the Holy Spirit" (Titus 3:5). Our sins are washed away, forgiven, by the water combined with God's Word.

God saved Noah and his family by keeping them safe on the ark. In the waters of Baptism, we are buried and raised again with Jesus Christ. God saves us through Christ's work on the cross. See **Romans 6:3–4**.

God delivered Noah and his family to a renewed creation. One day, He will deliver all believers to "new heavens and a new earth" forever (2 Peter 3:13).

Connections

Water Saves

The account of the flood may look a lot more like destructive water than life-giving water. But when Moses wrote this section, he didn't title it "The Destruction of the World"—he named it "The Generations of Noah." Moses' focus was on how God saved Noah, and therefore saved generations to come, through the One who would come from Noah's descendants.

The apostle Peter connected the flood with Baptism. Read **1 Peter 3:20–21** below. Then talk about how the flood saved and how Baptism saves.

God's patience waited in the days of Noah, while the ark was being prepared, in which a few, that is, eight persons, were brought safely through water. Baptism, which corresponds to this, now saves you, not as a removal of dirt from the body but as an appeal to God for a good conscience, through the resurrection of Jesus Christ.

THE FLOOD SAVED | **BAPTISM SAVES**

Timeless Truth Connection

God has redeemed me to be His own. Are we any better than those people who died in the flood? "Of course!" we might be tempted to say. But the truth is that we're not, and neither was Noah. God saved Noah not because Noah was so good, but because God is so good. God provided a way for sinners to be saved through Jesus Christ. Noah trusted in God's promise. We trust in God's promise too, and He redeems us to be His own.

Christ Connection

God safely delivered Noah and his family from the destruction of the world. In Christ, God has promised His forgiven people a new creation when Jesus comes again. God saved Noah and his family by keeping them safe on the ark. In the waters of Baptism, we are buried and raised again with Jesus Christ. God saves us through Christ's work on the cross.

28

Checks for Understanding

Before your learners leave, consider ways you can give them feedback for next week.

- **Exit Ticket:** Ask learners to write a question or comment they have about the lesson on a sheet of paper to leave with you. Review the questions so that you can address them in your next class.
- **Learning Log:** Ask learners to make a connection between God saving Noah from the flood and God saving us through the waters of Baptism.

Abraham to Jacob

Timeless Truth

God has called me to be His own.

Lesson Focus

The learner will be able to make connections between the narratives of Abraham, Isaac, and Jacob, and will share how God worked in them to carry out His promise to send a Savior.

Pair up students to talk through this question, or work together as a group. Ask students or willing pairs to share with the whole group.

7 Abraham to Jacob

Consider This

God's Mercy

Think of a time when you deserved punishment but you received mercy, or forgiveness, instead. What happened? How did it make you feel? Share with a partner or write your thoughts below.

In this section of narratives, we will see how God showed mercy to Abram and his descendants. They didn't deserve to become God's people. Neither do we. But God's love for us is great, and so is His mercy.

The Big Picture

God chooses Abram from the line of Shem to carry on God's promise of a Savior. God calls Abram out of his country to go to the land He will show him. God promises Abram that, even though Abram and his wife, Sarai, are childless and old, He will make Abram's descendants into a great nation. All nations will be blessed through him. Though Abram and Sarai sometimes falter in their faith, God keeps His promise, and Isaac is born when Sarah is ninety and Abraham is one hundred. Abraham shows great faith when God tells him to sacrifice his and Sarah's only son, Isaac, intending to follow God's command—but God stops him. Abraham finds a wife for Isaac from his family back in his homeland. Isaac marries Rebekah, and they have twin boys, Jacob and Esau. Though Esau is the firstborn, God chooses Jacob to continue the line of the promised Messiah.

The narratives in this section are found in the **Book of Genesis**, chapters 12–27. These narratives took place roughly between 2166 and 1930 BC.

The account of Job also took place around the time of the Patriarchs—Abraham, Isaac, and Jacob. The **Book of Job** is one of the Books of Wisdom and Poetry, along with the books of Psalms, Proverbs, Ecclesiastes, and Song of Solomon. The Book of Job was most likely written by Job or a contemporary.

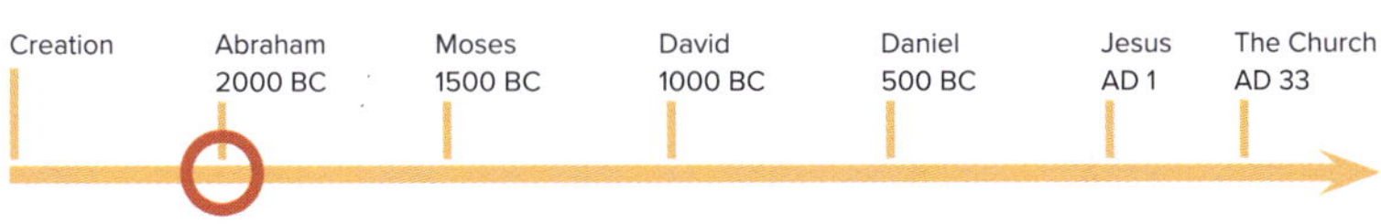

I can make connections between the narratives of Abraham, Isaac, and Jacob, and I can share how God worked in them to carry out His promise to send a Savior.

29

Unit 2: The Beginning — God has called me to be His own.

One definition of *mercy* is "a blessing that is an act of divine favor or compassion."

Abraham, Isaac, and Jacob were held in high regard by the Israelite people as the fathers of the faith. But they were sinners, just as we are. In His mercy, God chose them to be the forefathers of the promised Messiah. As we read about their faith and their failures, and God's forgiveness and faithfulness, we can be encouraged. God's love and mercy for His people is great.

In the time after the flood, the human race again began to turn away from God and worship other gods. Abram's family also worshiped idols (Joshua 24:2).

God promised Abram that he would be the father of the nation through which all nations would be blessed. Jesus was a descendant of Abram, and by His death and resurrection, all nations are blessed.

This section about Job will take a little explaining to students, as some may not know who Job is. If time is short, touch on this only briefly, so that at least students know where Job falls in the Old Testament timeline.

The account of Abram and Melchizedek is an interesting one to discuss, but if you are running short on time, you could save this discussion for another time.

DIGGING DEEPER

GENESIS 12–27
JOB

THE CALL OF ABRAM

Abram's father, Terah, took his family from Ur to Haran (see map). God called Abram out of Haran, and out of idolatry, to become the father of a great nation—God's chosen people.

Read **Genesis 12:1–9**. What did God promise Abram? God also told Abram that in him, all families of the earth would be blessed. How would that happen?

EGYPT

Abram listened to God and journeyed with his wife, Sarai, and his nephew Lot to the land of Canaan, the land promised to his descendants (Genesis 12:7). He settled near there between Bethel and Ai. But soon a famine made them go down to Egypt. There, Abram showed a lack of trust in God's care. Read **Genesis 12:10–20**. What did Abram do? What was the result?

THINK ABOUT IT . . .

God blessed Abram and Lot, and their flocks became so large that their herdsmen quarreled (Genesis 13). Abram decided to part ways and let Lot choose the land he wanted. In doing this, Abram showed trust in God's promise—he didn't guard his land jealously. When is it hard for you to give up something to someone else?

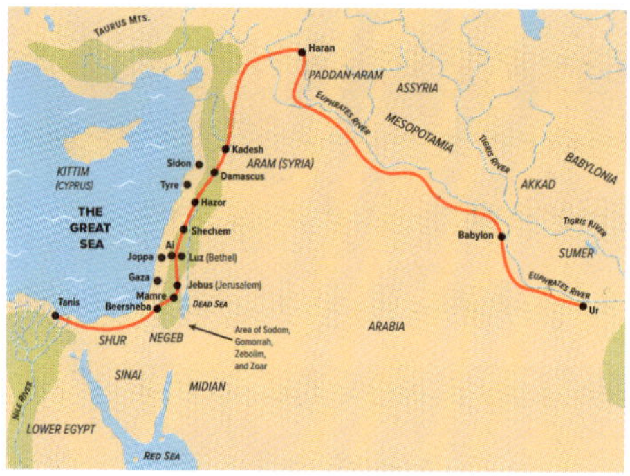

JOB

Job was not one of the patriarchs, but he does give us an example of faith and hope in suffering. In the Book of Job, God shows us that He is our Redeemer, even as we suffer in this world. Our suffering may be a trial permitted by God for our good or the good of another. Job could not understand or explain his suffering, but in the end, God led Job to sincere repentance and renewed faith in God's mercy. Job prophesied about Jesus and the resurrection when he declared, "I know that my Redeemer lives, and at the last He will stand upon the earth. And after my skin has been thus destroyed, yet in my flesh I shall see God" (Job 19:25–26).

Did You Know?

After Abram's battle to save Lot and his family (see **Genesis 14**), Melchizedek, described as "king of Salem" (Jerusalem) and the "priest of God Most High," came out to meet him. He brought food for Abram's men and gave God the glory for the victory. Abram gave him a tenth of the spoils. Melchizedek was a picture, or type, of Jesus—a different order of priesthood—both a priest and king. See **Hebrews 5:6** and **7:11–17** and **Psalm 110:4**.

30

GOD'S COVENANT WITH ABRAM

Abram wondered how God would make his family great when he had no children. Would his servant be his heir? No, God said, Abram would have a son from his own body. Then God pointed him to the stars and said, "So shall your offspring be." Read **Genesis 15:1–6**. What was Abram's response?

THE COVENANT OF CIRCUMCISION

Ishmael was thirteen years old, and Abram ninety-nine, when God appeared to Abram again. God renewed His covenant with him and gave him a new name: Abraham, "father of nations." God told Abraham that all his offspring from that time forth were to be circumcised. God gave Sarai a new name as well: Sarah. What other news did God have for Abraham? Read **Genesis 17:15–21**.

SARAI AND HAGAR

Ten years after God called Abram to leave his homeland and gave him the promise that he would be the father of many nations, Abram and Sarai were still childless. Sarai decided to take things into her own hands and gave her Egyptian servant Hagar to Abram as a second wife. Read **Genesis 16:1–6** and talk about what happened as a result.

THE BIRTH OF ISAAC

Twenty-five years after God promised Abraham a son, Isaac was born. Look back at **Genesis 17:15–17** and read **Genesis 21:1–7**. The name *Isaac* means "he laughs." Talk about why was this an appropriate name for Isaac.

ABRAHAM AND ISAAC

Read or listen to **Genesis 22:1–19**. Does this account remind you of another Father and Son?

God did sacrifice His only Son, Jesus, so that we could be with Him in heaven one day. Talk about the ways that this account points us to Jesus' sacrifice for us on the cross.

JACOB AND ESAU

Abraham had his servant find a wife for Isaac from his family in Haran. Isaac married Rebekah, and they had twin boys, Jacob and Esau. Esau was the firstborn, but God told Rebekah that Esau would serve the younger twin, Jacob. Esau despised his birthright, giving it up for a bowl of stew. Later, Rebekah and Jacob tricked Isaac into giving Jacob the blessing for the firstborn. Esau was angry enough to kill Jacob, so Jacob went to live with Rebekah's brother Laban for a time (Genesis 25, 27–28).

31

Abram believed God. He said, "Amen!" to God's promise. In **Romans 4:19–21**, the apostle Paul described Abram's faith, saying, "He grew strong in his faith as he gave glory to God, fully convinced that God was able to do what He had promised" (vv. 20–21).

Abraham offered up his son Isaac, and God the Father offered up His Son, Jesus.

Both sons carried wood: Isaac carried wood for the sacrifice, Jesus carried the wood of the cross.

A ram took Isaac's place and saved him from death, and Jesus, the Lamb of God, took our place and saved us from eternal death.

The sacrifices also took place near each other: Abraham offered Isaac on Mount Moriah, and Jesus died for our sins just outside the city (Jerusalem) that was built on that same mountain.

Option: Instead of going through each section as an entire class, where the teacher talks and the students listen and follow along, assign pairs of students to work on an individual box and then present what they learned to the class. If you have room and time for each pair to make a visual representation of their section, have students put those up on the wall in chronological order.

If you have a smaller class, have pairs of students do more than one box of information.

Discussion Helps

Question: Why would Sarah give Abraham her servant as a second wife?

Answer: It was a custom of the day for a barren wife to give her female servant to her husband as a second "wife," with the understanding that any children she would bear would belong to the first wife.

This was a sin, and it showed a lack of faith in both Sarah and Abraham. Much pain and suffering came from this sin.

Question: What about circumcision?

Answer: When God renewed His covenant with Abraham, He added a physical sign—circumcision. Every Israelite boy would be circumcised at eight days old. It would be a daily reminder to every male of God's promise to His people. The shedding of blood pointed to the shedding of Christ's blood on the cross for our redemption.

Connections

Patriarchs and Promises

Abraham, Isaac, and Jacob are called the patriarchs, literally the "fathers" of God's people, the Israelite nation.

Look back at the narratives on the previous pages. What did you find interesting? Did something surprise you? Did anything give you a new or better understanding of how God was keeping His promise of a Savior through the lives of these men and their families? Jot down your thoughts below.

Timeless Truth Connection

God has called me to be His own. God called Abraham, Isaac, and Jacob to be the fathers of His people Israel. God has called you to be His own as well. It was God who took action in the lives of Abraham, Isaac, and Jacob. God takes the initiative in our lives also, calling us through His Word and blessing us with the Holy Spirit to hear and believe the promises He gives us in Jesus.

Christ Connection

God promised Abraham land, offspring, and the blessing of the nations—that is, in Abraham, all nations would be blessed. How would all nations be blessed in Abraham? Through the descendant who would come from Abraham about two thousand years later: Jesus. Jesus descended from the line of Abraham and the Israelite people, but Jesus' work on the cross was for all people, all nations.

32

If time is short, or if writing is a barrier for students, wrap up with a discussion rather than having students jot down their thoughts. Doing both is also an option, depending on your time.

Checks for Understanding

Before your learners leave, consider ways you can give them feedback for next week.

- **Paired Discussion:** Have learners turn to a partner and share one thing they didn't know before this lesson. Listen in on conversations.
- **Learning Log:** Students should choose one patriarch: Abraham, Isaac, or Jacob. How did he show he was a sinner? How did he show faith in God?

Israel to Joseph and Egypt

Timeless Truth

God invites me, His redeemed child, to daily receive His gifts and commend my life to His care.

Lesson Focus

The learner will be able to describe how God guided Jacob, Joseph, and their families through difficult times. The learner will share that God is also with him or her in difficult times and gives hope in Jesus.

It shouldn't be too difficult for students to think of things that are unfair in this world. Ask willing students to share, and add your own response as well.

Both Jacob's and Joseph's life stories are fascinating: Jacob, the deceiver, ends up being deceived. Joseph, the dreamer, ends up the interpreter of dreams.

Both men are richly blessed with material blessings and the blessing of God's hand in their lives. Both experience suffering and hardships. Both men are blessings to others—Jacob, Israel, fathers the tribes of Israel, and Joseph keeps many from starvation. Of course, the greatest blessing that would come from them would be Jesus, the promised Savior.

8 Israel to Joseph and Egypt

Consider This

Not Fair

Sometimes, life just doesn't seem fair. People cheat and get away with it, bullies pick on those who are smaller and weaker, and others are punished when they don't deserve it. Think of something that's unfair and write it below.

In many of the narratives in this section, things happen that just don't seem fair. But through it all, God is present and active. He is faithful to His people, even when they disobey Him. He makes good come from evil. And He works in the lives of His imperfect people to continue His perfect plan to send a Savior.

The Big Picture

After tricking his father into giving him the blessing of the firstborn, Jacob flees to his uncle's house in Haran to escape his brother Esau's murderous rage. On the way, Jacob has a dream where the Lord Himself renews the covenant promise that was made to Abraham and Isaac. In Haran, Jacob meets the love of his life, Rachel, and works seven years to earn permission to marry her. But the deceiver is deceived by his uncle, and Jacob unwittingly marries weak-eyed Leah. Jacob works seven more years to marry Rachel. Rachel and Leah compete for who can bear the most sons. After another seven years, Jacob and his large family leave Laban and return to face Esau, who surprisingly, has forgiven Jacob. Jacob plays favorites and gives Rachel's son Joseph a coat of many colors. Joseph dreams that his brothers and parents will bow down to him. His brothers are understandably upset. They overreact by selling him to traders, who sell him to an Egyptian officer, Potiphar. Joseph is unfairly accused and thrown into prison, but God is with him and he rises to power as second in all of Egypt. Through God-given wisdom, Joseph saves thousands of people from famine, including his own family, who eventually come to live in Egypt. Joseph forgives his brothers, saying, "As for you, you meant evil against me, but God meant it for good, to bring it about that many people should be kept alive, as they are today" (Genesis 50:20).

This section is found in the **Book of Genesis**, chapters 28–50. These events happened approximately between 1930 BC and 1806 BC.

I can describe how God guided Jacob, Joseph, and their families through difficult times, and I can share that God is also with me in difficult times, giving me hope in Jesus.

33

God invites me, His redeemed child, to daily receive His gifts and commend my life to His care.

Unit 2: The Beginning

Digging Deeper

Genesis 28–50

Jacob's Dream

After tricking his father, Jacob fled to Haran to stay with his uncle Laban until Esau cooled off. Jacob laid down for the night in a field, with a stone as his pillow. He dreamed of a ladder (or staircase) with angels going up and down. Then the Lord Himself spoke to Jacob. Read **Genesis 28:10–22**.

What did the Lord say to Jacob? What was Jacob's response?

God gave the same promise to Jacob that He had given to Abraham and Isaac. Jacob realized that God was with him. He promised to place his trust in God.

Jacob Marries Leah and Rachel

Read or skim **Genesis 29:1–30**. When Jacob arrived at his uncle Laban's house near Haran, he fell in love with Laban's daughter Rachel. Jacob promised to work seven years as a bride price for Rachel. But when seven years were up, Laban tricked Jacob and gave him Leah, Rachel's sister, instead. Laban gave Rachel as a wife to him as well, but Jacob had to promise to work another seven years for Laban.

How does it feel to be tricked? Jacob willingly worked another seven years for Laban. Why do you think he did this?

God trained Jacob to change his deceitful ways. Jacob had to deal with deceitful Laban. He continued to work for Laban, trusting that God would provide for him and his family. His love for Rachel made the many years seem short.

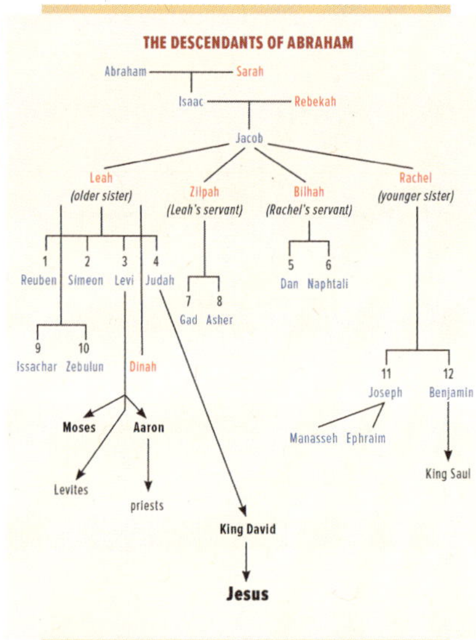

Sibling Rivalry

Jacob ended up with two wives, Leah and Rachel. But he loved Rachel more. God had mercy on Leah and gave her four sons. Rachel became jealous because she couldn't have children, so she gave her servant to Jacob as a wife. The servant had two sons. Then Leah gave her servant to Jacob, and that servant had two sons. Leah had two more sons and a daughter. Finally, God granted Rachel a son—Joseph. (Later, Rachel would have another son, Benjamin, but she would lose her life in childbirth.)

Look at Jacob's family tree. What names do you recognize? Through which of Jacob's sons would the Messiah come?

34

God blessed Leah with sons to ease her pain of being loved less by Jacob. Leah's fourth son, Judah, would be the one through whose line the Messiah would come.

The Bible never condones polygamy. God created marriage to be between one man and one woman (Adam and Eve; Mark 10:6–8).

God does not approve of everything He tolerates.

The Bible points out the pain and evil that comes from polygamy.

There is quite a bit of Bible reading in this lesson. Here are some options for making it more accessible to students:

Use a Bible app to listen to readings.

Break the long readings into shorter chunks for reading.

Pull out the key verses and put those on index cards, allowing students to focus on only those.

Jacob Fears Esau

After fourteen years of working for his uncle, Jacob left Laban to go to his homeland. But he was afraid that Esau would still be angry with him. So he prayed to God for help and then made a plan, splitting up his people into two groups, sending a gift of livestock on before him, and sending his immediate family over the river ahead of him.

Meanwhile . . .

Jacob Wrestles with God

After Jacob sent his wives and children across the river ahead of him, he was alone for the night. A man came to wrestle with him until morning. In the morning, the man touched Jacob's hip socket and put it out of place, but Jacob would not let go of the man. Recognizing that this was no mere man, Jacob asked for a blessing. So the Lord God blessed Jacob and gave him a new name, Israel, which means "He strives with God."

Jacob and Esau Are Reconciled

Jacob, limping from his encounter with God, humbled himself as he drew near to Esau, bowing seven times to his brother. But instead of being angry, Esau ran to meet him, weeping tears of joy and forgiveness. Read **Genesis 33:1–11**.

Think of a time when someone forgave you. How did that feel? What difference did it make in your relationship with him or her?

You may want to let learners pair up or get in small groups to talk over this question. Forgiveness is powerful, especially God's forgiveness. We sin against God every day, yet He still loves us and welcomes us back with open arms. Help your learners know the forgiveness they have in Jesus.

Joseph

Joseph was son number eleven for Jacob, but because he was the son of Jacob's favorite wife, Rachel, he was his father's most-loved son. Jacob gave him an expensive coat of many colors, and Joseph dreamed that his brothers and parents would bow down before him. As you can imagine, all this made Joseph's ten older brothers hate him. One day, they did something about this dreamer. Read or listen to **Genesis 37:17–36**.

Talk about what Joseph's brothers did and whom it affected.

Joseph Forgives His Brothers

Joseph had every reason to take revenge on his brothers. They had sold him into slavery, separated him from his family, and caused his father to be heartbroken. But Joseph trusted God. He saw how God worked through bad situations to bring about good. Joseph forgave his brothers. After their father died, they were afraid that Joseph would hurt them. But Joseph said to them,

> *As for you, you meant evil against me, but God meant it for good, to bring it about that many people should be kept alive, as they are today. (Genesis 50:20)*

God at Work

Joseph's life started off easy as the favored son, but he soon faced trial after trial. Through it all, Joseph recognized God's hand in his life.

Take a look at how God worked through the circumstances in Joseph's life:

Genesis 39:1–2

Genesis 39:19–23

Genesis 41:56–57

Genesis 45:5–8

Genesis 46:2–4

Options: Read through all these verses together, or divide up and give each group or pair of students a verse. Then have groups share their reflections.

35

The Lord was with them. **Genesis 28:15** records the promise the Lord made to Jacob when He appeared to him in a dream: "Behold, I am with you and will keep you wherever you go." **Genesis 39:2, 23** tells us that Joseph prospered in Egypt because the Lord was with him.

Connections

Hope in Hardship

Jacob, Joseph, and their families encountered hardships and heartache in their lives. They brought some of the hardships on themselves by their actions, but some things they suffered because of the actions of others. Through it all, what gave them hope? See **Genesis 28:15** and **39:2, 23**.

Do you have hardships in your life? God is with you, just as He was with His people long ago. He offers you His comfort and strength as you face difficult situations. We have hope too—the hope of forgiveness and everlasting life through faith in the promised Messiah, Jesus. Write a prayer below, asking God for help in your hardships and thanking Him for the hope that He gives you.

As we read about God's people in the Bible, we see that though they often had great faith, they also were great sinners. They had joyful times and hard times. Through it all, God was faithful to them, forgiving them and giving them hope. We can find comfort as we read these accounts. We, too, sometimes show faith and sometimes fail. We have good times and hard times too. God promises to be with us, His children, also. He forgives us for Jesus' sake and gives us hope.

Timeless Truth Connection

God invites me, His redeemed child, to daily receive His gifts and commend my life to His care. God called Jacob, the second born of Isaac, to carry on the promise of the Savior. God stayed faithful to His people and His promise, even when they sinned and hurt one another and themselves. He called His people back to Himself. We also turn from God and try to make it on our own. God calls us back to Him—He calls you to be His own and trust in Him alone.

Christ Connection

God worked through the lives of His chosen people to fulfill the promise of the Messiah many years later. Jesus understands the suffering that we go through in our lives. Jesus suffered so that we could have eternal life. Jesus demonstrated that God can salvage our brokenness and offer us free forgiveness and eternal life. God is faithful.

36

Checks for Understanding

Before your learners leave, consider ways you can give them feedback for next week.

- **Summary:** Give each learner a note card on which to write (or tell you so you can write) the reason he or she has hope, even in hard times.
- **Learning Log:** Have learners write down (or tell you) one new thing they learned about Jacob and one new thing they learned about Joseph. Read their responses during the week, and leave a short, encouraging note for them in their books.

Unit 3: The Exodus and Conquest

Essential Questions

Who is God?

What is God's plan for His people, including me?

How does God show His faithfulness to His people?

Focus Statements

9. The learner will be able to express that the God of Abraham, Isaac, Jacob, and the Israelites is also his or her God, and will describe who God is using words and events found in His Word, the Bible.
10. The learner will be able to give examples of God's plan for His people and will share how God is faithful to His promises, even when we disobey Him.
11. The learner will be able to relate God's faithfulness to the Israelites to the faithfulness He shows us as His redeemed children, and will commit his or her life to His care.
12. The learner will be able to describe the cycle of sin and deliverance of God's people in the Book of Judges, and relate it to his or her own sin and daily need for repentance and deliverance in Christ.

Assessment Options

1. **Preassessment Options**

   Before you begin, have each learner spend a few minutes writing down answers to these questions.

   - When Moses asked God for His name, what did God say?
   - What did God do for His people who were enslaved in Egypt?
   - How did God use judges to help His people?

   After learners have written their answers, either collect the answers to read and leave feedback or quickly go over them together as a class. You'll get a good idea of where each learner is coming from as you begin.

2. **Formative Assessment Options**

   Formative assessments are ways to monitor student learning. Choose from the following:

   a. Checks for Understanding: These lessons cover a lot of information. Check how well your learners understand the content by using one of the "Checks for Understanding" at the end of each lesson.

   b. Weekly Summaries: Learners can write a two- or three-sentence summary of the events of the lesson. Get your learners in the habit of writing these summaries and reviewing them as you go through the different narratives.

   c. Learning Log: This is located at the back of the student book. Ask learners to write down one important fact or question from the lesson in their Learning Log. There is also a place for you to give feedback.

   d. Reflection Tools: These may include sermon notes, memory work, and self-reflections. As you move through the unit and your learners do these formative assessments, consider asking questions like these: How is memorizing Bible passages helping you? What connections are you making between sermons and the lessons as you take sermon notes? How is your understanding of the Bible and God's plan of salvation growing?

3. **Summative Assessment Options**

   Summative assessments evaluate student learning at the end of an instructional unit. Choose from the following assessment methods:

   a. Learning Portfolio: Have students complete a variety of formative assessments over the course of this unit. At the end of the unit, have learners compile at least one of each type of formative assessment, along with completed lesson notes and other samples you require. If they've completed these tasks to your satisfaction over the course of the unit, you can use their work as a great summative assessment. *Note:* At the beginning of the unit, make a list of samples you will collect so there are no surprises at the end.

b. Written Responses: You can check for understanding by asking your learners to write short answers to several questions. This could be done inside or outside of class, and the length of the answers can vary. However, this is not a good option for students who struggle academically. Remember, your goal is to identify what students have learned, not how well they can write, so allow modifications as needed. For example, some students could dictate answers to an adult or into a recording device.

   You may write your own questions or use the following questions based on the unit:

   - Who is God? How does He reveal Himself to us?
   - How was God faithful to His promises, even when His people disobeyed Him?
   - In what ways are we similar to the Israelites?

Teacher Tips

1. This unit covers a lot of ground. If you feel that you will not be able to cover all the material, choose beforehand which narratives you want to focus on in each lesson.
2. You may want to use additional visual supplements for these lessons. Look online or in Bible story books for visuals that match the narratives.
3. Because all these units cover large sections of Scripture, there will be a lot of reading and discussing. But your time together doesn't have to be dry or uninteresting! Your attitude will set the tone for the class. Show your interest and enthusiasm for God's Word. Encourage learners to ask questions and add to discussions. Allow your learners to move around your space, pair up with a partner to reflect, or work in small groups as you read and discuss. Be creative in your examination of the text together.
4. Keep in mind that your learners will vary in their knowledge and understanding of the Bible. You may be teaching this course to learners who have heard many of these Bible narratives before. Others may have a general idea of the narratives and message of the Bible. For others, these Bible accounts may be completely new. You can help all learners feel more comfortable by asking for volunteers to read, marking Bible passages with a bookmark ahead of time, and grouping those who are familiar with the Bible with those who less familiar with it.
5. You will have students with special needs in your class. You may or may not have a good understanding of what those special needs are. Talk with parents to gain insight into what their child needs in order to learn most successfully. Be flexible with reading and writing requirements. Do some research to find ways for these students to access this content and share their knowledge most effectively.

Color Key for Teacher Notes

Tan = Specific additional assessments

Blue = Extra activities or questions

Green = Educational tips and directions for specific activities

Gold = Explanations of theological concepts or background for the teacher

Moses and the Exodus

Timeless Truth

God has called me to be His own.

Lesson Focus

The learner will be able to express that the God of Abraham, Isaac, Jacob, and the Israelites is also his or her God, and will describe who God is using words and events found in His Word, the Bible.

9

Moses and the Exodus

Consider This

Who Is God?

How do you get to know somebody? Turn to the person next to you and see how much you can find out about him or her in two minutes.

We get to know other people by talking with them, asking questions, and listening. But how do we get to know God? Think about it for a minute and write down your thoughts below.

God shows us a little of who He is through His creation, but we really get to know God when we hear or read about Him in His Word, the Bible. The narratives in this lesson show us many aspects of who God is: powerful, loving, patient, almighty, and so much more.

The Big Picture

Jacob moves his eleven sons and their families to Egypt to join Joseph and escape the famine in Canaan. There, the sons of Israel multiply and prosper. But after three hundred years, a new king of Egypt arises who doesn't remember Joseph. Pharaoh sees how many Israelites there are in the land (over two million by now), and he is afraid. So he decides to make them slaves. Pharaoh mistreats them. He makes a law to kill all newborn Hebrew boys. Life is hard for the Israelites. In fact, life is horrible. They cry out to God, and God answers them by raising up Moses, an Israelite who actually grew up in Pharaoh's palace, thanks to God's special intervention. Through Moses, God tells Pharaoh, "Let My people go!" Pharaoh says, "No!" After ten plagues on the Egyptians, ending with the death of Pharaoh's firstborn, Pharaoh finally says, "Go!" God leads His people out of Egypt and across the Red Sea. They are on their way to the Promised Land.

The narratives in this lesson are found in the **Book of Exodus**, chapters 1–15. Moses is the author. These events happened approximately between 1526 and 1446 BC.

Creation	Abraham 2000 BC	Moses 1500 BC	David 1000 BC	Daniel 500 BC	Jesus AD 1	The Church AD 33

I can express that the God of Abraham, Isaac, Jacob, and the Israelites is also my God, and I can describe who God is using words and events that I find in His Word, the Bible.

GOD HAS CALLED ME TO BE HIS OWN.

UNIT 3: THE EXODUS AND CONQUEST

37

You may want to give some guidelines or helpful hints about what to ask to get to know someone. Try these questions to start: How many people are in your family? What's your favorite thing to do? What's something you can't stand?

Walk around and listen in to get to know your learners a little better.

God's incredible creation shows us His power and creativity, but we can only get to know God on a personal level through His Word, the Bible. It is only in the Bible that we come to know about God's love for us and His plan of salvation, fulfilled in Jesus Christ, our Savior.

There is a lot going on in this narrative. As you read, have students highlight or circle all the main characters' names: Jacob, Pharaoh, Moses. This will help students begin to get an idea of who these narratives are talking about and how they are connected. You could even draw stick figures to represent different people in these narratives.

Pharaoh was afraid of the number of Israelites living in the land (around two million at the time). His solution? Enslave them. Make them work hard and make their lives miserable. But God was with His people, and the more they were oppressed, the more they grew in number!

As a last resort, Pharaoh commanded that every son born to a Hebrew should be thrown into the Nile. This set the stage for the events surrounding Moses' birth.

An interesting part of this account is found in **Exodus 1:15–21**, when Pharaoh told the Egyptian midwives to kill all the boys that are born. But the midwives "feared God" and did not kill the boys. When asked why they didn't obey, they said that the Hebrew women gave birth before they could get there, and they were not questioned further. This is a good example of obeying God rather than men (as Peter proclaimed in Acts 5:29).

Pharaoh's plans were thwarted. God is in control, not Pharaoh.

DIGGING DEEPER

EXODUS 1–15

JOSEPH TO MOSES

Jacob, his eleven sons, and their families (about seventy people in all) moved from the land of Canaan to Egypt to escape the famine. The Pharaoh gave them the best land, and they lived in security and prosperity. The Israelites multiplied until they filled the land. Three hundred years after the death of Joseph, a new Egyptian king rose up who forgot Joseph. He grew afraid of the number of Israelites in the land.

Read or listen to **Exodus 1:8–14**. What did Pharaoh do? What was the result of his action?

But that wasn't the worst thing Pharaoh did to the Israelites. What did he command next? Read **Exodus 1:22**.

THINK ABOUT IT . . .

The Hebrew title for the second book of the Pentateuch is taken from the words "these are the names." These first words of Exodus are identical to Genesis 46:8. The list of Jacob's sons that follows reminds readers that the Israelites God brought out of Egypt were the descendants of Abraham, Isaac, and Jacob. The English title for the book, Exodus, emphasizes Israel's departure from Egypt.

THE BIRTH OF MOSES

Moses' mother would not submit to Pharaoh's evil law to kill all Hebrew baby boys. She hid her newborn son, Moses, for three months. Then she made a basket, waterproofed it, put baby Moses in it, and set it in the Nile. She instructed Moses' sister to stay nearby to see what would happen. Pharaoh's daughter happened to come to the Nile to bathe that day. When she saw baby Moses, she had pity on him. She decided to break her father's law. She not only saved this Hebrew boy but also paid Moses' mom to nurse him! Then she adopted Moses as her own son, and he grew up in the Egyptian palace (Exodus 2:1–10).

Get together with a partner and talk about how you see God at work in this account of Moses.

MOSES AND THE BURNING BUSH

When Moses was forty, he killed an Egyptian who was abusing a fellow Hebrew. Afraid, he fled from Egypt to the land of Midian, where he became a shepherd. Forty years later, he was tending a flock when he saw a crazy sight—a bush burning, but not burning up. Then he heard a voice from the bush calling him: "Moses, Moses!" Wisely, Moses answered, "Here I am." The voice introduced Himself, saying, "I am the God of Abraham, the God of Isaac, and the God of Jacob." God told Moses that He had heard His people's cry for help and had seen their suffering. God told Moses He was going to deliver His people from Egypt, and Moses was going to lead them. Moses had lots of questions, including this big one: "If the people say, 'What is His name?' what shall I say to them?"

How did God respond? Read or listen to **Exodus 3:9–15**.

Now look up **John 8:57–59**. What was Jesus saying? Why did the people want to stone Him?

38

God humbled Moses before calling him to lead His people out of Egypt; for forty years, Moses herded sheep for his father-in-law.

"I AM WHO I AM." There is no one like God.

Yahweh or LORD—this is God's special name. Israel would use this name in prayer and worship.

When the Jews sarcastically asked if Jesus had seen Abraham, Jesus answered them, "Before Abraham was, I am" (John 8:58). "I am" is God's name!

Did You Know?

The name that God revealed to Moses at the burning bush was "I AM." This name is four letters in the Hebrew language יהוה and has been translated "YHWH," "Yahweh," or "Jehovah." This, God's Old Testament covenant name, is referred to as the *tetragrammaton*. *Tetra* means "four" in Greek, and *grammaton* refers to the letters of the alphabet. The tetragrammaton appears as "LORD" (small caps) in many English Bibles.

The Plagues

God's plan to rescue Israel involved sending ten plagues on Egypt to punish them for enslaving God's people. God sent plague after plague, but Pharaoh remained stubborn and proud. He hardened his heart and decided that he would not give in to the Israelites' God. Finally, when the tenth plague took his firstborn son, Pharaoh gave in and said to Moses, "Take your people, your flocks and herds, and go!" (See Exodus 7–11.)

Look at the list of plagues below. How horrible it must have been to see and experience them! Pharaoh saw the results of his sins, but he hardened his heart and would not listen to God.

Talk about how people today also sometimes harden their hearts against God. What is the earthly result? What's the result for those who completely reject God?

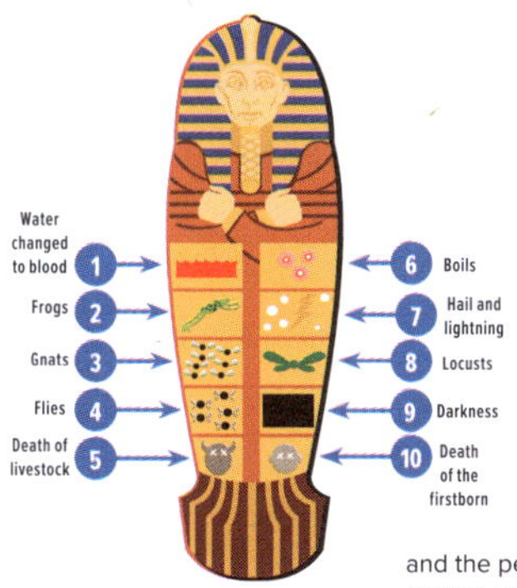

The Passover

God sent plague after plague to warn Pharaoh to set his people free, but Pharaoh hardened his heart against God. Then God sent the final plague: all the firstborn people and animals in the land would die.

But God protected the people of Israel. He told them to kill a lamb and spread its blood around the doors of their houses. They were to cook and eat the lamb for dinner, along with bitter herbs and unleavened bread, dressed in traveling clothes, ready to flee Egypt.

God's people listened, and the angel of death passed over their houses—but it struck the Egyptians' homes, including the Pharaoh's firstborn. A great cry rose up, and finally Pharaoh said to Moses, "Up, go out from among my people!" (See Exodus 12:1–32.)

The Passover lamb pointed to our Savior, Jesus. Read **1 Corinthians 5:7** and **1 Peter 1:18–19**. Talk about Jesus as our Passover lamb.

The Exodus and Crossing the Red Sea

Moses led God's people out of Egypt. The angel of God, a huge pillar of fire, and a pillar of cloud guided them.

But Pharaoh changed his mind again. He went after the Israelites. The people were terrified. But Moses told them not to fear—they would see the salvation of the Lord. God would fight for them.

The people came to the Red Sea. They were trapped! Or so they thought. God told Moses to stretch his staff over the waters. The water divided, and the people went across on dry land! Then the Egyptians started coming across, but God had Moses stretch out his staff again, and the waters closed over the Egyptians, drowning them all. God had saved them! (See Exodus 13:17–14:31.)

Together, read some of Moses' and Miriam's songs of praise to God in **Exodus 15:1–2, 20–21**.

39

To harden your heart against God is to refuse to listen to or believe in Him. When people harden their hearts against God and His Word, they reject His laws and His promises. Jesus called this the sin against the Holy Spirit (Mark 3:28–29). People do this when they refuse to let the Holy Spirit help them feel sorry for their sins and when they refuse to look to Jesus to save them. The earthly result is that they break God's laws and sin against Him and others. The result for those who completely reject God is eternal separation from Him when they die.

Jesus, like the Passover lamb, died so that we can live. The Israelites continued to celebrate the Passover to remember how God saved them, both from death and also from slavery in Egypt. In Holy Communion, Jesus gives His body and blood for the forgiveness of our sins. We remember how He died so that we can live eternally with Him. Jesus freed us from slavery to sin, death, and the devil.

There is a lot of print on these pages. This might be overwhelming and intimidating for students who struggle with reading. Use half sheets of paper to block off parts of the page that you aren't reading and make a sort of frame, or window, around the one part that the class is looking at.

There are several events in the life of Moses to keep track of here. Find a visual way to represent these for students by using stick figures or writing one big idea for each event on the board in a timeline fashion to help all students keep track.

One of the unique and wonderful things about our God is that He makes Himself known to us. Our God forms a personal relationship with us.

Encourage learners to look back at the lesson and in God's Word to find words and word pictures that describe who God is. Assist them as needed, giving prompts such as these: What does God do for you each day? How does the Bible describe God's love? What are some characteristics of our God?

As a review, have students consider the events of Moses' life as episodes of a television show. Students can give each episode a catchy title to help them remember and connect to each piece of the life of Moses.

CONNECTIONS

KNOWING THE LORD

In Exodus 5:2, Pharaoh asked Moses, "Who is the LORD?" The people of Israel learned about the Lord God through the words He spoke through Moses and through His saving actions. We get to know our Lord God through the words of Scripture, where we learn what God has done for His people, including us. In the space below, draw or write what you know about God and what He has done for you.

TIMELESS TRUTH CONNECTION

God has called me to be His own. God chose Israel to be His very own people. God told Moses to tell the people, "I will take you to be My people, and I will be your God" (Exodus 6:7). God has chosen you to be His own also. First Peter 2:9–10 says,

> *But you are a chosen race, a royal priesthood, a holy nation, a people for His own possession, that you may proclaim the excellencies of Him who called you out of darkness into His marvelous light. Once you were not a people, but now you are God's people; once you had not received mercy, but now you have received mercy.*

CHRIST CONNECTION

God delivered His people from slavery in Egypt, promising to lead them into the Promised Land. God has delivered us also from slavery to sin, death, and the devil, through the death and resurrection of Jesus, our Passover Lamb. Just as God fought for the Israelites when the Egyptians came after them, Jesus fought for us when He died on the cross and rose to life again.

40

CHECKS FOR UNDERSTANDING

Before your learners leave, consider ways you can give them feedback for next week.

- **Learning Log:** Ask students to describe who God is in one or two sentences in their Learning Logs.
- **Question:** Have learners, either on a piece of paper or in their Learning Log, write down a question they have about what was covered in this lesson. Read the questions during the week and try to address them in the next class.

Wilderness Wanderings and the Law

Timeless Truth

God has a plan for me as His human creature.

Lesson Focus

The learner will be able to give examples of God's plan for His people and will share how God is faithful to His promises, even when we disobey Him.

Brainstorm together as a group, or let students break into small groups to discuss these questions.

Some things that people look to are money, technology, popularity, and education.

As with the last lesson, there are many events in this swath of Scripture. As you read "The Big Picture," draw pictures to illustrate the events of the narrative. Use simple line drawings, or have students do the drawings. Perhaps have different students illustrate quickly and simply the different events described here.

10 Wilderness Wanderings and the Law

Consider This

Who Is Your God?

Whom do you trust to keep you safe and give you all that you need? We all want to feel safe and secure. What do people think will keep them safe and give them a good future?

In this lesson, we will see how God is training His people to obey and trust in Him above all things. God alone will keep them safe and secure and give them a future. God gives us that same promise.

The Big Picture

God sets His people free from slavery in Egypt. Now Moses leads them into the wilderness, slowly heading toward the Promised Land. Very soon, the people begin to grumble against Moses and Aaron, saying they are thirsty and hungry. This is just the beginning of the complaints that God's people will hurl at Moses and Aaron and God. God is patient, giving them quail and daily manna to eat and water to drink. Moses brings the Israelites to the base of Mount Sinai. Moses goes up to God on the mountain while the people stay below. With cloud and smoke and fire, God renews His covenant with the people. He tells them how they are to live as His chosen people. God Himself writes His Law on two stone tablets: the Ten Commandments. The people grow impatient when Moses takes a little longer than they would like on the mountain with God. They break commandment number one: "You shall have no other gods." God is angry with the Israelites, but Moses intercedes for them, and God shows mercy. God tells Moses and the people to build a sanctuary, the tabernacle, where God will dwell with His people.

The events and accounts in this lesson are found in chapters 16–40 of the **Book of Exodus**, and in the books of **Leviticus**, **Numbers**, and **Deuteronomy**. These events happened between 1446 and 1406 BC.

Creation | Abraham 2000 BC | Moses 1500 BC | David 1000 BC | Daniel 500 BC | Jesus AD 1 | The Church AD 33

I can give examples of God's plan for His people and share how God is faithful to His promises, even when we disobey Him.

The gift of manna in the wilderness foreshadowed the gift of Jesus as the bread of life. Jesus references the giving of manna to the Israelites in John 6, clarifying that it was God, not Moses, who gave them the manna. Jesus is the source of real life. Unlike the manna, which perished after a day, the life that Jesus gives lasts forever.

God would test His people by giving them specific instructions on how they were to gather the manna. God was teaching His people to obey His rules and trust in Him for His daily care of them.

Digging Deeper

Exodus 16–40, Leviticus, Numbers, Deuteronomy

God Provides

Not two months after the Israelites had been delivered by God from slavery in Egypt, they complained against Moses and Aaron, saying they wished they had died in Egypt rather than be hungry in the wilderness. God used the situation to test His people.

Read or listen to **Exodus 16:1–31**. How did God test the Israelites? What did He want them to learn?

God's Covenant

Moses led the people to the base of Mount Sinai. They encamped around the mountain while Moses went up to talk with God. God renewed the covenant promise that He had made to Abraham, Isaac, and Jacob: that Israel would be God's chosen people; they would inherit the promises given to the patriarchs; they would be a holy nation and a "kingdom of priests." Read or listen to **Exodus 19:1–6**.

The Old Testament priests acted as go-betweens, or mediators, between God and the people.

What did God mean when He said that the nation of Israel was to be a "kingdom of priests"?

Read **1 Peter 2:9**. How is the Church's vocation today similar to that of the nation of Israel?

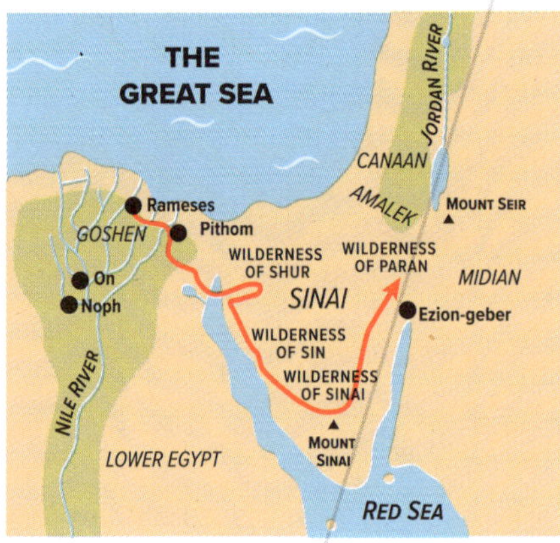

The Ten Commandments

The Israelites camped around Mount Sinai, but they were not to touch the mountain. God showed His presence with thick clouds, thunder and lightning, smoke, fire, and a loud trumpet blast. The people's sinfulness prevented them from approaching God directly, but God spoke to them through an intermediary, Moses. Through Moses, God gave His Law to the people.

Read or listen to **Exodus 20:1–17**. These commandments were written with the finger of God Himself on two tablets of stone (Exodus 31:18).

We often talk about the two "tables" of the Law: Commandments 1–3 (Exodus 20:1–11) and Commandments 4–10 (Exodus 20:12–17). How are these two sets of laws different?

The Golden Calf

Read or listen to **Exodus 32**. The Israelites grew tired of waiting for Moses to come down from the mountain. They started to doubt God's promises to them, and they demanded that Aaron build an idol to lead them. Aaron caved and gave them what they wanted, making a golden calf out of their own jewelry.

God threatened to destroy the people, but Moses interceded for them, and God relented.

When Moses came down and saw the people worshiping the calf, He burned it and scattered its ashes on the water. Then he made the people drink it.

Talk about times when we grow impatient with God or doubt His promises.

42

God's covenant establishes more than Israel's status; it shows them their vocation. Israel is to be a "kingdom of priests" to nations, God's missionaries to the world. Israel was to obey God's Law. As they obeyed God, they would show themselves to be God's people. The nations would see that relationship, and some would become part of God's chosen people by faith.

Commandments 1–3 describe our actions and behavior toward God, and Commandments 4–10 describe our actions and behavior toward other people.

Did You Know?

The ark of the covenant, the most holy piece in the tabernacle, was a box covered with gold and adorned with two cherubim with wings that covered the ark. It had two poles so it could be carried and contained the stone tablets of the Ten Commandments, a jar of manna, and Aaron's rod. The ark received the blood of sacrifice made on the Day of Atonement, which pointed to the ultimate and final sacrifice of Jesus Christ for all the sins of the world.

The Tabernacle

Read or listen to **Exodus 25:1–9**. God told Moses to build a sanctuary in which He would dwell. The people voluntarily gave toward building it. God was present everywhere, but He promised to be found in the tabernacle.

Skim through **Exodus 25–27**. God gave specific instructions about how the tabernacle was to be built and furnished.

God concluded His instructions for building the temple with a command to keep the Sabbath.

Read or listen to **Exodus 31:12–17**.

What was the Sabbath? Why did God want the people to keep it?

The Sabbath would be a day holy to the Lord. The people would not work on the Sabbath; it was to be a day of rest and worship to the Lord. God created the Sabbath on the seventh day of creation, when He "rested" from His work of creation.

The Spies and Forty Years of Wandering

Read or listen to **Numbers 13:1–14:10**. God commanded Moses to send twelve men, one from each tribe of Israel, into Canaan to spy on the land. After forty days, they returned with a report that the land flowed "with milk and honey" (13:27). But ten of the twelve spies were so intimidated by the size and strength of the people in Canaan that they refused to go in and conquer the land.

Only Caleb and Joshua showed trust in the Lord and His ability to give the land to the people.

Read **Numbers 14:34–38**.

What was God's punishment for the people's unbelief in God's promise? What happened to Joshua and Caleb?

All who were twenty years and older would not see the land God had promised them; they would die in the wilderness. But Joshua and Caleb and the next generation would inherit the land.

Leviticus

The Book of Leviticus is God's manual for the tabernacle. In it, God teaches His people about faithful and orderly worship.

The Book of Hebrews uses a lot of the same language as Leviticus: *atonement*, *sacrifice*, *redemption*. The sacrifices in Leviticus foreshadow Jesus' sacrifice on the cross and the peace and freedom we have in the Gospel.

Numbers

The Book of Numbers covers the thirty-nine-plus years that the Israelites spent wandering in the wilderness after they refused to enter the Promised Land. The accounts of water from the rock, the bronze serpent, and Balaam and his donkey are recorded in this book. As Israel complained and longed to return to Egypt, God stayed faithful to His people and His promise.

Deuteronomy

The Book of Deuteronomy begins on the plains of Moab, as God's people prepare to enter the Promised Land after forty years of wandering in the wilderness. Deuteronomy clarifies and explains the Law for a new generation of Israelites.

43

Because of the large amount of content to cover in this section of Scripture, there isn't much room for students to write on these pages. Discussing and not writing is fine. Or if you want students to have notes to refer back to, ask learners to bring a spiral notebook to use for writing notes and answers.

Option: Discuss these questions out loud together before asking learners to write their thoughts on the page.

Consider looking up the First Commandment in *Luther's Small Catechism with Explanation* (2017 edition) and reading "The Central Thought" to your group.

Connections

In Whom Do You Trust?

We usually think of the Ten Commandments and God's Law simply as God's demand on us—"Do this," "Don't do that." But God's Law teaches us that He wants to be our God, our only God. He wants to free us from the evils of this world, and He wants to provide us with all that we need.

Martin Luther's explanation of the First Commandment, "You shall have no other gods," is this:

What does this mean? We should fear, love, and trust in God above all things.

Look back at this lesson. What difference would it have made if the Israelites had feared, loved, and trusted in God above all things?

What about you? What difference would it make in your life if you feared, loved, and trusted God above all things? Write down your thoughts on both questions below.

Timeless Truth Connection

God has a plan for me as His human creature. "Oh how I love Your law!" says Psalm 119:97. How can the psalmist say that he loves God's Law? He tells us in verse 105, "Your word is a lamp to my feet and a light to my path." Through the Ten Commandments, God shows His will for us in our daily lives. And through God's Law, we see our failings and our need for a Savior.

Christ Connection

God commanded Moses to build a sanctuary, a tabernacle, where He would dwell among the people. In John 1:14, we read,

And the Word became flesh and dwelt among us, and we have seen His glory, glory as of the only Son from the Father, full of grace and truth.

Jesus, the Word, true God, came down from heaven to dwell with His people.

44

For students who have difficulty getting their ideas into writing, allow them to text you their responses or use some other digital communication device for their exit ticket. The other option is to have your student tell you their thoughts and you write it on a slip of paper.

Checks for Understanding

Before your learners leave, consider ways you can give them feedback for next week.

- **Quiz Question:** Ask students to write one quiz question to give to the class the following week. Remind them not to make it too difficult, since they will be taking the quiz also!
- **Exit Ticket:** Have learners write down on a slip of paper one example of how God is faithful to His promises. Have them leave the slip with you.

The Conquest of the Promised Land and the Tribes

Timeless Truth

God invites me, His redeemed child, to daily receive His gifts and commend my life to His care.

Lesson Focus

The learner will be able to relate God's faithfulness to the Israelites to the faithfulness He shows us as His redeemed children, and will commit his or her life to His care.

If students have trouble thinking of good leadership qualities, remind them of leaders they are familiar with, such as coaches, parents, church leaders, and political leaders.

11 The Conquest of the Promised Land and the Tribes

Consider This

Looking for a Leader

What makes a good leader? Make a list of the qualities that you think a good leader should have. Then exchange books with a partner and compare your lists.

God chose Joshua to be the next leader of Israel after Moses died. Joshua would lead the Israelites into the Promised Land and in the conquest of the land. But the real leader of the Israelites was God. He would go before His people and give them the victory.

The Big Picture

The Book of Joshua begins with Joshua taking over leadership from Moses, who has died. The book covers an intensive seven-year conquest of Canaan. During those years, Joshua leads the people of Israel in three campaigns against the people of Canaan to occupy the land. However, Israel did not completely remove the Canaanite people from the land. In some places, Israelites settled among the Canaanites. This was against God's will and His command, and it would cause many problems down the road for the people of Israel.

The purpose of the Book of Joshua is to record how God fulfilled His promise to give the land of Canaan to the Israelites as an inheritance. This book also describes how the land was divided among Israel's tribes, and Israel's recommitment to the covenant that God had given them at Sinai.

The accounts in this lesson are found in the **Book of Joshua**. The author is traditionally understood to be Joshua, but it may have been written by an unknown author. The events in Joshua happened between 1406 and 1375 BC.

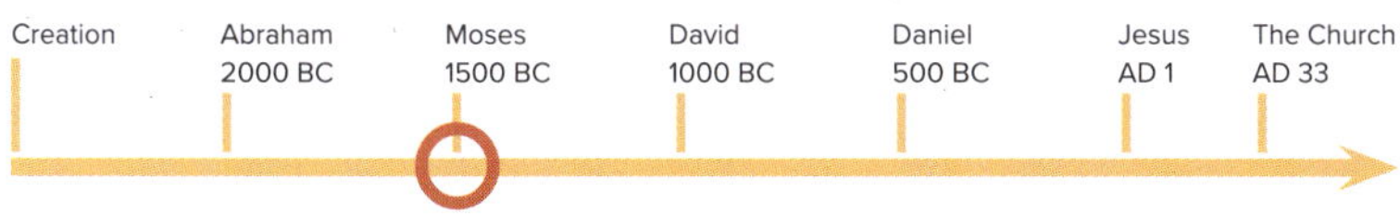

I can relate God's faithfulness to the Israelites to the faithfulness He shows me as His redeemed child, and I can commit my life to His care.

God worked through a prostitute to keep the spies safe and to give Israel courage as they entered the Promised Land. God gave Rahab, a non-Israelite and a prostitute, faith in Him. God desires that all people would be saved.

This time, the people would trust in God. They followed God's command, staying away from the ark that led them, and the hundreds of thousands of Israelites crossed over on dry land.

Joshua set the stones to be a sign, a memorial, so that when Israel came back to that place and the children asked what the stones meant, their parents would remind them how God led them through the Jordan and into the Promised Land.

Today we remember the good things that God has done for us with celebrations at Easter, Christmas, and other times during the year.

Joshua and the people listened to God and obeyed His instructions, circling the city once a day for six days and circling seven times on the seventh day. God gave them the city. It was His victory for His people. God keeps His promises; He is trustworthy.

DIGGING DEEPER

JOSHUA

RAHAB AND THE SPIES

God made Joshua the leader of Israel after Moses died. Joshua knew that to enter the Promised Land, they would have to first conquer the city of Jericho. So he sent two spies into Jericho. They sneaked in and went into the house of a woman named Rahab. Unfortunately, someone found out there were Israelite spies in Jericho. Soldiers came to Rahab's house and questioned her. But Rahab believed in the Lord, the God of Israel. She hid the spies and told the soldiers they were gone. Rahab knew God was going to give Jericho to the Israelites. She told the spies that all Jericho was in fear of the Israelites and their God. She asked the spies to protect her and her family when they came back to take the city. What did the spies do?

Read **Joshua 6:22–25**. How does this account show God's mercy and love for all people?

ISRAEL ENTERS THE PROMISED LAND

It was finally time. The Israelites stood on the bank of the Jordan River, ready to cross over the land that God had promised to give to Abraham, Isaac, and Israel. But there was a problem. The Jordan was overflowing its banks and anyone who stepped into it would be caught up in the foaming, swirling water and carried away. Forty years before, the fathers of these Israelites had not trusted that God would give them the land. Would they trust now?

Read or listen to **Joshua 3:7–17**.

Joshua commanded one man from each tribe to take a rock from the middle of the river. They carried them to the shore and Joshua set them up. Why did he do this?

Read or listen to **Joshua 4:1–7**.

What does the Church do to remember what God has done for us?

JERICHO

The people of Jericho were scared of the Israelites whose God had made the waters stop so they could pass through. But they had tall, thick walls to protect their city. How would the Israelites break down those walls? They wouldn't. God would. His plan: The Israelite army would circle the city, with the priests leading the way, carrying the ark and blowing trumpets. Then they would return to camp. This went on for six days. What happened on the seventh day?

Read or listen to **Joshua 6:15–21**. What did this victory show the Israelites?

Did You Know?

Jericho was about nine to twelve acres, with a circumference of a half mile to a mile. A large group could circle the city in less than an hour.

46

There isn't much room for writing lengthy answers on this page. If you want students to write answers, consider having them use a notebook or other paper to write responses. Questions can also be used for discussion only. This student book is to guide and stimulate thinking, not for grading correct answers.

Think About It . . .

Joshua and Caleb were the only two of their generation who went into the Promised Land. Joshua was Moses' assistant in the wilderness. He led the Israelites into the Promised Land and in battle against their enemies. Joshua's name means "the Lord saves" in Hebrew. In Greek, the same name is Jesus. Joshua's life pointed to Jesus, our Savior. Jesus fought all our enemies on the cross. On the Last Day, Jesus will come back to take us to our promised land, our forever home with Him.

The Land Is Divided among the Tribes of Israel

Joshua 13–22 recounts the dividing of the land among the tribes. The borders of each tribe's territory are given in detail. The Lord also told Joshua to appoint six cities of refuge. What were these cities for?

Read or listen to **Joshua 20:1–9**.

How did the appointment of these cities show both God's justice and His mercy?

Peoples in the Land of Canaan

The people who lived in Canaan worshiped false gods, like Baal and Asheroth. God told the Israelites to clear out these people so they wouldn't tempt the Israelites to worship their gods. These are the main groups the Israelites met in Canaan.

Canaanites—descendants of Noah's son Ham; they may have created the first alphabet

Amorites—also descendants of Noah's son Ham

Jebusites—their capital city was Jerusalem

Hittites—scholars think these people may have come from Russia; Esau married a Hittite woman

Hivites—these people made a treaty with Joshua

Girgashites—also descendants of Noah's son Ham

Perizzites—very little is known about these people

Philistines—originally from the island of Crete, they controlled access to iron

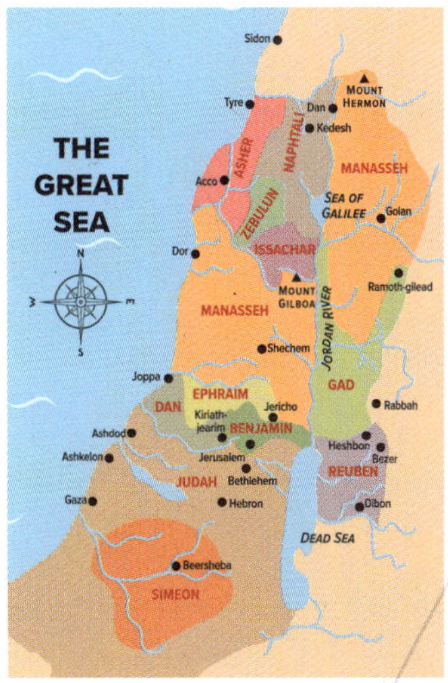

Q. Did the sun really stand still in the sky?

A. Joshua 10:1–15 tells us that after the capture of Jericho, five kings came against Israel. But Joshua surprised them and they ran off in fear. God sent down hailstones that killed many soldiers. But night was coming and Joshua was afraid the armies would get away, so he asked God to stop the sun in the sky so he could finish the battle.

Could the God who made the sun, moon, and stars stop the earth spinning for a time? Yes, our God can.

47

God has authority over life and death. The Fifth Commandment tells us, "You shall not murder." However, those who killed a person unintentionally would have a God-ordained legal right to safety in a city of refuge, and a full trial.

Some people are quick to discount miracles in the Bible, such as the parting of the Jordan, the destruction of the walls of Jericho, and the stopping of the sun. They look for natural causes and explanations. But the God who created all things certainly has power over His creation to do what He wishes. God's Word is truth.

If students are distracted by so much print on the page, help them to block off the parts of the page that you aren't using by covering those parts with a piece of paper or a note card to focus on one section at a time.

The names of the groups of people that the Israelites met are tricky to read. There's no need for students to stumble and be embarrassed by not being able to read them. Read the names out loud and help the students pronounce them correctly after you say them.

Option: Give learners blank index cards and markers or colored pencils so they can copy down Joshua 1:9. Encourage them to make one card for themselves and one card to give to a friend or family member.

Connections

Promises Kept

God kept the promises that He had made to the people of Abraham, Isaac, and Israel. He brought them into the Promised Land and gave them victory over their enemies. God gave them every reason to put all their trust and hope in Him. God also gives us every reason to commit our lives to His care. God's promise to Joshua is for you also:

> **Have I not commanded you? Be strong and courageous. Do not be frightened, and do not be dismayed, for the LORD your God is with you wherever you go. (Joshua 1:9)**

Let this Word of God strengthen you this week. Write it on a slip of paper and carry it with you. Make a copy and give it to a friend. Remember that God is with you, and He loves and cares for you.

Timeless Truth Connection

God invites me, His redeemed child, to daily receive His gifts and commend my life to His care. God promised to be with Joshua as he led the Israelites into the Promised Land. God kept His promises to give His chosen people land and victory over their enemies. God has chosen us to be His people, and He gives us the gift of salvation in Jesus, our Savior. Through Jesus, He gives us the victory over sin, death, and the devil.

Christ Connection

After Joshua led Israel across the Jordan and before Jericho, he saw a man standing before him. When asked who he was, the man replied, "The commander of the army of the LORD. Now I have come" (Joshua 5:14). He told Joshua he was on holy ground, and He allowed Joshua to worship Him. This was the Son of God in His preincarnate state (before He came to earth as a human baby). God Himself came down, ready to fight for His people; He would win the battles. Jesus promises to be with us as well. He has won the final battle for us, the battle against sin, death, and the devil. He will lead us into the new promised land when He comes again.

48

Checks for Understanding

Before your learners leave, consider ways you can give them feedback for next week.

- **Learning Log:** Ask students to write a question they have about the lesson in their Learning Log. Read the questions during the week and try to address them next time in class.
- **Paired Discussion:** Have each learner turn to a partner and share with that person one new thing that he or she learned from this lesson. Listen in on these conversations.

The Judges

Timeless Truth

God has a plan for me as His human creature.

Lesson Focus

The learner will be able to describe the cycle of sin and deliverance of God's people in the Book of Judges, and relate it to his or her own sin and daily need for repentance and deliverance in Christ.

Students may not feel comfortable sharing their personal situations. Allow them time to think and share as they feel comfortable. You could share your own situation as a way to help students open up.

To help students follow along with this narrative, make a numbered list of the events on the board or a large sheet of paper. Shorten each statement to just a few words, visual cues or symbols, or a combination of words and pictures. If some students are good at making those types of visuals, let them do the illustrating.

---

12 The Judges

Consider This

Doing the Right Thing

Think about a time when you just did what you felt like doing without thinking about the consequences. What happened?

When we act on our feelings, we can end up doing the wrong thing. We need someone to guide us and to help us do the right thing.

In today's lesson, we see what happened when the Israelites did whatever they felt like doing. They ended up doing the wrong things—forgetting God, worshiping idols, doing evil. God continually called them back through punishments and deliverers, but they just kept on going back to doing the wrong thing.

The Big Picture

The Book of Judges begins by listing the various tribes of Israel that did not complete the conquest of the land. Instead, they make some Canaanites serve them as slaves (which went against God's command), and they allow other Canaanites to stay in the land and live among them (which also went against God's command). This causes the Israelites to fall into a sorry cycle: (1) The people fall away from God and adopt the culture and idols of the Canaanites. (2) God allows another nation to invade them. (3) The Israelites call on God to deliver them. (4) God raises up a judge to deliver them. (5) The judge dies; Israel turns back to their evil, idolatrous ways; and the cycle starts over. Things become worse and worse as "everyone did what was right in his own eyes" (Judges 17:6; 21:25).

This narrative can be found in the **Book of Judges**. The author of the book is unknown. The timeline of this book is 1375–1080 BC, between Joshua's death and the rise of Israel's monarchy.

Creation | Abraham 2000 BC | Moses 1500 BC | David 1000 BC | Daniel 500 BC | Jesus AD 1 | The Church AD 33

I can describe the cycle of sin and deliverance of God's people in the Book of Judges, and I can relate it to my own sin and daily need for repentance and deliverance in Christ.

The Spirit of the Lord came upon Othniel. The Spirit changed the hearts of the judges to do God's will. The Holy Spirit is at work in believers' hearts today also, helping us do what is good and God-pleasing.

The account of Deborah and the reluctance of Barak to go into battle without her shows a loss of male military and spiritual leadership.

Teaching Option: Assign a judge to pairs or small groups of students to research and present to the class. Students can make a poster to show more about their judge, or they can make a digital presentation.

When they are finished, have them choose another judge until you cover them all.

If time is short, you can present about some judges and students can present about others.

Digging Deeper

The Judges

The Book of Judges describes how God's people kept going further away from Him. Because they did not completely remove the Canaanites from the land, they gave in to the temptation to worship false gods and practice evil. Time and again, God let other nations rise up against Israel so they would come back to Him. Then Israel would cry out to God, and He would raise up a judge to deliver them. But Israel kept turning back to idolatry and evil, falling deeper and deeper into great sinfulness.

Many of the judges were unusual, and some were unsavory characters. Again we see how God chooses the unlikely, the weak, and the despised to accomplish His saving purposes. There are six "major" judges and six "minor" judges. The major judges have longer narratives.

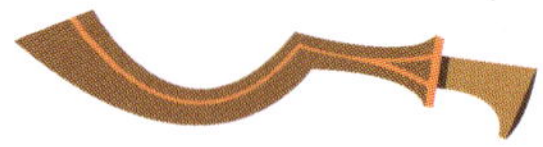

Othniel vs. Mesopotamia

Othniel

(Tribe of Judah)

This first judge of Israel is the only one who is not called out for immoral behavior or wrong motives. He defeated the king of Mesopotamia, who had ruled over Israel for eight years.

Read **Judges 3:9–11**.

What do these verses say about Othniel? Why is this important?

Ehud vs. Moabites

Ehud

(Tribe of Benjamin)

When Othniel died, Israel again practiced evil, and God allowed Moab to overtake them. After eighteen years, the people cried out to God, and He raised up Ehud. One of the first things we learn about Ehud is that he was left-handed. He used this trait plus his quick wit and agility to kill the king of Moab.

Read this colorful story in **Judges 3:12–30**.

Deborah vs. Canaan

Deborah

(Tribe of Ephraim)

Deborah was a prophetess who judged Israel when the Canaanites ruled over them. She told Barak, the Israelite commander, to go into battle as God had commanded him, but he would not go without her. Because of this, she told him that the honor of the victory would go to a woman. Look up **Judges 4:17–22** to see what this woman, Jael, did.

How is this account a negative reflection on Israel at that time?

Did You Know?

The title for this book in Hebrew means "to rule or govern." It can also mean "to judge" in the sense of "deliver." In many cases, the judges that God gave to help Israel were military deliverers.

Minor Judges

Shamgar (not called a judge, may not have been an Israelite; 3:31)
Tola of Issachar (10:1–2)
Jair of Gilead (10:3–5)
Ibzan of Bethlehem (12:8–10)
Elon of Zebulon (12:11–12)
Abdon of Ephraim (12:13–15)

As students are working, make yourself available to answer questions and keep students on task. If reading these Scripture passages becomes a stumbling block, encourage students to listen to them on a Bible app.

Gideon vs. Midianites

GIDEON

(Tribe of Manasseh)

The angel of the Lord came to Gideon, calling him to lead an army against the Midianites. But Gideon was afraid. He asked God for two signs, which God patiently provided. Then God showed Gideon and the Israelites that their only hope was to trust in the Lord for victory.

Read about the unusual way that God gave Gideon the victory in **Judges 7:2–22**.

Things went from bad to worse after Gideon. Though Gideon refused to become king, his wicked son Abimelech (son of his Canaanite concubine) made himself king after Gideon died.

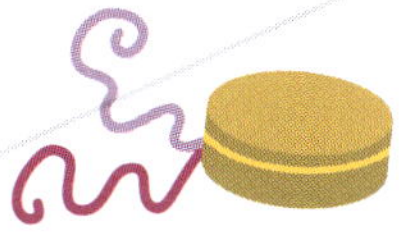

Jephthah vs. Ammonites

JEPHTHAH

Jephthah was a rough character, the son of an Israelite man and a prostitute. But he was a mighty warrior and was chosen to lead Israel against the Ammonites. Jephthah is remembered most for the rash vow he made to God. He vowed that if he won against the Ammonites, he would sacrifice the first thing that came out of his door. He returned victorious, and his daughter came running out with a tambourine to meet him. (Read the full story in **Judges 11:1–12:7**.) The accounts in the Book of Judges warn us against many things. What does this account teach us?

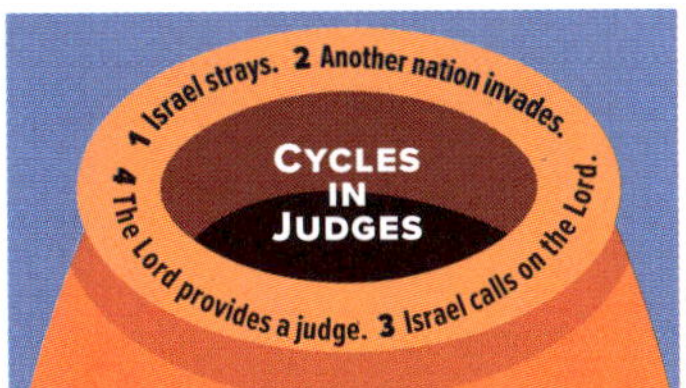

This diagram shows what repeatedly happened to Israel during the three-hundred-year period of the Judges (Judges 2:11–3:6).

Samson vs. Philistines

SAMSON

(Tribe of Dan)

Samson was set apart before birth to be a Nazirite. A Nazirite was not to cut his hair during the time that he served God, and Samson was to serve God his whole life, so when he cut his hair, the Holy Spirit left him and he lost his great strength. Samson was to deliver Israel from the Philistines, but instead, he often killed the Philistines for personal revenge. Samson killed many Philistines. Once he killed a thousand with a donkey's jawbone. But Samson had a weakness for women. One woman named Delilah was his final downfall. Read or listen to **Judges 16** for the whole account.

In the end, Samson gave up his life to destroy the temple of the false god and deliver his people. Read **Judges 16:28–30**.

Why was Samson able to regain strength in the end?

51

God whittled down the Israelite army from 32,000 to 300. Armed with trumpets, clay pots, and torches, they surprised the Midianites, who fought themselves in their confusion.

Gideon had multiple wives and many children. Abimelech was the son of his Canaanite concubine. Once again, the evils of polygamy are brought to light.

We should not make foolish vows or swear in God's name or in uncertain conditions.

Finally, Samson repented and called on the true God to help him. He asked that God would strengthen him one more time so he could be what God had meant him to be: a deliver for Israel.

This lesson covers a large span of years and specific content. You know how much of this your students can handle. If your time is short or if your students get easily overwhelmed, choose just one or two people to focus on to illustrate the larger message of the judges.

In today's society, many feel that people should be able to think and do whatever they feel is right for themselves, as long as it isn't hurting anyone. But because of our sinful nature, the things we feel are right are oftentimes wrong and against God's will, and they do end up hurting others.

Connections

Right in Whose Eyes?

Twice in the Book of Judges, we read these words: "Everyone did what was right in his own eyes." In fact, the book ends with that sentence, emphasizing how far away from God and immoral the nation of Israel had become. Think about our society today. Are people doing what is right in God's eyes or what they feel is right in their own eyes? Now think about yourself.

If we're being honest, we know that we often do what we want to do and not what God wants us to do. But just as God was faithful and patient with the Israelites, He is patient and faithful with us, for the sake of His Son, our Savior, Jesus. Take a moment to write a prayer of thanks to God for His unfailing love and forgiveness given to you for Jesus' sake:

Timeless Truth Connection

God has a plan for me as His human creature. The accounts in the Book of Judges show us how quickly sin and evil spreads when people turn away from God and forget His will for our lives. God's Law guides us and shows us how we are to live under Him and with one another. When we stray, He calls us back to Himself, offering love and forgiveness in Jesus.

Christ Connection

The "Angel of the Lord," the same messenger who appeared to the patriarchs, appeared to the Israelites at the beginning of the Book of Judges and also to Gideon and to Samson's parents. This, again, was the preincarnate Christ. Israel felt a need for a king, though they found out later that an earthly king was not the answer. Jesus Christ, the promised Messiah, the King of kings and Lord of lords, would fulfill Israel's need. He ushered in the kingdom of God, fulfilled His rule at the cross, and will reign forever and ever in the new heaven and new earth (Revelation 11:15).

52

Alternate Review Option: This lesson has some very interesting and action-packed stories of the judges. Close by asking students to share their favorites and why, either with the class or on this page. Students could say, write, or draw their response.

Checks for Understanding

Before your learners leave, consider ways you can give them feedback for next week.

- **Summary:** Ask students to write two or three sentences in their Learning Logs or on a sheet of paper describing one judge and how God used him or her. Have them leave this summary with you so you can review it for next time and see what they learned.
- **Question:** Have learners, either on a piece of paper or in the Learning Log, write down a question they have about what was covered in this lesson. Read the questions during the week and try to address them in the next class.

Unit 4: The Kings

Essential Questions

What has God done for me?

How is God faithful to people even when people are unfaithful to God?

How do the narratives of the kings point me to Christ?

Focus Statements

13. The learner will be able to summarize the narratives of Samuel, Saul, and the early life of King David, expressing how God was faithful to His people even when they were not faithful to Him.
14. The learner will be able to paraphrase the narratives of the kingdom of God's people under David and Solomon and design his or her own prayer asking God for forgiveness and wisdom.
15. The learner will be able to summarize why the kingdom split, what happened in the kingdom of Israel, and why the Israelites were conquered and went into exile.
16. The learner will be able to identify some of the faithful kings in Judah and how God was faithful to His people in their weaknesses even when they weren't faithful to Him.
17. The learner will be able to explore the Books of the Prophets in the Old Testament and explain the role they played in God's salvation story during the time of the kings.
18. The learner will be able to explain how God's people trusted in His promises during their time of exile, and how He is faithful to His promises to us today in Jesus.
19. The learner will be able to paraphrase the period between the return from exile and the birth of Christ and empathize with those who had to wait for the coming of the Messiah.

Assessment Options

1. **Preassessment Options**

   Before you begin, have each learner spend a few minutes writing down or telling you answers to these questions.

   - What do you know about the Bible kings Saul, David, and Solomon?
   - What do you know about other kings of Israel in the Bible?
   - What is a prophet? What do you know about the prophets in the Bible?

   After they have written these down, either collect the answers to read and leave feedback or quickly go over them together as a class. You'll get a good idea of where each learner is coming from as you begin.

2. **Formative Assessment Options**

   Formative assessments are ways to monitor student learning. Choose from the following:

   a. Weekly Summaries: As you go through the lessons in this unit, there's a lot of information. One of the checks for understanding common to each lesson in this unit is a two- or three-sentence summary of the events of the lesson. Get your learners in the habit of writing these summaries and reviewing them as you go through the different narratives.

   b. Learning Log: After each class, the students write in their Learning Log one important thing they learned in that class.

   c. Reflection Tools: These may include sermon notes, memory work, and self-reflections. As you move through the unit and your learners do these formative assessments, consider asking questions like these: What is easiest and most difficult about memory work? What have you learned about sermons from taking sermon notes? How have you grown as a learner through the first three units?

3. **Summative Assessment Options**

Summative assessments evaluate student learning at the end of an instructional unit. Choose from the following assessment methods:

a. Learning Portfolio: Have students complete a variety of formative assessments over the course of this unit. At the end of the unit, have learners compile at least one of each type of formative assessment, along with completed lesson notes and other samples you require. If they've completed these tasks to your satisfaction over the course of the unit, you can use their work as a great summative assessment. *Note:* At the beginning of the unit, make a list of samples you will collect so there are no surprises at the end.

b. Written Responses: Check for understanding by asking learners to write a short-answer paper with three to ten questions. This could be done inside or outside of class, and the length of the answers can vary. Know your students. Some will manage only the concrete questions; others will be ready for abstract thinking. The point is not to frustrate students with questions but to help them demonstrate what they've learned. Here are some sample questions based on this unit:

- What happened during the time of kings Saul, David, and Solomon?
- What happened in the Northern Kingdom?
- What happened in the Southern Kingdom?
- What were the main messages of the prophets?
- What happened during the exile and return?
- What have you learned about how God has created, redeemed, and called you to be His own?
- What have you learned about how God's Word is living and active in your life?

Teaching Tips

1. As mentioned in previous units, consider building a visual timeline in your learning space, each week adding important events, people, and the books of the Bible mentioned in the narratives. This can be as simple as putting a piece of masking tape across an open wall and each week taping note cards with the name of the lesson, books of the Bible, and major characters and events. A visual organizer is a great way to keep learners on the same page.
2. This unit covers a lot of ground quickly. The books mentioned in this section cover roughly one-fourth of the text of the Bible, and the narratives span hundreds of years. Many of these narratives, sadly, often get overlooked just for the sake of time. Because of this, these lessons mention a lot of details. Be extremely mindful of your time; pick and choose which narratives you focus on, and move on. Each lesson has a central narrative (outlined in a special box) that is given more attention than the rest. If you're choosing to pare down each lesson, consider focusing mostly on this narrative with your learners. The end goal is that your learners will see the big picture of what happened during the period of the kings, from Saul to the return from exile. Most important, the central focus is that your learners will see how God was faithful, in all of the political and religious turmoils of the time, to fulfill His promise in sending the Messiah to redeem the world.
3. There is a lot of reading and not as much activity in this unit. Encourage your learners to move around your space, pair up with a partner to reflect, or work in small groups as you read and discuss. Be creative in your examination of the text together.

Color Key for Teacher Notes

Tan = Specific additional assessments

Blue = Extra activities or questions

Green = Educational tips and directions for specific activities

Gold = Explanations of theological concepts or background for the teacher

Samuel to King David

Timeless Truth

God has redeemed me to be His own.

Lesson Focus

The learner will be able to summarize the narratives of Samuel, Saul, and the early life of King David, expressing how God was faithful to His people even when they were not faithful to Him.

13 Samuel to King David

Consider This

Who Knows Best?

Have you ever done anything that everyone else thought would be foolish but you did it anyway and it ended badly for you? What was it? Write it below and then share with a partner.

In today's lesson, we'll look at how God's people thought they knew better than Him and it went poorly. Yet God still salvaged the situation and gave His people a king after God's own heart.

The Big Picture

At the end of the time of the judges, God appoints the great prophet and priest Samuel to lead His people. The people, however, demand a king in order to be like other nations. Though He warns them that bad things will happen, God gives them a king: Saul. Saul is a mighty warrior but rejects God, so God sends Samuel to choose a new king. God picks David, a young shepherd of the tribe of Judah to be the next king after Saul. David has a heart after the Lord's own, and God uses David to do great things. While still a young man, God uses David to defeat the enemy's champion, Goliath, in battle. David becomes a court musician and war leader, as well as son-in-law to Saul. Saul becomes jealous and tries to kill David, so David must run away. Saul later dies in battle along with his son (and best friend of David) Jonathan. After Saul's death, there is a war between David's followers and Saul's descendants, with David eventually prevailing and being anointed the next king.

This section comes from the books of **1 Samuel**, **2 Samuel**, **1 Chronicles**, and **Psalms**. The narrative occurred between roughly 1060–1009 BC.

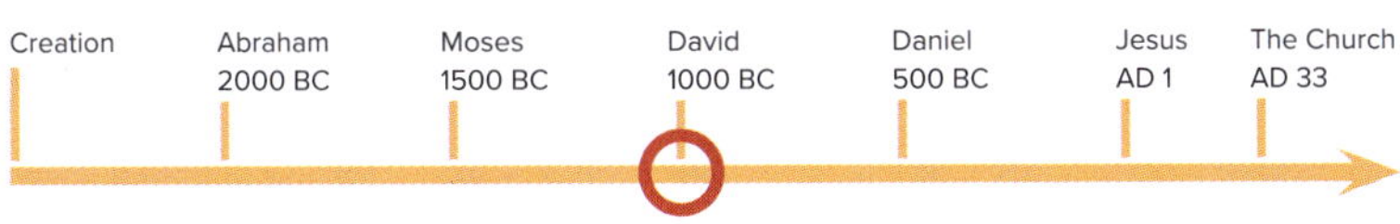

I can summarize the narratives of Samuel, Saul, and the early life of King David, expressing how God was faithful to His people even when they were not faithful to Him.

Unit 4: The Kings — God has redeemed me to be His own.

53

This particular question can either be fun or rather personal. It will be important to understand your particular group. If you suspect that they may start bragging about getting away with foolish things or say something that gets them into trouble, consider giving them a disclaimer and warning them to only write something they'd be willing to share with the entire group. The point is to get them to consider how God must think of us when we do foolish things.

As always, this is a sizable block of text. Read the text and, if you have time, have your learners underline or highlight one word or phrase that sticks out to them about this summary. Then they can share with a partner why it sticks out to them.

Option: If you have a developing timeline on a wall in your space, consider adding the lesson number and name, dates, and books of the Bible to your timeline at this time.

Saul did not trust in the Lord and the Lord's timing, especially when it didn't make sense politically. He took the priest's job into his own hands, which was displeasing to God, who desired for Saul to trust Him.

God, through Samuel, gave many warnings to the people that a king would take away their freedoms. We can be like the Israelites in that we know what God's will is for His human creatures, and that He warns us about the consequences of sin, yet we often think we know better and disobey God. Praise the Lord He is patient and merciful with us!

Option: Divide your class into teams of two or three and give them a couple of minutes to read over the text and figure out a quick way to act out this scene for the class. Each member has to participate in one role. Then either pick one bold group to perform or have each group perform a quick skit of this scene.

Digging Deeper

Think About It . . .

What is God's desire for us when we disobey Him? What does God desire that we receive? How do we make the same kind of mistakes as Saul?

God's People Demand a King

After a series of mistakes, God's people were tired of having judges lead. They demanded a king, just as other nations had. Read **1 Samuel 8:10–22**. What did God say would happen if they got a king?

How are we sometimes like the Israelites?

Saul

It didn't take too long before the king, Saul, did something bad. Read **1 Samuel 13:8–14**. What was it that Saul did that was really so wrong? Write it down in your own words here.

God Chooses Saul

God chose Saul to be king. Saul was tall and strong, just like the people wanted.

Samuel

God spoke to Samuel and called him to lead His people as both prophet and priest. When Samuel grew up to be the great priest of the people, God did great things through Samuel. Read **1 Samuel 7:3–11**. What would it have been like, do you think, to have been there for this?

Hannah

This section began with a woman, Hannah, who was unable to have children. She went to the temple to pray for a child and received a promise from God that she would have a son. She had a child, named him Samuel, and gave him to serve in the temple his whole life. Samuel became a great prophet and priest. Hannah prayed a powerful song of thanks. Read **1 Samuel 2:1–10**. What does her prayer tell us about who God is and what He does?

54

Writing in these undefined spaces may be a struggle for some students. Writing is not essential to these activities—you could just discuss these questions as a group. But for some students, writing really helps them process information. Make sure that students know that complete sentences and perfect spelling are not necessary. Another option is to provide paper or a notebook as an alternative to writing in the student book.

This section tells us how God tends to raise up the lowly and humble. He does this for us lowly sinners in Jesus. In addition, you may note that Mary's song later echoed a lot of similar ideas (Luke 1:46–56).

David

After defeating Goliath, David grew in popularity. He became a war leader of God's people. What did Saul think? What did he do? Read **1 Samuel 18:6–16**. For most of the rest of Saul's reign, David would be an outlaw on the run from the king.

God's Purposes

Though Saul didn't know it, God was still using David for His purposes. Read **1 Samuel 16:14–23**. What was so special about David?

After Saul's Death

After many years, and failing to follow God, Saul was killed in battle. After Saul's death, there was a war between Saul's followers and David's for who would be the next king. In the end, God gave the victory to David. Read **2 Samuel 5:1–5**. From the text, what is one thing that sticks out to you about David's anointing as king?

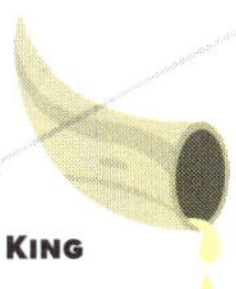

Samuel Anoints a King

While Saul was still king, God talked to Samuel, the prophet, and told him to go anoint (set aside for a special purpose) a new person who would become king after Saul. Read **1 Samuel 16:1–13**. What is one thing that sticks out to you about this? What does this tell you about how God works, and how that is different from how people work?

David and Goliath

Perhaps David is most famous for a battle he fought against the giant Philistine enemy named Goliath. While Saul was at war with the enemy Philistines, the enemy sent a champion to fight. In this combat, each side presented a champion, and whoever won would show the other side that their god was more powerful. Read **1 Samuel 17:4–11**. What was Goliath like?

David heard and would not let this stand. He was God's anointed! What did David say to Goliath's mockery of God? Read **1 Samuel 17:26–27**.

David confronted Goliath on behalf of God's people and defeated him. Read **1 Samuel 17:41–51**. How was Goliath defeated?

55

Saul showed his selfish and jealous heart by trying to kill David. The rest of their relationship would be one of David running from Saul while still trying to honor his king.

Option: Have learners quickly sketch out things they notice from David's anointing and share with a partner.

Saul had done wrong and had to face the consequences. Yet God used simple means, the songs of a shepherd, to calm the king. Many of these songs are recorded in Psalms, and God's Word still speaks comfort to us.

Goliath was intimidating, a real champion who looked and sounded like a great warrior out of legend. David looked far less imposing, yet David understood that what Goliath was doing was mocking God. Through David, God overpowered and killed Goliath. It was not really about David at all. In this way, David serves as a kind of messiah: one who is called by God to be His agent of salvation. Jesus, the ancestor of David, is the true Messiah, and this narrative helps us understand God's power against the ancient enemies of the devil, the world, and our sinful flesh.

God doesn't look at outward appearances the way we do. He looks at the heart. He saw that David, though a sinner, would not turn to worshiping idols and would turn to God in repentance when he sinned. We are to look at people through God's eyes. We are all sinners in need of a Savior.

Here are some connections between David and Jesus: Both were part of the family line of the Messiah, both were born in Bethlehem, both were shepherds (David a shepherd of sheep, Jesus the Good Shepherd of people), both were kings of God's people, both were champions who fought God's enemies, both were anointed by God for service.

Jesus, though, is far greater. He is the Savior and King of all.

If you have time, divide your learners into small groups. Have them read one of the psalms and summarize what it says (fifteen words or so). If you don't have time in class, consider making this a homework assignment or going over this section at the beginning of the next class. It's important that your learners at least can identify where the Psalms are located in the Bible and have a general idea of what they contain.

Connections

The Greater King

King David's descendant would be Jesus. Jesus often referred to Himself as the Son of David, the greater King who did greater things than David.

Are there any other connections you can make between David and Jesus? What are they?

Timeless Truth Connection

God has redeemed me to be His own. In the Scripture for the lesson, God's people demanded a king, directly going against God's will for His Old Testament people. He wanted them to trust and serve Him alone. God was patient though. Saul, the first king, disobeyed God. Even so, God raised up a new king, David, who served Him alone. God anointed (set aside) David to do His work of rescuing, or redeeming, His people from the Philistines, Goliath, and the Israelites' desire to serve idols.

Christ Connection

God used David to rescue His unfaithful people from their enemies. In a greater way, the Father would one day send Jesus to rescue His unfaithful people from the enemies of the devil, the world, and our sinful flesh.

Psalms

The Book of Psalms is the songbook of God's people in the Bible. It contains 150 different songs (the word *psalm* means " sacred song") written by a number of different people over the time of the Old Testament. David wrote many of them, but Moses even wrote one (Psalm 90), as did other writers. Throughout the Old Testament, in Jesus' day, and even today, the Psalms have been an important part of the worship life of God's people. They express things like thanks to God, laments, prayers, and even prophecies about Christ!

Look up and read one or more of these famous psalms, and summarize it in the margin or out loud with a partner: **Psalm 2**, **Psalm 23**, **Psalm 46**.

56

Checks for Understanding

Before your learners leave, consider ways you can give them feedback for next week.

- **Summary:** Pass out note cards and have each learner write a two- or three-sentence summary of God's narrative of salvation in this lesson. Have them leave this summary with you so you can review it for next time and see what they learned.
- **Learning Log:** Have your learners write down one thing from the lesson about how God is faithful to His people even when they were not faithful to Him. Have them leave this with you in their Learning Log to review before next time.

DAVID TO SOLOMON

TIMELESS TRUTH

God invites me, His redeemed child, to daily receive His gifts and commend my life to His care.

LESSON FOCUS

The learner will be able to paraphrase the narratives of the kingdom of God's people under David and Solomon and design his or her own prayer asking God for forgiveness and wisdom.

14 DAVID TO SOLOMON

CONSIDER THIS

TRUE WISDOM

How would you define the word *wisdom*?

Who is one person in your life whom you would consider wise? Jot down some details about this person in the space below. Then share.

In today's lesson, we will see God granting wisdom to Solomon. We will find, however, that true wisdom comes from God as we receive the gifts of His Word, as well as forgiveness, life, and salvation.

The Big Picture

After David becomes king, he establishes his kingdom in Jerusalem. There, David desires to build a temple to the Lord, but God tells him that David's descendant would build Him a temple and David's throne would last forever. David continues to rule as king, and though he has a heart for the Lord, he is far from perfect. David commits adultery and has a friend killed to cover up his sin. God confronts David, and David repents and is forgiven. David's troubles continue as one of his sons tries to overthrow him (and nearly does) and David must fight a war against him. After David dies, his throne goes to his son Solomon, to whom God grants great wealth and wisdom to rule. Solomon builds a temple to the Lord and writes three Books of Wisdom that are found in the Bible. As Solomon's power increases, however, he marries many foreign women, who bring their idols and false worship into Israel. Sadly, near the end of his reign, Solomon worships many false gods. God cannot let these horrific sins pass, and so, after Solomon's reign, life for God's people will be different in Israel.

This section comes from the books of **2 Samuel** and **1 Kings**, as well as **Proverbs**, **Ecclesiastes**, and **Song of Solomon**. The narrative occurred between roughly 1009–931 BC.

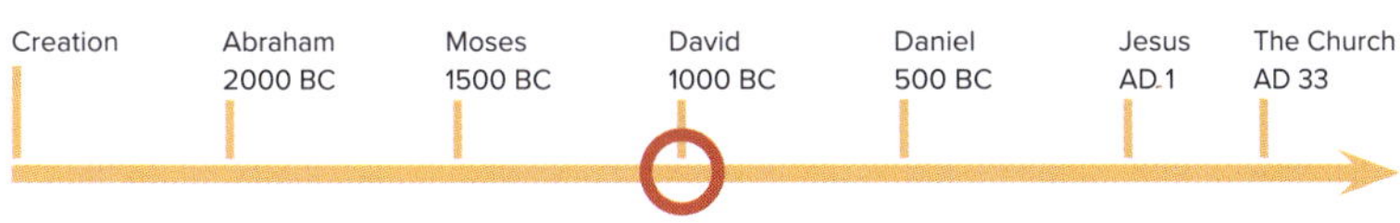

I can paraphrase the narratives of the kingdom of God's people under David and Solomon and design my own prayer asking God for forgiveness and wisdom.

GOD INVITES ME, HIS REDEEMED CHILD, TO DAILY RECEIVE HIS GIFTS AND COMMEND MY LIFE TO HIS CARE.

UNIT 4: THE KINGS 57

Active Option: Have each learner write down his or her name and a definition of the word *wisdom* on a note card. Then they will secretly hand it to you. Shuffle the cards and read off the definitions one by one. After each, the learners have to guess who wrote the definition. At the end, the person who guessed the most correct wins. Then look up a definition of the word *wisdom* online or in a dictionary. The point of this is to get the learners thinking about wisdom, which should help prepare them to think about this section of the narrative when wisdom literature was written.

If your learners are familiar with these narratives, ask them to find one new detail they didn't already know. As you go through the lesson, challenge learners to find the text and dig deeper into this new learning.

Option: If you have a developing timeline on a wall in your space, add the lesson number and name, dates, and books of the Bible to your timeline at this time.

Digging Deeper

David Wants a Temple

After David finally got a break from his wars and settled down in his new capital city of Jerusalem, he wanted to build God a permanent temple. Read **2 Samuel 7:4–17**. How is God's Word here about David's son, and how is it also about Jesus?

Absalom

David's troubles continued when one of his sons, Absalom, rose up to try and overthrow his father and take the throne. After some fighting, Absalom was killed in battle. Read **2 Samuel 18:33**. What do we learn about David's heart here?

David's Terrible Sins

Some time later, David committed a terrible sin. He committed adultery with the wife of one of his faithful soldiers. She became pregnant, and though David tried to cover it up, he ended up having her husband, Uriah, killed in battle. God sent the prophet Nathan to confront David about his sin. Though he would have to suffer loss, David repented and was forgiven. David wrote **Psalm 51** about the experience. Read the psalm, pinpoint one thing that sticks out to you about what we can learn from David about prayer, and write down why.

Solomon Becomes King

Before David died, he gave instructions to Solomon before Solomon became king of Israel. Read **1 Kings 2:1–4**. In your own words, summarize what David told Solomon to do as king.

Solomon's Books in the Bible

Solomon authored three Books of Wisdom in the Bible (summarized on the scrolls). These are all grouped with the Books of Poetry and can be found after the Book of Psalms (much of which his father, David, wrote). These books each have their own message, but their central purpose is to teach wisdom. Read **Proverbs 1:1–7**. Rephrase it in your own words below.

Ecclesiastes
Life without God is empty; the only rescue comes from God as He leads us to fear, love, and trust Him and His Word.

Proverbs
This book describes God's wisdom by contrasting the actions of wise and foolish people.

Song of Solomon
Though married love is wonderful, God's love for you in Christ is the greatest love of all.

58

Solomon would build the temple and would be a great king. The Messiah would be a king forever, and His presence among God's people in the flesh would be greater than God's presence in the temple. These are very abstract ideas. Not all learners are abstract thinkers yet. Doing this section together can help bridge that gap.

This can be a very personal thing. Perhaps first read this out loud as a group, answering questions about vocabulary. Then each learner can take a couple of minutes to reflect, thinking about his or her own sins and comparing them to David and David's hope in God's forgiveness.

David's heart broke when his rebellious son was killed. David was capable of forgiveness, even when betrayed. Jesus' heart for forgiveness of His people led Him to the cross for us.

If time is short, reflect on this question as a group out loud. David instructed Solomon to fear, love, and trust in God above all things.

For longer Bible readings, consider having students use a Bible app to listen to rather than read the Scripture.

Option: Pause here and have your learners identify these books in their own print Bibles. They can find where the books are and flip through them for a minute before moving on to the other narratives. Note that the Song of Solomon has a lot of mature material about the love between husbands and wives and how this reflects Christ's relationship with the Church. Measure your learners' maturity here. Remember, however, that this book is one of the books of the Bible and you and your learners need to be able to talk about the actual content of the Bible together.

God Comes to Solomon

Once Solomon became king, God came to him in a vision. Read **1 Kings 3:3–15**. What did Solomon ask for? Why do you think it's so pleasing to God?

Solomon Turns Away from God

Even though Solomon built a beautiful temple and gained great wealth through his wisdom, he also did great evil. Read **1 Kings 11:1–8**. In your own words, explain what happened with Solomon and why he turned from God. How can this happen to us?

Solomon Builds a Temple

Solomon was finally able to build a beautiful temple to the Lord. He moved the ark of the covenant into the Most Holy Place. Look at the artist's rendering below. What is one observation about the dedication of the temple that sticks out to you?

When Solomon dedicated the temple, something incredible happened. Read **1 Kings 8:10–11**. What do you suppose was the meaning of this? Where have you seen this in the Bible before? What does it mean?

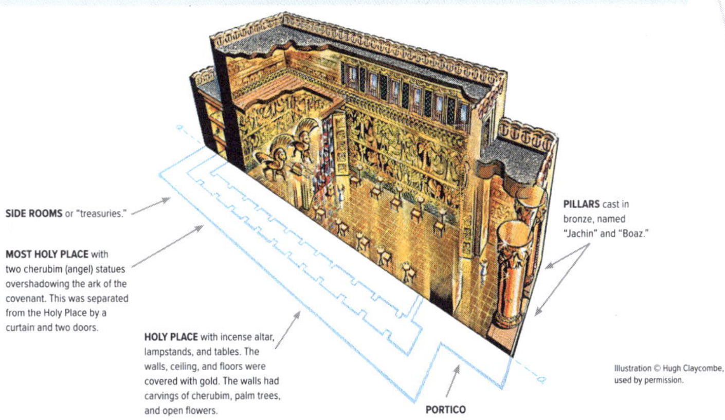

Illustration © Hugh Claycombe, used by permission.

59

Solomon asks for wisdom to serve God's people. God is pleased with this because it means Solomon is taking his role as God's anointed servant seriously. We should be mindful to consider how we can serve God wisely as well.

This can be a very difficult thing to discuss. Solomon had great wisdom but forgot what it was to be used for. Solomon married many woman and was influenced by them to allow the worship of idols. We should be careful about who we associate with, especially in marriage. God desires that we marry only fellow believers. We are to, together, continually return to worship to receive the gifts of God's Word and then continue to cling to God's Word in our daily lives. In these, God strengthens and keeps us firm in the faith. Be sensitive to students who may have a parent who is an unbeliever.

God's presence was often shown in fire or in a cloud of glory during the time of the exodus. Here, at the dedication of the temple, God's glory reappears. This shows God's presence and His pleasure at the new temple.

Option: Solomon's temple is an amazing thing to investigate, and an illustration does not do it justice. Look up artists' renditions of Solomon's temple online for more detail.

This lesson has had a lot of reading and writing. It may seem like a lot to add a writing element at the end, but it doesn't have to be. If your learners are not great writers, or if they are tired of sitting at their spaces, consider moving locations—like going outside or to the sanctuary to reflect. Even if your learners don't write, encourage them to sit quietly and think or pray apart from their neighbors for both the "Timeless Truth Connection" and "Christ Connection."

Connections

Praying for Wisdom

In the Scripture for this lesson, we see two kings, David and Solomon, who were both given great things by God: wisdom, wealth, and power. Write down your own prayer in the space below, asking for wisdom from God.

Timeless Truth Connection

God invites me, His redeemed child, to daily receive His gifts and commend my life to His care. God, in Christ, has called you to be His own. He has given you the gift of eternal life and is your King forever. Yet the devil, the world, and our sinful flesh present so many temptations to us each day. Use the prayer you wrote above to ask God daily for the wisdom to faithfully receive His gifts and commend your life to His care.

Christ Connection

In this lesson, we see two kings, David and Solomon. They both disobeyed God, yet only one, David, confessed his sins, repented, and received forgiveness. This is God's desire for us: that as we sin, we repent, freely receive the gift of forgiveness, and then try to live according to His will, or plan, for us. Solomon, though wise, ultimately did not fear, love, and trust God above all things in the end. Though we sin, Jesus did not. He is always there to forgive us.

God made a promise to David that his descendant would be a king forever, and Jesus is the fulfillment of that promise. Jesus is not only our King, He is also our High Priest, lives in us as we are the temple of the Holy Spirit, and gives us all good things.

Think About It . . .

How can you honor Jesus as your King and High Priest this week?

60

Checks for Understanding

Before your learners leave, consider ways you can give them feedback for next week.

- **Exit Ticket:** Have learners write down one question they still have after this lesson on a piece of paper and leave it with you. Read through questions during the week so you can address them the next time you meet.
- **Reflection:** For the final activity on the "Connections" page, encourage your learners to create their own prayer, in writing or via video or a medium they choose, asking God for wisdom to faithfully receive His gifts and commend their life to God's care. Have them share it with you either before leaving or sometime throughout the week.

The Divided Kingdom in the North

Timeless Truth

God has a plan for me as His human creature

Lesson Focus

The learner will be able to summarize why the kingdom split, what happened in the kingdom of Israel, and why the Israelites were conquered and went into exile.

Many of these lessons and questions require sitting, so encourage your learners to first write out or sketch their thoughts in the space provided, then get up and find someone they're not sitting near to share their experiences. Talk in pairs about the biggest fights they've ever gotten into and what it felt like before coming back together.

Fighting can also be a sensitive topic, especially for students who have been bullied or for those who live in homes where fighting is common. Be careful not to glorify fighting, nor to ask students to share uncomfortably. Know your students and what will best get them interested in this lesson.

15 The Divided Kingdom in the North

Consider This

Broken Relationships

Think of the biggest fight you've ever gotten into. Was it with a friend or a brother or sister or someone from school? You don't have to write the event, but jot down or sketch below all the things that getting into that fight made you feel. Go!

Today's lesson is all about a big split in God's people. Though they had to suffer the consequences of broken relationships, God was still faithful to bring about His plan of salvation for them.

The Big Picture

After Solomon's death, things don't go well for God's people. Because of Solomon's sins, Israel is divided. Some people want to follow Solomon's foolish son Rehoboam, while others want to follow Jeroboam, one of Solomon's leaders. So God's people split the Promised Land into two nations: Israel in the north and Judah in the south. The nation of Israel is bigger both in land and the number of tribes that belong to it, but its kings all turn away from the Lord and don't follow Him. In fact, the kings of Israel all reject the one true God, setting up idols and worshiping false gods. Over the next two hundred years, God keeps sending prophet after prophet to go and speak to the kings of Israel in the north, warning them of God's Law and calling them to repent and be forgiven. Major prophets during this time include Elijah and Elisha, who, along with their students, warn the wicked kings of God's wrath and even perform mighty miracles where God shows His power. Yet, in the end, Israel does not listen, and God sends an invading empire, the Assyrians, to conquer them. Many in the Northern Kingdom are either killed or exiled to faraway lands. Though the Northern Kingdom falls, God remains true to His people, and some kings in the Southern Kingdom still remain true to God in Jerusalem.

This section is found in the books of **1 Kings**, **2 Kings**, and **2 Chronicles**. The narrative occurred between roughly 931–722 BC.

Creation	Abraham	Moses	David	Daniel	Jesus	The Church
	2000 BC	1500 BC	1000 BC	500 BC	AD 1	AD 33

I can summarize why the kingdom split, what happened in the kingdom of Israel, and why the Israelites were conquered and went into exile.

GOD HAS A PLAN FOR ME AS HIS HUMAN CREATURE.

UNIT 4: THE KINGS

61

This is a sizable block of text. Read the text and, if you have time, have your learners underline or highlight one word or phrase that sticks out to them about this summary. Then they can then share with a partner why it sticks out to them.

Option: If you have a developing timeline on a wall in your space, consider adding the lesson number and name, dates, and books of the Bible to your timeline now.

God appointed Jeroboam, a foreman of Solomon's building projects. Though not royalty, he would have understood the daily lives of God's people. God expected him to faithfully follow and worship Him alone.

Active Option: Write down these three questions on the board or a big piece of paper. After reading, divide the learners into three groups and assign each group one question. Groups will answer their question and come up front to write down and explain their answer to everyone else.

This may be a good time to take a step back and have a conversation about popularity and why people do foolish or sinful things to be more popular. Consider doing a group brainstorming session of all the things people to do become popular; then talk about whether those things are in line with God's plan for His human creatures, as found in the Ten Commandments.

Digging Deeper

A New Leader

Before Solomon's death, God appointed a new leader for ten of the tribes of His people. Read **1 Kings 11:28–39**. Who was this man, why did God give him leadership of ten tribes, and what did God expect him to do?

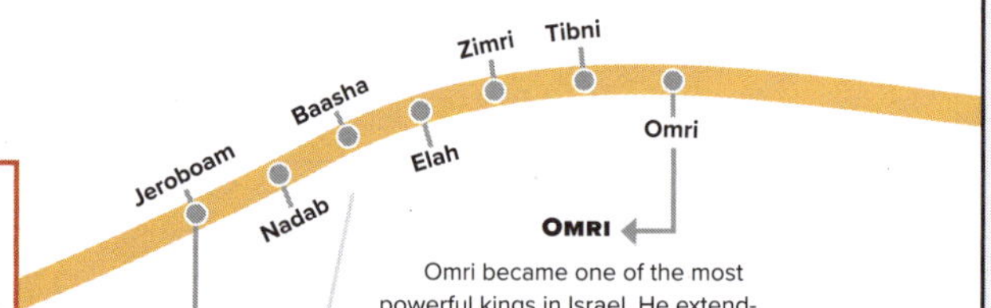

A Big Debate

After Solomon's death, there was a big debate. People wanted to know if Solomon's son Rehoboam would make a good king or would make the same mistakes as his father. With Jeroboam at their side, the leaders of God's people confronted the heir to the throne, Rehoboam, asking if he would make their work easier or more difficult. Rehoboam listened to his foolish friends and said he'd make their work harder when he was crowned king. Read **1 Kings 12:16–24**.

How did the people respond?

How did Rehoboam respond?

How did God respond?

Jeroboam

Right after Jeroboam became king in the north, he did something wicked. Like Solomon, he built idols and temples to worship false gods throughout his new kingdom. Read **1 Kings 12:25–30**. In your own words, why did Jeroboam commit these sins?

What do people do today for popularity, even when it goes against what is right? How can we avoid falling into temptations like these?

Omri

Omri became one of the most powerful kings in Israel. He extended the border; created the new capital city, Samaria; and even became somewhat famous outside of Israel. Yet, for all his power, he only gets eight verses in the Bible. Why do you think that is? Read **1 Kings 16:25–26** for clues.

62

This timeline has a lot of names, but is designed to give your learners a general idea of the number and names of the different kings of the Northern Kingdom of Israel in order. Consider reading the names out loud, and as you do so, encourage your learners to flip through 1 Kings, starting at chapter 12, and find the names of the different kings of Israel. Omri is an example of a powerful king who did not faithfully worship the true God. Most likely, he is given so little space in the Bible to show what God thinks of this sort of earthly power without faithfulness.

ELISHA

God took Elijah to heaven in a fiery chariot, and Elijah's student, Elisha, took over as God's prophet. God worked many miracles through Elisha and spoke His Word to the kings through him. The kings of Israel continued to worship false gods.

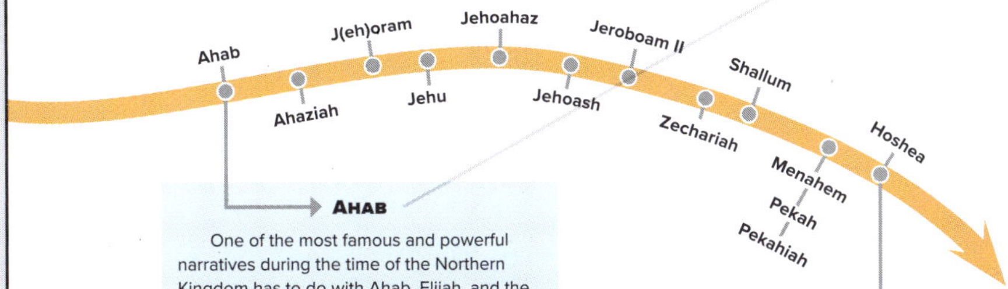

AHAB

One of the most famous and powerful narratives during the time of the Northern Kingdom has to do with Ahab, Elijah, and the prophets of Baal. King Ahab inherited a strong kingdom from his father, Omri. Read **1 Kings 16:29–34**. What kind of person was Ahab?

During this time, God called a man named Elijah to be His prophet to the wicked King Ahab. Read **1 Kings 17:1–6**. What was Elijah's message to Ahab?

While Elijah was on the run, God used him to do some amazing miracles, including raising a widow's son from the dead. But after three years, God used Elijah for a showdown against Ahab's false gods. God showed everyone who He is. Read or listen to **1 Kings 18:17–40**. Then in the space below, jot down what happened in the narrative.

HOSHEA

Hoshea was the last king of the Northern Kingdom of Israel. Read or listen to **2 Kings 17:6–20**. In your own words, summarize who conquered Israel and, according to the text, why it happened.

WHAT ARE THE BOOKS OF 1 AND 2 CHRONICLES?

These books (originally just one scroll) give a similar narrative retelling of the books of Samuel and Kings. Much of the information is the same, but there are some additions. This narrative history focuses more on the rule of King David's family tree and God's faithfulness to them throughout the generations.

63

This is a key narrative in the lesson. If your group is outgoing, let them discuss the first two questions as a group before dividing them into two teams and having them act out the events (rather than writing it in the space). Award the winning team based on participation of everyone in the group, accuracy to the text, and overall creativity. The goal is not to make light of the event, but to help learners really dig into the details of the narrative.

A major point is that God's people failed to obey His plan for them, and they turned from true worship to false worship. There were and still are consequences for our sins. This is why we need Jesus' forgiveness.

Option: We won't look much in the books of Chronicles, but if you have a spare moment, encourage your learners to identify them in their Bibles. Have your learners page through these books and see if they can identify any narrative sections they've already read during their lessons so far.

For students who have difficulty focusing on just one part of these pages at a time or who are easily distracted by all the text on the pages, help them to block off the rest of the page with pieces of paper to build a frame around each individual section as you discuss it.

If your learners have been sitting for a long time, encourage them to get up and move around the room for this activity. If you want them to work in groups, consider having each group write down or draw their answers on big sheets of paper instead of their student books.

Or consider bringing out some magazines or advertisements (preview them first) to identify or make a collage of different things people trust in or rely on in difficult times. If you break up into groups to do this, make sure that you are walking around and paying attention to their writing or collage-making so they stay on task. Give them five minutes to do this before returning together.

CONNECTIONS

WHAT ARE YOU WORSHIPING?

A god can be defined as anything that people trust in or rely on to help them in times of need. Brainstorm all the different things people trust in or rely on in difficult times; then note them or sketch them in and around the figure below.

Now try to categorize these things people worship as gods. Which ones are similar? Try to come up with two or three categories, or types, of false gods we rely on in times of need.

You see, we're not really different from the ancient Israelites. They worshiped idols and false gods like Baal and Molech. To them, these represented things that would help them in life, like money or power. Satan, the father of lies, was behind all of it then, and he's still behind all of it today.

TIMELESS TRUTH CONNECTION

God has a plan for me as His human creature. In the narratives about the Northern Kingdom of Israel, we see that God's people and the kings who ruled them worshiped false gods. God had a plan that they worship Him alone, but they did not listen. They did not follow God's plan, or will, for how they should live and whom they should worship. God's plan for us human creatures is that we worship and serve Him alone.

CHRIST CONNECTION

The amazing thing through all of this narrative is that though God's people continually turned their backs on Him, worshiped idols, and did terrible things in the name of their false gods, the Father was patient with them. In the end, there was justice and the people were conquered. Yet God did not give up on His people even when they were unfaithful to Him.

God was faithful to His promise to send the Savior even when God's people were unfaithful. Jesus is faithful to forgive our sins even though we are often unfaithful to Him.

64

CHECKS FOR UNDERSTANDING

Before your learners leave, consider ways you can give them feedback for next week.

- **Summary:** Pass out note cards and have each learner write a two- or three-sentence summary of God's narrative of salvation in this lesson. Have them leave this summary with you so you can review it for next time and see what they learned.
- **Learning Log:** Have your learners write down why the Northern Kingdom of Israel was conquered and went into exile. Then have them reflect on the question "What is God's plan for us as His human creatures?" and see what answer they give.

The Divided Kingdom in the South

Timeless Truth

God invites me, His redeemed child, to daily receive His gifts and commend my life to His care.

Lesson Focus

The learner will be able to identify some of the faithful kings in Judah and how God was faithful to His people in their weaknesses even when they weren't faithful to Him.

This icebreaker is also a quick review, but don't dwell too long on it. Instead, use it as an early check for understanding or formative assessment. Pay attention to what your learners are saying to one another to see what you may need to review moving forward.

16 The Divided Kingdom in the South

Consider This

Chaotic Kings, Faithful God

In one sentence, summarize everything you've learned about the time of the kings up to this point over the last three lessons. Go!

Talk to a partner about what you wrote. What do you have in common? What do you have that's different? Why is that?

There's a lot to this section of Scripture about the divided kingdom, but it's important to know in order to understand God's great plan of salvation. Though there's a lot to think about in this lesson, know that through it all God was faithful to His promises.

The Big Picture

After the death of Solomon, God's people in the Promised Land experience a split. Though the Northern Kingdom of Israel has more power and people, the Southern Kingdom of Judah has the royal city of Jerusalem, the temple, and the kings of the line of the Messiah. It would be through David's heir, from the Southern Kingdom of Judah, that the Savior of the world would one day be born. Just because the south has the kingly line does not mean that the kings or the people always serve the Lord. In fact, many of the kings of Judah worship false gods and idols, just like their neighbors in the north. Yet there are kings of the Southern Kingdom who do trust in the one true God and who work to bring repentance to God's people. Kings like Asa, Jehoshaphat, Joash, Hezekiah, and Josiah trust in the Lord, and God delivers them from their enemies, even when the Northern Kingdom of Israel is defeated and destroyed. Yet, eventually, God's people in Judah are also defeated, but this time by the Babylonian empire. There are consequences for their ongoing sin of unfaithfulness. In the midst of this, even after defeat and exile, God is still at work to preserve a faithful group of His people from Judah, most notably the royal line of David, the ancestors of Jesus.

This section is recorded in the books of **1 Kings**, **2 Kings**, and **2 Chronicles**. The narrative occurred between roughly 931–587 BC.

I can identify some of the faithful kings in Judah and how God was faithful to His people in their weaknesses even when they weren't faithful to Him.

God invites me, His redeemed child, to daily receive His gifts and commend my life to His care.

Unit 4: The Kings 65

Read the summary (or have a volunteer read it), and ask your learners to compare what happened in the South to what happened in the North (in the previous lesson). Perhaps even, after first glance, have them identify broad similarities and differences between the two nations of God's people and consider how that plays out in the rest of the lesson.

Option: If you have a developing timeline on a wall in your space, consider adding the lesson number and name, dates, and books of the Bible to your timeline at this time.

Help students follow along as you read by using a bookmark or piece of paper to cover up the rest of the narrative and move down line by line.

It may be useful here to flip back to the last lesson and compare the look of that page to this lesson. Notice that the last lesson followed the northern "branch." These kings ruled during the same time period, just in the southern "branch," and often the two kingdoms interacted.

Option: As you read through the names of the different kings out loud on the timeline, challenge your learners to flip through 1 and 2 Kings to find as many names of the kings of Judah as they can in the headings of their Bibles. Note that the names of the kings of Judah are interspersed with the names of the kings of Israel. Their narratives sometimes weave together, as they were all happening around the same time.

The narrative of King Hezekiah and the Assyrian invasion is pretty epic. After wiping out Israel, Assyria not only threatened to destroy Jerusalem but also claimed that the true God was not powerful enough to stop them. God responded by sending a message to Hezekiah and by defeating the Assyrians with His almighty power. An angel slew the invading army and the rest went back home.

Digging Deeper

Northern Kingdom

In the last lesson, we looked at the Northern Kingdom, called Israel, that was led by Jeroboam. The kings after him followed Jeroboam in worshiping false gods and idols and turning away from the one true God. Eventually they were destroyed by the Assyrians.

Isaiah

This lesson, we look to the kingdom to the south, called Judah. These kings were not all faithful, but they had one thing in common: they were of the messianic line.

One of the greatest prophets during this time was Isaiah, who famously served during the reign of King Hezekiah (find him on the timeline). Isaiah wrote a book of prophecy, and it is filled with prophecies about this future king who would come from the line. Read **Isaiah 9:2–7**. Pick out the different words that describe this promised king and write them down in the border surrounding this page.

Hezekiah

After the Assyrian invaders crushed Israel in the north, they headed down to also invade and conquer Judah in the south. Hezekiah, a faithful man of God, was king in Jerusalem at the time, and the city was completely surrounded by at least 185,000 Assyrian soldiers. Read or listen to **2 Kings 18:28–39**. Summarize in five words what the Rabshakeh (messenger from Assyria) says to Hezekiah.

Read **2 Kings 19:6–19**. How does God respond to the threats of Assyria?

In five words, summarize how Hezekiah responds.

Read **2 Kings 19:35–36**. What is one thing that sticks out to you about how God ended up defeating the Assyrians? Why is that?

Samaria

Read **2 Kings 18:9–12**. What happened to Samaria (the capital city of the Northern Kingdom) during the reign of Hezekiah? How do you think the people in Judah felt when this happened?

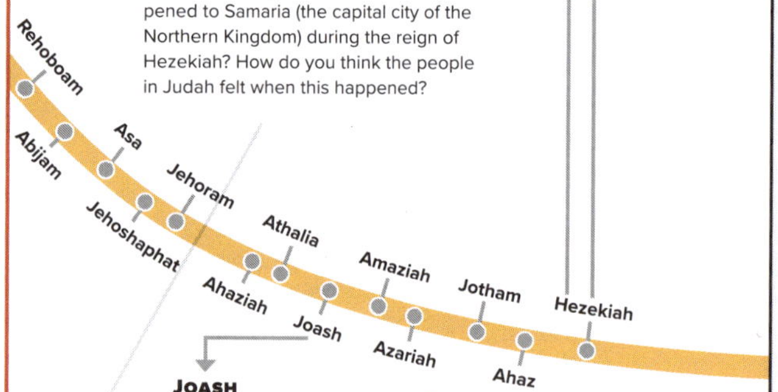

Joash

Good king Joash was only seven years old when he became king. As a baby, he was almost killed by a wicked queen, but God spared his life and he grew up in the temple before taking the throne.

66

If students struggle to write in these small, undefined spaces, have them use a spiral notebook or other paper to write their answer or doodle about these lessons. The student book is for thinking and processing information, not for grading, so there is no need to worry about writing complete sentences or spelling perfectly.

The nations of Israel and Judah were right between the empires of Babylon and Egypt. God's people lived along a strategic roadway between Africa, Asia, and Europe, so big nations valued having control over this area.

Did You Know?

During this period in the ancient world, large empires with huge armies started fighting for control over the land. First, Assyria and Egypt fought for power.

Circle Jerusalem on the map. Where is it in relationship to Assyria and Egypt?

When Assyria had been the big power for a couple of centuries, Babylon rose up and conquered Assyria and Judah. Circle Babylon (the capital of Babylonia) on the map.

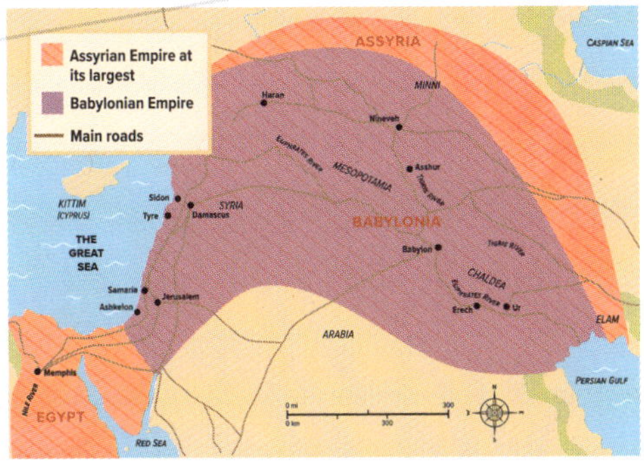

Think About It . . .

What do you think it would have felt like to be part of Israel or Judah when it was conquered? Why do you think that? How could this have challenged the people's faith in God?

Worship life in Judah was terrible by the time of Josiah. Possible descriptors include *wicked*, *sinful*, *wrong*, and *terrible*. Judah would have to suffer the consequences of their sins, but for Josiah's sake God staved off that destruction for a generation.

Josiah

Josiah was the last good king of Judah. Jeremiah (the man who wrote the books of Jeremiah and Lamentations) was Josiah's prophet. Read **2 Kings 22:1–13**. What one word, in your mind, summarizes what Judah's worship life was like when Josiah took over as king?

Josiah then went to inquire of the Lord what should be done. God responded through a prophetess. Read **2 Kings 22:16–20**. How did God respond to Josiah's repentance?

The Babylonians

In the end, God's people once again turned from Him and had to suffer the consequences. The Babylonians invaded and conquered Judah. Read **2 Kings 24:18–25:11**. Compare this to what happened to Israel 150 years before. How are they similar and different?

Similar	*Different*

Manasseh — Amon — Josiah — Jehoahaz — Jehoiakim — Jehoiachin — Zedekiah

Israel and Judah were both conquered by foreign empires as a direct result of their turning away from God. But they were conquered by different empires at different times, and we see God still working His plan of salvation through Judah, even after they are conquered and sent into exile.

Manasseh

Manasseh was described as the most wicked king ever in Judah. He turned from God and sacrificed his son to idols. Yet God does something incredible for him. Read **2 Chronicles 33:1–17**. What happened to Manasseh? Discuss with a partner.

67

In this almost footnote of a narrative, we witness one of the most incredible turnarounds in the Bible. We cannot overstate the wickedness of Manasseh, yet God was able to turn his heart to repentance and faith as he was held captive to the Assyrians. God does all the work in bringing us to faith and salvation. Also note that even though Assyria was defeated at the time of Hezekiah (Manasseh's father), the trouble of the foreign empires did not go away. Assyria, Egypt, and Babylon were constantly battling, bullying, and troubling God's people throughout the period of the kings.

This "Connections" page is more guided than many others because this lesson covers some serious themes. On one hand, God makes it clear that His people must face the consequences of their actions and, in so doing, suffer greatly. On the other hand, God makes it clear that He is faithful to them in preserving a remnant and promising the Messiah. We often focus on knowing where the line is between acceptable and unacceptable, forgetting the big picture of how God's Law and Gospel work to show our sin and show our Savior. Though scripted, this activity is meant to get the learners back to the basics of God's great plan of salvation.

CONNECTIONS

FINDING GOD IN THE BROKENNESS

Think about something that happened in your life. Something bad. You didn't know why God allowed it to happen, and you wondered where He was in all of this. It can be hard to remember these things. Draw or write about this bad thing in the mirror below.

TIMELESS TRUTH CONNECTION

God invites me, His redeemed child, to daily receive His gifts and commend my life to His care. The people in Judah had some faithful kings but also many unfaithful kings. The people, overall, turned from God to worship false gods. Though God had promised to be with His people, He allowed bad things to happen to them. We experience this too. Sometimes it's because we sin, sometimes it's just because others sin and the world is broken. Sometimes we know why, sometimes we won't know why.

In your mirror image above, draw cracks over the images or words, like the whole mirror is cracked.

CHRIST CONNECTION

Though many bad things happened, God had not let go of His promise. He was still with His people.

As the line of Judah was now conquered and many were led into exile, God did not abandon them. He was still going to fulfill His promise to send a Savior. When we go through tough times, God does not abandon us. He has sent the Savior, Jesus, who forgives us, gives us new life, and is with us no matter what happens.

Draw a cross over your drawing on the mirror image above. Because we are God's people, Jesus is with us and is faithful to us even when terrible things happen. As His people, we go through every struggle in prayer, receiving His gifts and commending our lives to His care.

68

CHECKS FOR UNDERSTANDING

Before your learners leave, consider ways you can give them feedback for next week.

- **Paired Discussion:** Have learners turn to a partner and share one thing they didn't know before this lesson. Listen in on several conversations.
- **Connection Activity:** Watch your learners as they complete the "Timeless Truth Connection" activity. Try to look at how they complete the activity, and encourage each learner to write down (or dictate to you or a helper) a prayer on a note card and leave that with you. It's personal, but if you pay attention you should be able to get a feel for what they understand.

The Place of the Prophets

Timeless Truth

God's Word is living and active in my life.

Lesson Focus

The learner will be able to explore the Books of the Prophets in the Old Testament and explain the role they played in God's salvation story during the time of the kings.

This lesson may seem a little overwhelming at first—your learners will be presented with a lot of options. Make sure to keep this icebreaker short. The most important thing is to help your learners understand that prophets speak God's Word. Sometimes it's prophecy about the future, sometimes it's speaking to present circumstances. Try to drive this home in the opening.

17 The Place of the Prophets

Consider This

God's Mouthpiece

Think of the different kinds of instruments that use a mouthpiece or that you use your mouth to blow through to make sound. Get in groups to brainstorm your answers and write them down in the space below. After one minute, the group with the most original answers wins! Go!

This lesson is all about the prophets of God and the Books of the Prophets in the Old Testament. Prophets are like the mouthpieces of God. He speaks through them to pass on His living and active Word to the world and His people. What sorts of things do you think God says through the prophets? Share.

The Big Picture

During the time of the divided kingdom, God sends many prophets who speak His Word to the people and the kings of Israel and Judah. Usually, God gives two messages: to repent of sins and to receive forgiveness. Also throughout, the prophets give many glimpses and details of the future hope of the Messiah. Even throughout the destruction of Israel by the Assyrians, the destruction of Judah by the Babylonians, the time of God's people in exile, and their return to the Promised Land, God speaks His Word of comfort and promise through the major prophets of Isaiah, Jeremiah, Ezekiel, and Daniel, and the twelve minor prophets.

This section is contained in the books of **Isaiah**, **Jeremiah**, **Lamentations**, **Ezekiel**, **Daniel**, **Hosea**, **Joel**, **Amos**, **Obadiah**, **Jonah**, **Micah**, **Nahum**, **Habakkuk**, **Zephaniah**, **Haggai**, **Zechariah**, and **Malachi**. The narrative occurred between roughly 875–430 BC.

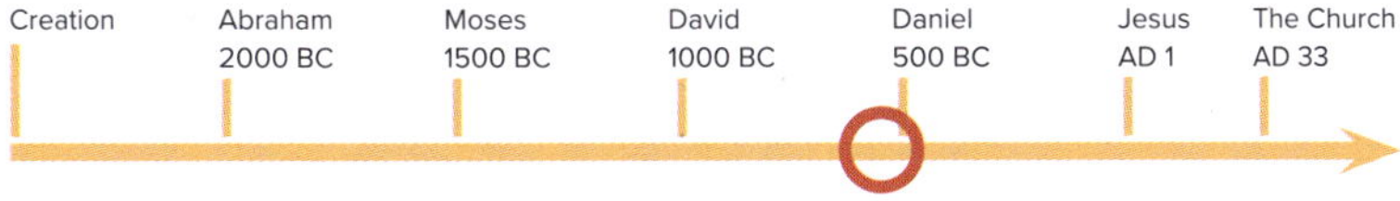

I can explore the Books of the Prophets in the Old Testament and explain the role they played in God's salvation story during the time of the kings.

Option: If you have a developing timeline on a wall in your space, add the lesson number and name, dates, and books of the Bible to your timeline at this time.

This page has a lot of information, so make sure to read the "Don't Panic" section out loud together to get started. Guide your learners to see the two different branches of the divided kingdom, and how some prophets spoke more to the kings in the north and some more to the kings in the south. Consider flipping back to previous lessons to review what happened in the north and in the south. Make sure to do all three questions here so your learners are engaged in the material.

Jonah knew that the Assyrians were a warlike people. He also knew that God wanted to bring these people to faith so He could save them too. Jonah ran away because he didn't want God to call them to faith. In the end, God did. This one book of the prophets helps illustrate a lot of what's going on in all these books. God is speaking His Word, which is able to accomplish what it says, into the nations of the world, calling them to repentance and to faith.

Digging Deeper

Don't Panic

There is a lot on these pages! This is because the Books of the Prophets take up about one-fifth of the entire Bible! (Find the section that begins with Isaiah and ends with Malachi in your Bible.) The prophets at the top of the page spoke more to the Northern Kingdom of Israel; those on the bottom spoke more to the Southern Kingdom of Judah.

Try doing these things to get a better idea of what these books are all about:

1. Look over the names of these books. On the next page ("Connections"), write down three thoughts that stick out to you about all of them.
2. Read over the Jonah section and answer the questions. This is a good example of what God called the prophets to do.
3. Pick two or more of the others. Look them up, read the key verses, and write your reflections on the "Connections" page.

NORTHERN KINGDOM

THE BIG SPLIT

SOUTHERN KINGDOM

Jonah (790 BC)

One of the first books of prophecy is the narrative of Jonah. It's short, but powerful. Its purpose is to help describe God's mercy toward the city of Nineveh, the capital city of Assyria. Remember, this was a warrior people bent on conquering the world! Read **Jonah 1:1–3**. Why do you think Jonah wouldn't do what God told him?

Jonah goes through many adventures, including a storm, being swallowed by a big fish, and being spit out before finally listening to God and going to Nineveh. Read **Jonah 3:1–10**. Summarize on your own or with a partner what happened.

Micah (750–686 BC)

Purpose: To call out false teachers and show God as the true shepherd of His people

Key Prophecy: **Micah 7:18–20**

Isaiah (740–681 BC)

Purpose: To comfort God's people with good news of God's plan to restore His people

Key Prophecy: **Isaiah 52:13–53:13** (looking to how Jesus would suffer and die to forgive our sins)

Joel (848–800 BC)

Purpose: To call God's people to repentance

Key Prophecy: **Joel 2:1–2, 12–13**

Nahum (663–612 BC)

Purpose: To remind God's people that God protects them

Key Prophecy: **Nahum 1:7–8, 15**

Habakkuk (605 BC)

Purpose: To show that God can even use bad things to accomplish His plan for His people

Key Prophecy: **Habakkuk 2:2–4**

70

If students are overwhelmed by all the print on these two pages, help them make a frame out of paper or index cards to show only the piece of content you are talking about.

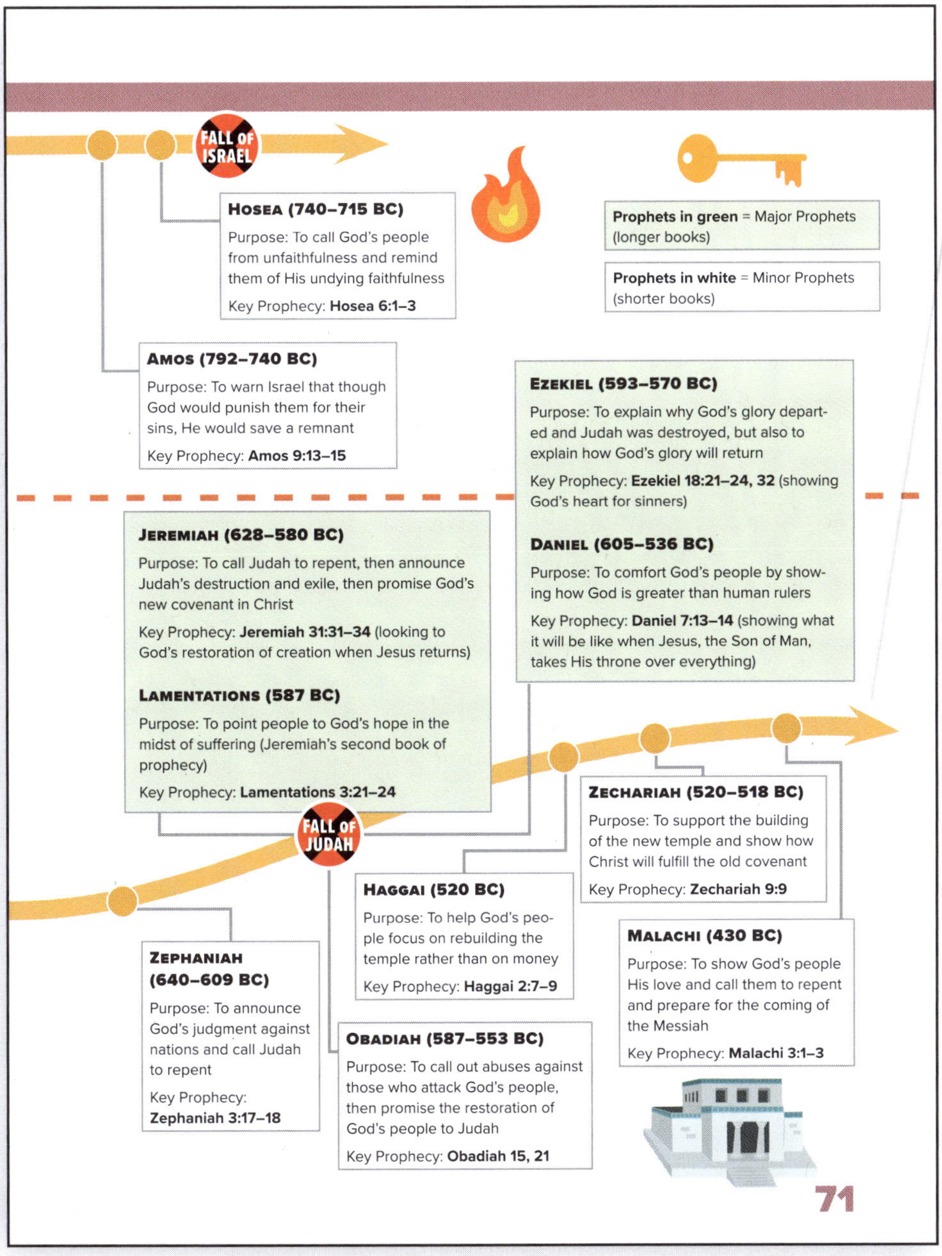

Options: Use one of these techniques to bring the timeline to life.

- Small Groups: Divide your class into small groups or pairs and give each group a set number of verses to look at and read. At the end of a set amount of time, each group will summarize their verses for the rest of the class.
- Timeline: Assign different books to different learners, and then give them note cards. The learners have to identify, read, and copy down the prophecies on their note cards. Place these prophecies on your timeline (if you have one in your space) or on a wall in your space. When all is done, have your learners work together to find similarities between the prophecies.
- Word Wall: Have your learners each pick a different book and read the key verses. Then they each pick one word or phrase that describes who God is and what God does in the prophecy and write it on the board or a large sheet of paper. Talk together about why they chose those words.

If you have younger students or students for whom this is too much to cognitively process independently, focus on the Jonah story and talk briefly about who all these names are.

Another option is to give your students these prophets prior to class and ask families to help students prep for the discussion at home.

Even if you used an alternative technique for the previous page, still have your learners write down their three things that stick out to them about these books and why. Have them share with a partner or small group. Listen in to hear what they've learned.

If you're short on time, skip this question.

Jesus Himself has had the final word on who God is and what He does for us. He sends the Holy Spirit, who works through God's Word to create and sustain faith in us. This living and active Word is received as we hear and read the Scriptures, and also as we receive and remember the Sacraments of Baptism and the Lord's Supper. God is not distant; He is as near to us now as He was at the time of the prophets.

Connections

Learning from the Prophets

On the previous page you were asked to read over the time of the Books of the Prophets and make some observations and reflections. Use the chart below to help.

What are three things that stick out to you about the Books of the Prophets? Why is that?	Which books did you look up and read the key prophecies? What did you learn about how God works in those prophecies?

Timeless Truth Connection

God's Word is living and active in my life. God's Word was living and active in the lives of His people during the difficult times of the kings. Think about it. What sorts of awful things did God's people have to live through during the time when God sent the prophets? Brainstorm with a partner.

Christ Connection

Yet through all of this, God was still speaking to His people. Often He told them to repent of their sins and be forgiven. Often what He said wasn't well received. But throughout it all, especially through these prophets, God's Word pointed to their ultimate hope.

Through the prophets, God promised His people a hope and a future. In Jesus, God has not only fulfilled His promises to send the Savior, but He has promised us a glorious hope and a future with Him forever in the new creation. This comes as God's gift to us in Christ.

Think About It . . .

*How does God still continue to speak to you? (Read **Hebrews 1:1**.)*

72

Checks for Understanding

Before your learners leave, consider ways you can give them feedback for next week.

- **Learning Log:** Have your learners write a few new things they've learned about the place of the prophets in their Learning Logs.
- **Personalized Prophecy:** Encourage each learner to pick one of the prophecies they read in the lesson today, write it down on a note card, and write why it matters to them. Watch as they do this to see whether they understand the meaning of the prophecy. Then encourage learners to stick them in their backpacks for the rest of the week, reading them a few times in their daily lives for encouragement in God's faithfulness to His people.

THE EXILE

TIMELESS TRUTH

God has a plan for me as His human creature.

LESSON FOCUS

The learner will be able to explain how God's people trusted in His promises during their time of exile, and how He is faithful to His promises to us today in Jesus.

18 THE EXILE

CONSIDER THIS

INVADED!

Just imagine . . . one day your hometown is invaded by an army. Many of your friends are either taken away or missing. You are separated from your family, put in handcuffs, and shoved into a van filled with other handcuffed people. After days of driving, you are unloaded into a town hundreds of miles away. You are given a new name and a new place to live, and you're told that you must now follow the rules of this new country. Hardest of all, you're told that you must now worship the new country's false gods, and if you don't worship those gods, you'll be put to death. What big questions would you have for God?

For this opening question, first have learners write down a question on their own. Then have each learner either share with the whole group out loud or write the question on a note card and put it up on the wall or the board. Once all the questions are up, compare the questions to find common themes. Keep one or more questions up for the duration of the class, seeing how God answers these questions for the people in exile.

This is a lot like the situation for God's people at the time of the exile into Babylon. Let's take a look at the timeline to see what happened to them, how the people responded, and how God responded to them.

The Big Picture

After Judah's continued sin, they must suffer the consequences. The great ancient empire of Babylon not only comes in and conquers the city of Jerusalem but also takes many of God's people hundreds of miles away to live with them throughout their empire. This small group, or remnant, includes some of the brightest young people of Judah, who are raised in Babylon to serve the king there. Among these are the young men Daniel, Shadrach, Meshach, and Abednego. While living far away from home, their faith is challenged time and time again. Yet they refuse to worship false gods in Babylon, and God miraculously rescues them. At the same time, God uses the great prophets Jeremiah and Ezekiel, among others, to speak words of repentance and the promise of restoration for His people during these seventy (and sometimes more) years in exile.

This section covers the books of **Daniel**, **Jeremiah**, **Lamentations**, and **Ezekiel**. The narrative occurred between roughly 605–538 BC.

Read the text and, if you have time, have your learners underline or highlight words or names that they remember from previous lessons. Have them identify those names in those previous lessons to see how the different narratives often overlap.

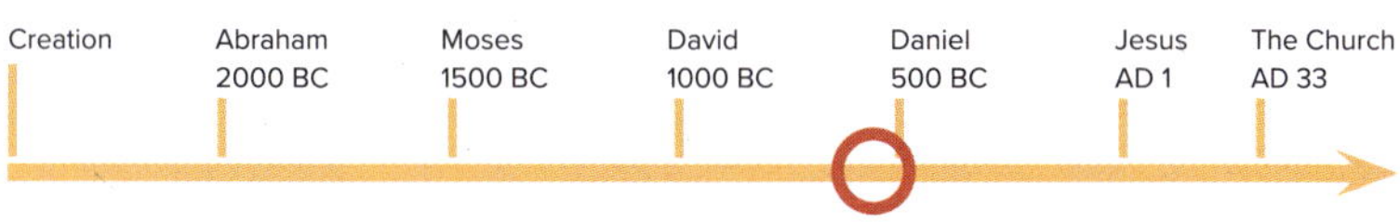

I can explain how God's people trusted in His promises during their time of exile and how He is faithful to His promises to us today in Jesus.

Option: If you have a developing timeline on a wall in your space, add the lesson number and name, dates, and books of the Bible to your timeline at this time.

Option: Look up these maps online to help find exact distances traveled or images of ancient Babylon.

Digging Deeper

Far from Home

In the map to the side, circle Jerusalem. This is where many of God's people were living before the exile. Then circle the city of Babylon. This is where many of God's people were brought. Then use the scale at the bottom of the map and follow the arrow to estimate the distance they were taken.

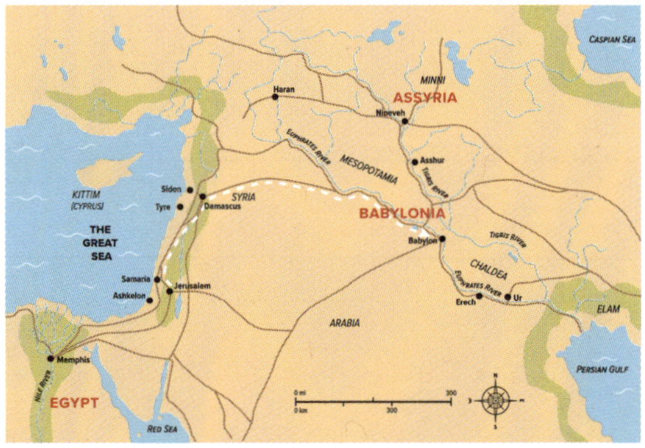

It was not uncommon in ancient empires for invaders to take capable young people and raise them to serve the empire. The young men here were no different. Their pressures, however, would be immense. They would be expected to abandon their old religion and culture and completely adopt the Babylonian culture. The world expects us to conform. As God's baptized, redeemed children, we are to find our identity and meaning in Christ.

God's Young Men

Read **Daniel 1:1–7**. Who were these young men? Why were they given such great treatment?

What sorts of pressures do you think these young men had to overcome?

Jeremiah

While some of God's people were in exile, others remained in Jerusalem. The prophet Jeremiah was one of them. (Write *Jeremiah* on the map next to Jerusalem.) God wrote a letter to His people, giving them instructions while they were in exile. Read **Jeremiah 29:1, 4–14**. What did God want them to do while in exile? (Pick three things.)

1.

2.

3.

What did God want them to remember while in exile? How is this really about Jesus?

Through Jeremiah, God comforts the people in exile, telling them to settle down and be productive, but to not forget His promises to them. His plan was to bring them back to Judea so that He could one day bring about the coming Messiah through them. We are to remember God's promises and faithfulness to us as we live out our lives among unbelievers, looking forward to the day when Christ will return.

Think About It . . .

What are other places in the Bible when God used dreams and gave His people the ability to interpret dreams? What do you think is the connection between these narratives?

Daniel

God gave one of these young men, Daniel, the ability to interpret the dreams that God sent to Nebuchadnezzar, the king of Babylon. What happened to Daniel and his friends after being appointed? Read **Daniel 2:46–49** for answers.

74

God most notably uses dreams to communicate during the time of the Patriarchs with Jacob, Joseph, and Pharaoh. For Joseph and Pharaoh, a connection is that these pagan foreign empires thought highly of dreams as ways their gods would communicate to them. The one true God used dreams to communicate His Word and His power over all things in these situations while God's people were in foreign lands.

Shadrach, Meshach, and Abednego

Daniel's friends, though given authority, found themselves in lots of trouble. Read **Daniel 3:1–12**. How big was the idol, and why do you think the punishment was so bad for not worshiping it?

But the three young men didn't worship the idol. Read what happened in **Daniel 3:16–30**.

Rephrase the young men's response to Nebuchadnezzar in five words below.

Is Nebuchadnezzar's response after the young men were saved surprising or not? Why?

Note: Many scholars throughout the centuries have thought that the fourth person in the fire might have been the Son of God, the Second Person of the Trinity. How does this add to the meaning of the narrative?

Daniel in the Pit of Lions

Like his friends, Daniel also got put into a difficult situation. The new king, now Persian, was tricked into making a decree that anyone who did not worship him would be thrown into a pit of lions. Daniel, still a trusted advisor of the king and worshiper of the true God, was thrown into the pit. The king, in distress over his friend, stayed up all night praying. In the morning, Daniel was found safe, as God had sent an angel to protect him. Read the king's response to Daniel's rescue in **Daniel 6:26–27**. How did God use Daniel's difficulty to witness who He is to the world?

How can God use our difficulties to witness who He is to the world?

Ezekiel

While Jeremiah was a prophet writing in Jerusalem, Ezekiel, another prophet, was brought into exile with Daniel. (Write *Ezekiel* next to Babylonia on the map.) Read one of God's messages to the exiles in **Ezekiel 36:24–28**. Discuss how many of these promises were fulfilled in the New Testament.

Daniel's Vision

God gave Daniel a mighty vision of the future, when the Son of Man (Jesus) will return and reign. Read **Daniel 7:13–14**. What's one detail that sticks out to you about this vision? Why is that?

75

The idol was massive (ninety feet tall). Not worshiping this idol was a sign of disobedience and treason against the king. The young men in exile were essentially slaves, so they really had little to no freedom to choose these things. Their response to their punishment is telling. They say God has the power to save but that even if He doesn't they won't bow. After they are saved, Nebuchadnezzar, for a brief period anyway, has a change of heart.

Assure your learners that we don't have to be happy when bad things happen to us. Most of the time, God doesn't tell us why (it's not for us to know), but He can use these things to help us witness His power to the world. We are to keep that in mind as we react to suffering in our lives.

The vision of the Son of Man is powerful and gives an impression of what Jesus will be like when He returns in glory. It may be useful to talk about how Jesus liked to talk about Himself as the Son of Man. When He does so, He is pointing everyone to how He is the figure in this passage.

You can point your learners to the images of Pentecost, where the Holy Spirit descends on many people. There God gathers people from all over the world and calls them to be His. The vision also points to the gift of Baptism, where God will wash away sins through the Sacrament. This vision from Ezekiel looks ahead to the future of the Church but also to the end of all things when Jesus returns to make all things new.

Some of this content is abstract and may be new for students. As necessary, focus on the basics and cut back on some of the details. By this time, you know your students and how much they can manage at a time.

Give your learners a few minutes to summarize these two questions in their own words. This serves as a check for understanding and a way to help them apply the big themes of the lesson to their own lives.

Again, this may be too abstract for some students to do independently. If needed, guide your students through these questions together.

Connections

Where Is God?

It's easy to ask ourselves, like God's people probably did in exile in Babylon, "Where is God in the midst of our pain and suffering?" When you look at the lesson for today though, you'll see that God was with His people the whole time! In each bubble, write down, in your own words, the answers to the questions from today's lesson (go ahead, you can look back).

Where was God when they were in exile?

How did God want them to live while in exile?

Timeless Truth Connection

God has a plan for me as His human creature. God's plan for us is that we love Him and serve our neighbor, even when things aren't going well for us, because that's what He designed us for.

Christ Connection

Though they had to live through terrible things and were in constant danger, Daniel, the young men, Jeremiah, Ezekiel, and the exiles all knew something. They remembered that they were God's people and nothing could separate them from God's promises. God's promises are still true today. God has created, redeemed, and called us to be His own.

In Christ, we know that we are God's people. As God's people, we can faithfully and joyfully love Him and serve our neighbor because we are His no matter what happens.

If your learners have their own Bibles, encourage them to underline or highlight Romans 8:38–39. If you have a little time, spread out to a different space for their prayer and reflection. Give them a few minutes of silence to pray. They may not have much understanding of or practice with the discipline of prayer, so this activity will help model it.

God's Word to Remember

Read **Romans 8:38–39**. This is God's promise to you! Write down or say a little prayer, thanking God for His mercy to you in Christ and how He called you to be His own, but also asking Him to give you strength to cling to the truth and follow His plan to love Him and serve your neighbor when bad things happen.

76

Checks for Understanding

Before your learners leave, consider ways you can give them feedback for next week.

- **Summary:** Pass out note cards and have each learner write a two- or three-sentence summary of God's narrative of salvation in this lesson. Have them leave this summary with you so you can review it for next time and see what they learned.
- **Big Questions:** Have learners, either on a piece of paper or in the Learning Log, write down in their own words (or tell you) how God was faithful to His people in exile and how He is faithful to us today in Jesus. Have them leave that paper with you before they leave.

The Return and the Intertestamental Period

Timeless Truth

God has created, redeemed, and called me to be His own.

Lesson Focus

The learner will be able to paraphrase the period between the return from exile and the birth of Christ and empathize with those who had to wait for the coming of the Messiah.

> This lesson has a little less content than others, so if you're used to rushing through the opening question, consider slowing down this time and taking another minute or two to build community through sharing.

19 The Return and the Intertestamental Period

Consider This

It's Hard to Wait!

Think of a time when you had to wait for something. What was the hardest thing about waiting for it? Why? Write down your answer in the space below.

In this lesson, we see God's people released from their exile and sent back home. Their waiting, in one sense, was over. In another, it was just beginning! Let's dig into this together.

> This is a sizable block of text. Read the text and, if you have time, have your learners underline or highlight one word or phrase that sticks out to them about this summary. Then they can share with a partner why it sticks out to them.

The Big Picture

After His people spend roughly seventy years in exile, God provides a new king, Cyrus the Persian, who sends many of the exiles back to the Promised Land. Under the watch of the governor Zerubbabel (who was part of the messianic line) and the priest Ezra, God's people rebuild the temple, though it was not as glorious as the one built by Solomon. But not all is well: the enemy neighbors scheme to halt their plans and destroy the people. Nehemiah, an advisor to the king of Persia, returns to Jerusalem not only to rebuild the surrounding wall and defend the city but also, along with Ezra, to help reestablish true worship of God among the people. At the same time, back in Persia, God raises up one of His people in exile, Esther, to be one of the queens of Persia. Through her faithfulness and courage, God stops a plot to kill all Jews in the Persian Empire. After all this, God stops speaking through the prophets, and we have no new books of the Bible for over four hundred years. During this time, however, much happens to God's people. They are conquered by Greek invaders, win their freedom for a time, and then are conquered once more by Roman invaders. It seems as if God is far away from His people, who wait for the Messiah to come and fulfill God's promises. Yet just around the corner, God is preparing His people for the coming of the Christ.

This section is found in the books of **Ezra**, **Nehemiah**, **Esther**, **Zechariah**, and **Malachi**. The narratives from these books occurred between roughly 538–430 BC.

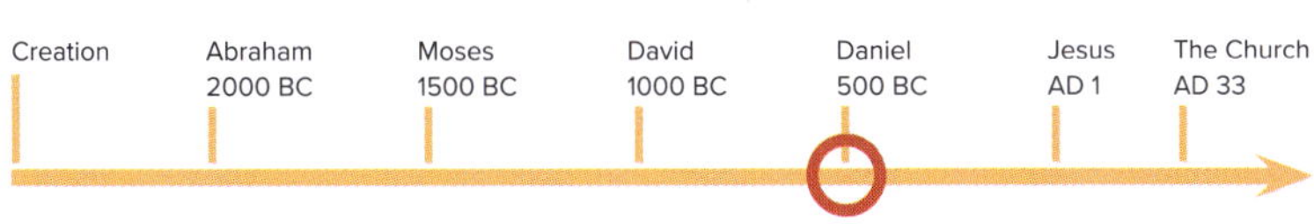

> **Option:** If you have a developing timeline on a wall in your space, add the lesson number and name, dates, and books of the Bible to your timeline at this time.

I can paraphrase the period between the exiles' return and the birth of Christ and empathize with those who had to wait for the coming of the Messiah.

The second temple, even though it had all the essential components of the first, was smaller and less spectacular. It reflected the reality that, though God's people were back from exile, things just weren't the same as they were when David and Solomon were kings.

God worked through the Persian king to provide not only freedom from their exile but also resources and a new temple in Jerusalem. When the temple was complete, there was both shouts of joy and weeping, indicating happiness that the temple was rebuilt but sadness that it wasn't as nice as the old temple. Also, you may note that the glory of the Lord didn't appear as it had with Solomon. God was with His people, but things were just not the same. They would have to wait for Jesus for the glory to return to the temple.

Nehemiah was brave and bold, and this little narrative is rich with details about how they defended themselves and rebuilt the wall. Today in the Church we both build one another up through God's Word and defend one another from the lies of Satan with God's Word.

Digging Deeper

Zerubbabel's Temple

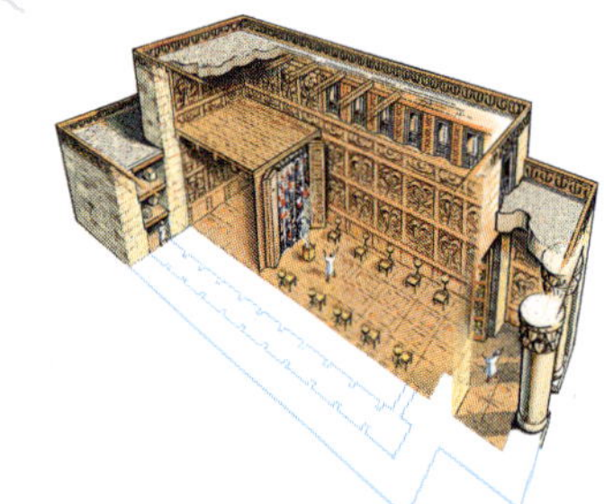

Illustration © Hugh Claycombe, used by permission.

The New (Second) Temple

Take a look at this drawing of what the new temple probably looked like. Compare it with the image of Solomon's temple on page 59. How are they similar and different?

Why do you think that is?

The Proclamation of Cyrus

If you remember from the last lesson, the tribes of Judah were led into exile by the Babylonians. During their time in exile, the Babylonian empire was conquered by the Persian empire. Under new leadership, something happened. Read **Ezra 1:1–5**. From the text, find all the ways God was working through the Persian king.

While the new temple was built (see the picture above), what happened? Read **Ezra 3:10–14**. Why do you suppose the people responded the way they did?

Nehemiah

Though the temple was eventually rebuilt, the enemy nations hated God's people returning. So Nehemiah, an exile and cupbearer to the king of Persia, got permission from the king to go to Jerusalem and rebuild their walls. Read **Nehemiah 4:14–23**. What is one thing that sticks out to you from this section?

Discuss how this is like the church today.

Esther

Around this time, back in Persia, God was doing something amazing. Esther, a young Jewish woman, was chosen to be one of the queens of the Persian king. This happened at the exact time a man in the Persian court was working to kill all the Jews in the empire. God used her to keep this from happening. Find the Book of Esther in your Bible, and read about their celebration in **Esther 8:16–18**.

Did You Know?

Around this time, God's people started being known less as Hebrews or Israelites and more as Jews—same people, different title.

78

Option: The narrative of Esther is also rich and powerful, but there's not room in this lesson to explore it fully. Challenge your learners to open their Bibles to the Book of Esther and page through it, looking for some details after reading the summary in the lesson. Have each learner share one detail that he or she notices while doing a quick overview of the Book of Esther.

NEHEMIAH'S PRAYER

After the walls of Jerusalem were totally rebuilt, Nehemiah (the leader) and Ezra (the high priest) held a big celebration. During this celebration, Nehemiah said a long prayer. In this prayer, he retold the entire narrative of the Old Testament.

Have someone (maybe your leader) read the entire section of this prayer, **Nehemiah 9:2–38**, out loud. (Or listen using a Bible app.) While this person reads, flip back through this workbook and try to follow along with the narrative timeline. If you have time, when you're done listening, try to identify which verses from Nehemiah's prayer summarize the narrative from each unit of this workbook.

UNIT 2

UNIT 3

UNIT 4

Discuss what is at the heart of Nehemiah's prayer. Why do you think this?

CONGRATS, YOU'VE MADE IT TO THE END!

The last book of the Old Testament is the last prophecy that God sent before John the Baptist came more than four hundred years later. It comes through the prophet Malachi. Read **Malachi 4:2–6**. Why do you think the Old Testament ends this way?

What do you think the "day of the LORD" is? What do you think it means that Elijah will come before the "day of the LORD" comes?

THE INTERTESTAMENTAL PERIOD, OR THE TIME BETWEEN THE OLD AND NEW TESTAMENTS (AKA GOD'S PEOPLE CAN'T SEEM TO CATCH A BREAK)

With a partner, brainstorm everything you know about ancient Greece or ancient Rome. You have thirty seconds. Go!

Ever wonder what happened after the end of the Old Testament? After the last prophet, Malachi, we have no more books of the Bible until the apostles give us the books of the New Testament, centuries later. This doesn't mean, however, that nothing happens to God's people! Lots happens in the ancient world. Great big ancient empires take turns fighting over who would rule the ancient world. And guess who was right in the middle of everything? God's people in Jerusalem. They got traded between different empires. Some left them more alone than others (like the Persians), some caused real problems (like the Greek ruler Antiochus IV Epiphanes). Below is a really simple timeline of events.

Persia (538–333 BC)	Greeks under Alexander the Great (332–323 BC)	Greeks under warring factions who fought over Judea (323–167 BC)	Period of independence when God's people fought off invaders (167–63 BC)	The Romans, the greatest empire of the ancient world (63 BC to the time of Jesus)

Discuss what it might have felt like to be one of God's people after so many invasions and being so mistreated by invading armies throughout so many centuries.

79

This is a very long passage, but it's a great summary of the entire narrative. Encourage your learners to stand while they listen. Unit 2 covers verses 6–8, unit 3 covers roughly verses 9–25, and unit 4 covers roughly verses 26–38. Nehemiah's prayer is a prayer of confession and thanksgiving, ultimately asking for God to continue to fulfill His promises to His people. Break up these long readings into smaller sections as you read, summarizing as you go.

The Old Testament ends with a warning and a promise. The prophet like Elijah would be John the Baptist, and the day of the Lord is ultimately the day of God's judgment. Jesus comes to offer forgiveness of sins so that, in Him, we can be free from God's eternal judgment. This anticipates that John the Baptist would precede Jesus, who is the final judge of the living and the dead.

There is a lot here, but this simple summary should give a general idea of the state of God's people in the Time between the Testaments. When Jesus started His ministry, God's people were tired of being occupied and were looking for a leader who would give them independence.

This activity allows students to demonstrate their understanding of the flow of the narrative of the Old Testament. If you want to expand the experience, after each learner makes his or her own timeline, divide your learners into groups and have each group make a big timeline on a large piece of paper and see what they have in common.

CONNECTIONS

IT WAS GOD'S PLAN ALL ALONG!

The time of the Old Testament—everything we've looked at so far—has been all about God's plan of salvation. From beginning to end, God has been working behind the scenes through His people and in the world to fulfill His promise to restore creation through the Messiah. You have just a couple of minutes, but in the space below, make a quick timeline of the big events of the Old Testament in order. Challenge yourself to write down as many as you can in just a few minutes. Go!

In the beginning . . .

TIMELESS TRUTH CONNECTION

So, yeah, it's hard, but it's a start! You've learned so much over these lessons. What's most important to remember is that the narrative of the Bible is about God's plan of salvation. It's all about Christ, and it involves you. **God has created, redeemed, and called you to be His own,** no more or no less than God's people in the Old Testament.

CHRIST CONNECTION

As we look to the New Testament in the next lesson, we look to how God finally, in His time, fulfills His promise to send the Savior of the world.

God's people in the Old Testament continually disobeyed God and worshiped false gods, yet the true God forgave them and promised to restore His creation one day. In Christ, God forgives us when we sin and promises to restore His creation for us.

THINK ABOUT IT . . .

How have you seen Jesus in the Old Testament?

80

Option: Instead of demonstrating this as a group, send this project as homework. This would not be busy work, but instead an end-of-the-Old-Testament project where each learner must creatively find a way to present a timeline of the narrative, hitting as many major events and people as possible from the Bible and the student book.

Checks for Understanding

Before your learners leave, consider ways you can give them feedback for next week.

- **Summary:** Pass out note cards and have each learner write a two- or three-sentence summary of God's narrative of salvation in this lesson. Have them leave this summary with you so you can review it for next time and see what they learned.
- **Timeline:** Use the above activity on the "Connections" page as a check for understanding, watching what your learners write down and what they miss so you can get a good idea of what they have learned about the overall narrative of salvation.

Unit 5: The Life of Christ

Essential Questions

Who is Jesus?

How did Jesus fulfill the Old Testament prophecies of the Messiah?

What was Jesus' purpose and mission?

What has Jesus done for me?

Focus Statements

20. The learner will be able to describe who Jesus is and will make connections between the Old Testament and the Gospels to show how He fulfilled the prophecies of the Messiah.
21. The learner will be able to express what the kingdom of God is and describe how Jesus is a different type of King.
22. The learner will be able to cite examples of how Jesus served others both physically and spiritually, pointing to His greatest act of service to humankind—His death and resurrection.
23. The learner will be able to give examples demonstrating that Jesus is both true God and true man and will explain why this truth is important for our salvation.
24. The learner will be able to describe the events of Jesus' Passion and connect them to the different messianic promises in the Old Testament.
25. The learner will be able to summarize the events of Jesus' crucifixion and express what that means for his or her life as God's redeemed child.
26. The learner will be able to paraphrase the events of the resurrection and connect Jesus' resurrection to his or her resurrection hope as God's redeemed child.

Assessment Options

1. **Preassessment Options**

   Before you begin, have each learner spend a few minutes writing down answers to these questions. Be careful that students don't get bogged down with these and take too much time away from instruction.

   - Why did Jesus come to this earth?
   - What did Jesus do during His ministry on earth?
   - Give a short summary of Jesus' death and resurrection.

   After they have written these down, either collect the answers to read and leave feedback or quickly go over them together as a class. You'll get a good idea of where each learner is coming from as you begin.

2. **Formative Assessment Options**

   Formative assessments are ways you can monitor student learning. Choose from the following:

   a. Checks for Understanding: These lessons cover a lot of information. Check how well your learners understand the content, using one of the Checks for Understanding at the end of each lesson.

   b. Weekly Summaries: Learners can write a two- or three-sentence summary of the events of the lesson. Get your learners in the habit of writing these summaries and reviewing them as you go through the different narratives.

   c. Learning Log: This is located at the back of the student book. Ask learners to write down one important thing or question from the lesson in their Learning Log. There is also a place for you to give feedback.

   d. Reflection Tools: These may include sermon notes, memory work, and self-reflections. As you move through the unit and your learners do these formative assessments, consider asking questions like these: How is memorizing Bible passages helping you? What connections are you making between sermons and the lessons as you take sermon notes? How is your understanding of the Bible and God's plan of salvation growing?

3. **Summative Assessment Options**

   Summative assessments evaluate student learning at the end of an instructional unit. Choose from the following assessment methods:

   a. Learning Portfolio: Have learners complete a variety of formative assessments over the course of this unit. At the end of the unit, learners will compile at least one of each type of formative assessment, along with any other work you have asked them to do. *Note:* At the beginning of the unit, make a list of samples you will collect so there are no surprises at the end.

   b. Written Responses: You can check for understanding by asking your learners to write short answers to several questions. This could be done inside or outside of class, and length of the answers can vary. However, this is not a good option for students who struggle academically. Remember, your goal is to identify what students have learned, not how well they can write, so allow modifications as needed. For example, some students could dictate answers to questions to an adult or into a recording device.

      You may write your own questions or use the following questions based on the unit:

      - Who is Jesus?
      - Give two examples of how Jesus fulfilled the Old Testament prophecies of the Messiah.
      - How does Jesus' suffering, death, and resurrection give you hope?

Teaching Tips

1. This unit covers a lot of ground. If you feel that you will not be able to cover all the material, choose beforehand which narratives you want to focus on in each lesson.
2. You may want to use additional visual supplements for these lessons. Look online or in Bible story books for visuals that match the narratives.
3. Because all of these units cover large sections of Scripture, there is a lot of reading and discussing. But your time together doesn't have to just be you talking and students listening. Allow your learners to move around your space, pair up with a partner to reflect, or work in small groups as you read and discuss. Your attitude will set the tone for the class. Show your interest and enthusiasm for God's Word. Encourage learners to ask questions and add to discussions. Be creative in your examination of the text together.
4. Keep in mind that your learners will vary in their knowledge and understanding of the Bible. You may be teaching this course to learners who have heard many of these Bible narratives before. Others may have a general idea of the narratives and message of the Bible. And for others, these Bible accounts may be completely new. You can help all learners feel more comfortable by asking for volunteers to read, marking Bible passages with a bookmark ahead of time, allowing students to use Bible apps to listen to Scripture passages, and grouping those who are familiar with the Bible with those who less familiar with it.

Color Key for Teacher Notes

Tan = Specific additional assessments

Blue = Extra activities or questions

Green = Educational tips and directions for specific activities

Gold = Explanations of theological concepts or background for the teacher

Jesus' Birth and Childhood

Timeless Truth

God has redeemed me to be His own.

Lesson Focus

The learner will be able to describe who Jesus is and will make connections between the Old Testament and the Gospels to show how He fulfilled the prophecies of the Messiah.

Based on your learners, choose whether to guide a whole group discussion or break into smaller groups for learners to talk about this question.

20 Jesus' Birth and Childhood

Consider This

Who Is Jesus?

The name of Jesus is one of the most recognizable names in all the world. But do people really know who Jesus is?

What have you heard people say about Jesus? Take a few minutes to talk about it.

Now write who *you* think Jesus is below.

God's people believed that He would send the Messiah. But many were looking for a political messiah, one who would establish an earthly kingdom. The Gospels show that Jesus was the fulfillment of the messianic prophecies. Jesus ushered in the heavenly kingdom of God. He would bring salvation not by earthly rule but by sacrificing Himself on the cross for the sins of the world.

The Big Picture

"When the fullness of time had come, God sent forth His Son . . ." (Galatians 4:4).

God's people have been waiting a long time for the promised Messiah—thousands of years, in fact. Finally, the time is right. God sends His only Son into the world to be born of a woman, to be born as one of us. Jesus Christ, the promised Offspring of King David, is born and raised not in a palace but in the humble towns of Bethlehem and Nazareth.

Jewish shepherds and Gentile Wise Men from the East come to worship the baby King. Faithful old believers Simeon and Anna thrill to see the infant face of the long-awaited Savior. The boy Jesus "grew and became strong, filled with wisdom. And the favor of God was upon Him" (Luke 2:40).

The four Gospels—**Matthew**, **Mark**, **Luke**, and **John**—all tell of the life of Jesus Christ. Jesus' birth and childhood is recorded only in the books of Matthew and Luke. The author of Matthew is the apostle Matthew (Levi), former tax collector turned disciple. The author of Mark is John Mark, cousin of Barnabas. Luke was a physician who was a contemporary of Paul (Luke also wrote Acts). John was written by the apostle John, the "disciple whom Jesus loved." The accounts in this lesson occurred around 2 BC–AD 14.

Creation | Abraham 2000 BC | Moses 1500 BC | David 1000 BC | Daniel 500 BC | Jesus AD 1 | The Church AD 33

I can describe who Jesus is, and I can make connections between the Old Testament and the Gospels to show how He fulfilled the prophecies of the Messiah.

Unit 5: The Life of Christ — God has redeemed me to be His own.

81

Make your way through the sections on these two pages together. You may read some sections, and volunteers may read other sections. Another option is to divide your group into pairs or trios and have each group work through one of the sections on these pages before presenting their section to the entire class.

Immediately at the beginning of his Gospel, John tells his readers who Jesus Christ is: God from eternity, fully God, but distinguished from the Father, come to bring life to the world.

Verse 14 tells us that the Word became flesh. The Son of God took on human nature. So Christ is true God and true man.

Jesus was a descendant of King David, from whose family the Messiah was to come. Abraham was the father of the Israelites, through whom all nations were to be blessed. Jesus was that blessing.

Jesus' ancestry is filled with sinners. Note in particular Judah and Tamar; Rahab; and David and Bathsheba. They needed a Savior, just as we do. Of course, Joseph was not Jesus' biological father, but His stepfather. Mary, too, came from the line of David.

Digging Deeper

The Gospels

Matthew, Mark, Luke, and John each tell the account of the earthly life and ministry of Jesus Christ.

Matthew, an eyewitness to much of what he recorded, emphasized that Jesus was the Son of David, true King of Israel, who fulfilled the prophecies of the Old Testament.

Mark's is a Gospel of action. He most likely drew from Peter's testimony. Mark emphasized the deeds of Jesus and Jesus' powerful words to perform deeds.

Luke "carefully investigated everything from the beginning" (Luke 1:3 NIV). Luke's Gospel was written for the Church to be used for teaching. Luke told the account of Jesus from birth to death and resurrection.

John recorded details and many of Jesus' difficult sayings, and also recorded that Jesus performed many "signs"—miracles that demonstrate that Jesus is the Messiah.

The reason and purpose of all four Gospels is stated by John: "Now Jesus did many other signs in the presence of the disciples, which are not written in this book; but these are written so that you may believe that Jesus is the Christ, the Son of God, and that by believing you may have life in his name" (John 20:30–31).

The State of the World

The time was ripe for the coming of Christ. Alexander the Great had spread the Greek language throughout the Middle East. The Maccabees had rid the Judeans of pagan worship practices. The world was at rest under the stable rule of the Roman Empire (the kingdom of iron prophesied in Daniel 2:40) and would stay at rest for centuries. The prevalence of the Greek language would aid the spread of the Gospel, as would the well-kept Roman roads.

The Word Made Flesh

The Gospel of John introduced Jesus Christ as the Word.

Read or listen to **John 1:1–4**. What does this say about who Jesus is?

Now read **John 1:14**. What other information is given about who Jesus is?

The Genealogy of Jesus Christ

Matthew's Gospel begins with a genealogy, or family line, of Jesus that traces the promise through the generations.

Skim through **Matthew 1:1–16**. What do you notice?

Did You Know?

Rome was the fourth kingdom that the prophet Daniel had described (see Daniel 2). The fifth kingdom that Daniel had foretold (Daniel 2:44), the eternal kingdom, the kingdom of God, would be ushered in by Jesus Christ.

82

The Birth of Jesus

Matthew mentions Jesus' birth, but only Luke records the events of Jesus' birth.

Read or listen to **Luke 2:1–7**.

Joseph and Mary arrived for the Roman census in Bethlehem, the hometown of their ancestor King David, just in time for Mary to give birth.

Read **Micah 5:2** and **2 Samuel 7:12–13**.

How were these Old Testament verses fulfilled?

Bethlehem was full of travelers! There was no room in the inn, so Mary gave birth to Jesus in a place where animals were kept and laid Him in a manger.

Read or listen to **Luke 2:8–14**.

Who were the first ones to hear about the birth of the promised Messiah? Shepherds, out in the fields, keeping watch over their sheep! What was the angel's message to them?

Read or listen to **Luke 2:15–20**.

Talk about the shepherds' response and Mary's response. What is our response to the Good News of Jesus, our Savior?

The Visit of the Wise Men

Only Matthew records the visit of the Wise Men.

Read or listen to **Matthew 2:1–12**.

The Wise Men were Magi—not kings, but advisors to kings. They were Gentiles, not Jews.

They came from "the east," most likely from Babylon, Persia, or Arabia.

The Wise Men knew that a king of the Jews had been born, but the text doesn't say that they knew this was the Son of God.

The star led them to Judea, then right to where Jesus' family was living in Bethlehem.

Herod and the Jewish leaders had no idea that the Messiah had been born.

The Wise Men presented Jesus with gifts of gold and frankincense and myrrh. They were the first of many Gentiles to worship Jesus.

How does this event show God's love for all people of the world?

The Presentation of Jesus

When Jesus was forty days old, Joseph and Mary took Him to Jerusalem to be presented to the Lord in accordance with Mosaic Law. An old man named Simeon, who was waiting for the Messiah, was there. The Holy Spirit had revealed to him that he would see the Christ before he died. Simeon took Jesus in his arms.

Read what Simeon said in **Luke 2:29–32**.

Jesus was the Messiah who would bring salvation to the world. He was the One of whom Isaiah prophesied. He would be "a light for the nations, that My salvation may reach to the end of the earth" (Isaiah 49:6).

The Boy Jesus in the Temple

The Gospels don't tell us much about the childhood of Jesus. But we do have one account (**Luke 2:39–52**). When Jesus was twelve, He went with Mary and Joseph and many families to Jerusalem to celebrate the Passover. On the way home, Mary and Joseph discovered Jesus wasn't among the families. They rushed back to Jerusalem, searching high and low until on the third day they found Him in the temple courts. He was sitting with a group of teachers, listening and asking questions. And they were amazed at His understanding. When Mary asked Him why He had treated them this way, He answered, "Why were you looking for Me? Did you not know that I must be in My Father's house?" (Luke 2:49).

What did Jesus mean by saying this to His mother, Mary? Talk about it.

83

It was well-known among the Jews that the Christ would come from Bethlehem. See **John 7:42**.

The message of the angel was "good news of great joy . . . for all the people" (Luke 2:10)—the Jews and the Gentiles (us).

What is the Good News? A Savior, Christ the Lord, is born—the promised Messiah had come!

The shepherds were given a "sign." The Savior would be wrapped in swaddling cloths and lying in a manger. This showed the fulfillment of another prophecy: **Isaiah 7:14**.

The shepherds rushed to Bethlehem to see Jesus. Then they told everyone the Good News.

Mary treasured all these things in her heart.

We hear the Good News and tell others about it, and we reflect on God's Word in our hearts. Both are genuine responses of faith.

Extra Discussion

Q. Was Jesus really born in a stable?

A. The only details we have from the Bible are that there was no room for Mary and Joseph in the inn and that Jesus was laid in a feeding trough for animals. Mangers are found where animals are fed, but we do not know if Jesus was born among animals.

Caves in the hills around Bethlehem were often used to house animals, and some historians say that animals were sometimes even kept in the same buildings where people lived. What is important is that Jesus was not born in a palace, but in a lowly place among the people He came to save.

Mary gently chided Jesus for not staying with them. His answer was a reminder to both Mary and Joseph that He was sent to the earth to do His Father's business—the salvation of the world. Mary and Joseph did not fully understand what He was saying.

Option: Divide into learners into three groups and have each group take one prophecy and fulfillment. Then have the groups share their thoughts.

Connections

Jesus Is the Promise Fulfilled

Jesus fulfilled all the Old Testament prophecies that were made concerning the promised Savior, the Messiah. Below are three of the many prophecies. Read the Old Testament prophecy on the left, then tell how Jesus fulfilled the prophecy on the right. Look up the Bible references to help you.

Micah 5:2

"But you, O Bethlehem Ephrathah, who are too little to be among the clans of Judah, from you shall come forth for Me one who is to be ruler in Israel, whose coming forth is from of old, from ancient days."

Matthew 2:1–6

Jesus was born in Bethlehem, the city of David.

Isaiah 7:14

"Therefore the Lord Himself will give you a sign. Behold, the virgin shall conceive and bear a son, and shall call His name Immanuel."

Matthew 1:20–23

Mary was a virgin—the angel told Joseph that the child in her, Jesus, was conceived by the Holy Spirit.

Genesis 12:2–3

"And I will make of you [Abraham] a great nation, and I will bless you and make your name great, so that you will be a blessing . . . In you all the families of the earth shall be blessed."

Matthew 1:1

Jesus was the Offspring of Abraham. In Jesus all nations would be blessed.

Keep your eyes open for more prophecies fulfilled by Jesus in the coming lessons.

Timeless Truth Connection

God has redeemed me to be His own. From the time of Adam and Eve, God's people were waiting on the promise that God had made to send a Savior, one who would redeem them from sin, death, and the power of the devil. Jesus is that Redeemer. He came to this earth to make you His own.

But when the fullness of time had come, God sent forth His Son, born of woman, born under the law, to redeem those who were under the law, so that we might receive adoption as sons. (Galatians 4:4–5)

Christ Connection

Jesus is the promised Messiah, the one of whom all the Old Testament prophecies spoke. Jesus is God, and yet He humbled Himself to come down from heaven to become like one of us so that He could take the punishment for our sins and bring us back to God.

84

There is a lot of print on these pages. Keep an eye out for students who seem overwhelmed by it all. Their anxiety may show itself in noncompliant behaviors or self-distraction. Help students to cover the parts of the page that they aren't working on to reduce the stress from so much print.

Checks for Understanding

Before your learners leave, consider ways you can give them feedback for next week.

- **Summary:** Give your learners note cards. Ask them to write down (or tell you so you can write for them) the reason Jesus came down from heaven. Have them leave this summary with you so you can review it for next time and see what they learned.
- **Learning Log:** Have your learners write down (or tell you) one new thing they learned about Jesus, the promised Messiah. Read their responses during the week, and leave a short, encouraging note for them in their books.

Jesus' Early Ministry

Timeless Truth

God has redeemed me to be His own.

Lesson Focus

The learner will be able to express what the kingdom of God is and describe how Jesus is a different type of King.

Ask willing learners to share their lists. Most people, if they were king for a day, would choose ways to be served with the best of everything. Some learners might add things they would do for others. Point out that Jesus is a king who serves others instead of having others serve Him.

If your group is small, you could also do this as an entire group, brainstorming ideas together and putting them into one big list on the board.

21 Jesus' Early Ministry

Consider This

To Be a King

Have you ever thought about what it would be like to be a king? How would you rule? How would you act? What decrees would you make? Take a minute to think about it, then make a list of what you would do if you were king for a day.

Jesus is the long-awaited Messiah, the King of the Jews. Jesus began His ministry proclaiming, "The kingdom of God is at hand!" (Mark 1:15). Throughout His ministry, Jesus sought to teach the people that His kingdom was not of this world, but a heavenly kingdom.

The Big Picture

The Gospel of Mark introduces us to "the voice of one crying in the wilderness, 'Prepare the way of the Lord'" (1:3). The voice is John the Baptist, Jesus' cousin. John calls on people to repent and be baptized for the forgiveness of sins. Then Jesus comes to be baptized—not for forgiveness, but to fulfill all righteousness so that He can take our sins upon Himself. Jesus then goes immediately into the wilderness for forty days and nights and is tempted by the devil. He resists the devil's temptations with the Word of God. Jesus seeks out and calls twelve men to be His inner circle of disciples. He does His first miracle at a wedding in Cana, turning water into wine. The disciples see this sign and believe in Him. Nicodemus comes to Jesus at night, afraid of what the other Jewish leaders might say. Jesus teaches about water and the Spirit, being "born again," and the great love of God the Father for the whole world.

These accounts come from the four Gospels—**Matthew**, **Mark**, **Luke**, and **John**. The accounts in this lesson occurred around AD 30–31.

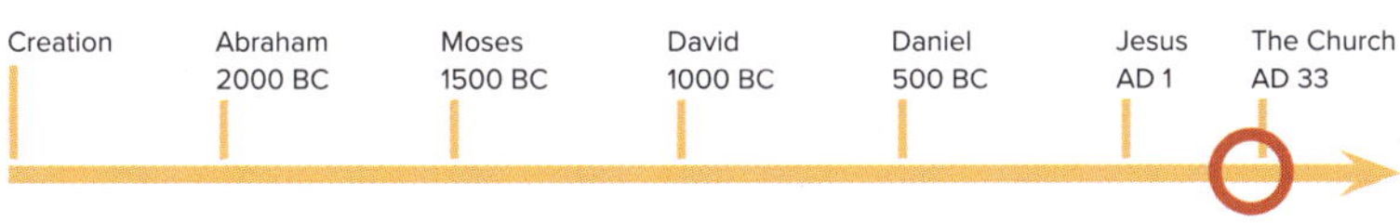

I can express what the kingdom of God is and describe how Jesus is a different type of King.

85

God has redeemed me to be His own.

Unit 5: The Life of Christ

John called for people to repent and be baptized, confessing their sins, to prepare them to receive their Savior. Our sin shows us our need for a Savior.

John told the people that the Messiah was coming!

Jesus would be baptized with the same Baptism as sinners to confirm His identity with sinners: Jesus is true man, but sinless. Jesus came to take on our sin and carry it to the cross. Jesus provides our righteousness.

"For our sake He made Him to be sin who knew no sin, so that in Him we might become the righteousness of God" (2 Corinthians 5:21).

After Jesus' Baptism, the Father spoke, declaring Jesus to be His beloved Son, and the Holy Spirit descended on Him.

These pages cover quite a bit of content. Consider dividing your class into smaller groups and assigning each group one of the boxes on the page to explore. After five to ten minutes, they will present their findings to the larger group.

Help students cover the sections of the page that they are not working on to reduce distraction.

Digging Deeper

John the Baptist

Mark's Gospel begins by proclaiming the fulfillment of the Old Testament prophecy of Isaiah 40:3: "Behold, I send My messenger before Your face, who will prepare Your way, the voice of one crying in the wilderness: 'Prepare the way of the Lord, make His paths straight'" (Mark 1:2–3).

John the Baptist was that messenger.

Read or listen to **Mark 1:4–8**.

What was John's message to the people?

What exciting news did he have to tell them?

(See also Matthew 3:1–12; Luke 3:1–17; John 1:19–28.)

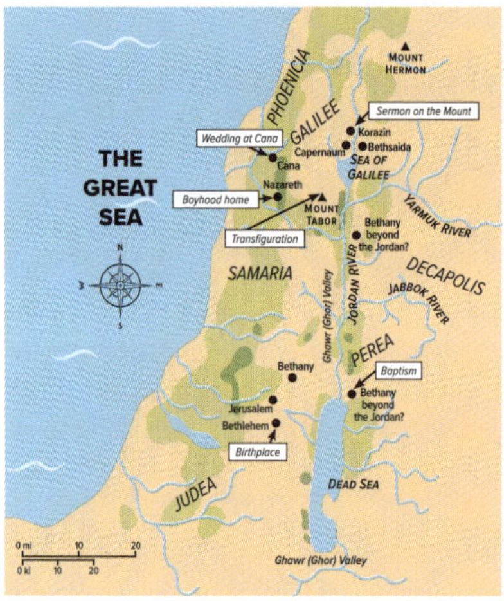

The Kingdom of God

Now after John was arrested, Jesus came into Galilee, proclaiming the gospel of God, and saying, "The time is fulfilled, and the kingdom of God is at hand; repent and believe in the gospel." (Mark 1:14–15)

Jesus ushered in the kingdom of God when He came to this earth. See more on the kingdom of God in the "Connections" section.

The Land of Jesus

Jesus spent most of His ministry in Galilee. Eleven of His twelve disciples were from this region. Jerusalem and the temple were in Judea, a region farther south. The territory between Galilee and Judea was Samaria.

Jesus' Baptism

Jesus' Baptism marked the beginning of His ministry and is recorded in all four Gospels.

John baptized many people for the forgiveness of sins. One day, he saw Jesus coming to be baptized. John knew Jesus was God's perfect Son, who had no need to have sin washed away.

Read or listen to **Matthew 3:13–17**.

What reason did Jesus give for being baptized?

What happened after the Baptism of Jesus?

(See also Mark 1:9–11; Luke 3:21–22; John 1:29–34.)

Jesus' Temptation

After Jesus was baptized, He spent forty days and nights in the wilderness. Afterward, He was tempted by the devil.

Read or listen to **Luke 4:1–13**.

How did Jesus respond to each of the temptations of the devil?

Why was Jesus tempted by Satan?

How does the fact that Jesus faced temptation and overcame the devil help us in times of temptation? See **Hebrews 4:14–16**.

(See also Matthew 4:1–11; Mark 1:12–13.)

86

Jesus used words from Scripture to reject the devil's temptations.

Adam and Eve gave in to Satan's temptation and disobeyed God. Their sin passed on to us. We all sin and deserve the punishment for sin: eternal death. Jesus did what we cannot do. He fulfilled the Law perfectly in our place.

Jesus was tempted, just as we are, but He did not sin. He knows the temptations and evil that we face in this world. When we are tempted, we can go to Him in confidence, knowing He will help us.

Jesus Calls the Twelve Disciples

After Jesus was baptized, He went to the region of Galilee. As He passed along the Sea of Galilee, He saw two sets of brothers who were fishermen.

Read or listen to **Mark 1:16–20**.

What did Jesus mean when He said, "Follow Me, and I will make you become fishers of men"?

Talk about the response of Peter, Andrew, James, and John. How does this surprise you or challenge you?

Read **Matthew 10:2–4** to find the names of the twelve disciples whom Jesus chose as His closest followers.

(See also Matthew 4:18–22; Mark 3:16–19; Luke 6:13–16.)

For God so loved the world, that He gave His only Son, that whoever believes in Him should not perish but have eternal life. (John 3:16)

Jesus Teaches Nicodemus

Nicodemus was a Pharisee and an important Jewish leader. He saw Jesus' signs and believed He was from God. He wanted to talk to Jesus, but he was afraid of the other Jewish leaders, so he came to Jesus at night. Nicodemus said to Jesus, "We know you are from God, because of the signs you do." Jesus answered, "Truly, truly, I say to you, unless one is born again he cannot see the kingdom of God." Nicodemus was confused! How can a person be born again?

Read or listen to **John 3:1–8** to hear what Jesus said.

What does it mean to be "born of water and the Spirit?"

How do we receive new life?
Read **John 3:16**.

Did You Know?

The word *disciple* is used in the Bible to describe all the people who followed Jesus and His teachings, including people in Acts who had never seen Jesus. In that sense, we are also disciples of Jesus. See **John 8:31–32**.

The Wedding at Cana

Jesus was attending a wedding in the town of Cana when His mother asked Him to help the wedding hosts, who had run out of wine. Jesus told the servants to fill six large jars with water, then draw some out to take to the master of the feast. The master proclaimed that this wine was far better than the first wine that was served.

Read or listen to **John 2:1–12**.

Who witnessed this, Jesus' first recorded miracle?

What happened as a result of this miracle?

Jewish Sects in Jesus' Time

Pharisees: Middle-class Jewish lay leaders. Accepted the whole Old Testament Scriptures, but added many man-made laws. Thought they could get to heaven by obeying the Law. Nicodemus was a Pharisee.

Sadducees: Ruling leaders; many were scribes and/or priests. Religious skeptics who denied the final judgment and resurrection. Accepted only the Pentateuch.

Zealots: More political than religious, they despised the Roman rule. One of Jesus' disciples was Simon the Zealot.

87

Jesus calls these men to leave their fishing profession and follow Him. They would share the Gospel and draw people into God's kingdom.

These men immediately left everything—their jobs, their boats and net, their father—and followed Jesus. They trusted Jesus.

"Jesus said to the Jews who had believed Him, 'If you abide in My word, you are truly My disciples, and you will know the truth, and the truth will set you free'" (John 8:31–32).

Mary, Jesus' disciples, and the servants were the only ones who witnessed Jesus' miracle. Jesus came for all—kings and servants alike. Like the shepherds at Jesus' birth, the servants see God's glory.

Jesus saved the wedding party from embarrassment. More important, this miracle "sign" showed Jesus' power and glory, and His disciples believed in Him.

Water and the Spirit point to Baptism. To be born of the flesh is our natural physical birth. We are born sinful. Our sinful nature has been passed down to us from the time of Adam and Eve. Through the Holy Spirit and water in Baptism, we are born again and receive the gift of forgiveness and new life in Christ.

John 3:16, the "Gospel in a nutshell," tells us that it is through the work of Jesus Christ that we are saved and have new life, eternal life, in Him.

Ask learners to share some differences with the rest of the group.

Point out that most people want to be served rather than to serve others. Jesus was a very different type of King. He came to serve others with His love.

Option: Look in *Luther's Small Catechism with Explanation* (2017 edition) at the explanation of Second Petition for more discussion on the kingdom of God.

These items are not meant to be read independently but shared together in your closing discussion. For students who are easily overwhelmed by a lot of print on a page, reassure them that they are not expected to read and know this information independently. On the other hand, for students who are strong readers and independent learners, they may enjoy looking ahead and reading this information on their own.

Connections

The Kingdom of God

Look back at the king-for-a-day list you made at the beginning of the lesson. Now look at some of the things that Jesus, our King, did when He came to this earth. What differences do you see?

Kingdom Facts

- The kingdom of God was promised in the Old Testament.
- It is different from any kingdom on earth.
- It describes the rule of God in the hearts of people through the Holy Spirit.
- Jesus often spoke of the kingdom of God (Matthew 4:17; 5:3; 6:33).
- The kingdom of God was the subject of many of Jesus' parables.
- The phases "kingdom of God" and "kingdom of heaven" appear almost a hundred times in the New Testament.
- It is identical to "the kingdom of heaven."
- We enter the kingdom of God through rebirth by water and the Spirit (John 3:3–5).
- The kingdom of God is received by believers in childlike trust (Mark 10:13–16) through the power of the Holy Spirit.
- Jesus ushered in the kingdom of God when He came to this earth.
- The kingdom of God will be complete when Jesus returns at His second coming.

Timeless Truth Connection

God has redeemed me to be His own. Jesus began His ministry on earth by proclaiming, "The kingdom of God is at hand!" Jesus ushered in that Kingdom when He came to earth. Jesus was the Servant-King on earth, healing and caring for His people. He was rejected as King, then willingly gave up His life to redeem His people. Jesus will come again to reign forever as King of all creation.

Christ Connection

Jesus is the King, the promised Messiah. He is the descendant of King David, but He is sinless. He obeyed His Father's will and overcame the temptations of the devil. He showed His power as He made water into wine, and He taught Nicodemus that it is through water and the Spirit that one enters the kingdom of God.

88

Checks for Understanding

Before your learners leave, consider ways you can give them feedback for next week.

- **Exit Ticket:** Have learners write down one question they still have after this lesson on a piece of paper and leave it with you. Read through questions during the week so you can address them the next time you meet.
- **Learning Log:** Have your learners write about the kingdom of God in their Learning Logs.

Jesus' Middle Ministry

Timeless Truth

God has redeemed me to be His own.

Lesson Focus

The learner will be able to cite examples of how Jesus served others both physically and spiritually, pointing to His greatest act of service to humankind—His death and resurrection.

> Have learners raise hands to show their choice or, if you want to get them active, stand on different sides of the room according to their choice.

22 Jesus' Middle Ministry

Consider This

Would You Rather?

Choose either A. or B.

A. Clean the bathroom? *OR* B. Vacuum the house?

A. Clean your brother's room? *OR* B. Help him with his homework?

A. Wash your sister's feet? *OR* B. Wipe her nose?

A. Babysit your little cousin? *OR* B. Change his diaper?

Did any of those options sound good to you? If we're being honest, most of us would rather be served than serve others. Not Jesus. He is the Servant who "came not to be served but to serve, and to give His life as a ransom for many" (Mark 10:45).

> Serving others doesn't come naturally to us—it is something we need to be taught. Often we will choose to serve based on what's easier or what's in it for us. However, we do sometimes serve out of our love for someone.
>
> Jesus served us out of obedience to His Father and His great love for us.

The Big Picture

Much of Jesus' ministry is centered in the area of Galilee, north of Jerusalem. As Jesus teaches, heals, and proclaims the kingdom of God, great crowds begin to follow Him. Jesus sees that the people are like sheep without a shepherd, and so He teaches them many things, especially about the kingdom of God. In what we know as the Sermon on the Mount, Jesus explains the intent of God's Law, talks about being blessed and being salt and light, teaches about prayer and not being anxious, and gives the Golden Rule. Jesus shows love for all people by speaking to a Samaritan woman, revealing that He is the promised Messiah. He feeds more than five thousand people—both spiritually and physically. He performs many miracles of healing, and He exhibits His power over the laws of nature. When He asks His disciples who they think He is, Peter confesses, "You are the Christ, the Son of the living God" (Matthew 16:16).

We find these accounts from the life of Christ in the four Gospels—**Matthew**, **Mark**, **Luke**, and **John**. The accounts in this lesson occurred around AD 31–32.

Creation | Abraham 2000 BC | Moses 1500 BC | David 1000 BC | Daniel 500 BC | Jesus AD 1 | The Church AD 33

I can cite examples of how Jesus served others both physically and spiritually, pointing to His greatest act of service to humankind—His death and resurrection.

If time is short, choose just a few portions of the Sermon on the Mount to go through together.

Matthew 5:13–16: We are to be witnesses of Christ in our words and deeds. Our "good works" point people to Jesus and lead others to glorify God.

Matthew 5:17–20: Jesus fulfilled all that was prophesied about Him in the Old Testament and kept the Law perfectly. All was accomplished in Jesus' work, especially in His death and resurrection.

Matthew 5:21–48: Jesus explains the Law spiritually. When we are judged by the true intent of the Law, we are not able to keep it. We need Christ.

Matthew 6:5–14: Jesus teaches us how to pray and gives a model for prayer that we follow today: the Lord's Prayer.

Matthew 6:25–34: First seek God's salvation, then entrust your daily life into His care.

Matthew 7:12–14: "Whatever you wish that others would do to you, do also to them"—this sums up how we are to be. We will fail, but we call on Jesus for forgiveness and ask Him to walk with us on the narrow way.

Digging Deeper

The Sermon on the Mount

Jesus went throughout Galilee, teaching, healing, and telling people about the kingdom of God. Great crowds followed Him. Seeing the crowds one day, Jesus went up on a mountain and taught them. The teaching of Jesus in Matthew 5–7 is known as the Sermon on the Mount. Jesus began by calling His disciples "blessed" because of what God had in store for them. Then Jesus called on His disciples to do good and to be good.

Look up a few of these passages and talk about their meaning.

Matthew 5:13–16—Salt and Light
Matthew 5:17–20—Christ Fulfills the Law
Matthew 5:21–48—The Intent of the Law
Matthew 6:5–14—Prayer
Matthew 6:25–34—Do Not Be Anxious
Matthew 7:12–14—The Golden Rule

The Samaritan Woman

On their way through Samaria, Jesus and His disciples stopped at a village. The disciples went to get food, and Jesus sat by a well. When a Samaritan woman came, Jesus asked her for a drink from the well. She was shocked that a Jew would talk to her. Jews despised Samaritans. But she was even more surprised by what Jesus said to her next.

Read or listen to **John 4:7–29, 39–42**.

What is the "living water" in verse 10?

What was the result of Jesus talking to the Samaritan woman?

Did You Know?

Who were the Samaritans? When Assyria conquered the Northern Kingdom of Israel in the eighth century, they took most of the people as captives. The Israelites who remained in the land intermarried with people from other countries. These people came to be known as Samaritans. Their Bible contained only the first five books, written by Moses. They built their own temple instead of worshiping in Jerusalem. The Jews regarded them as unclean and despised them so much they traveled around, instead of through, Samaria.

Jesus Feeds the Five Thousand

All four Gospels record the feeding of the five thousand. A crowd of at least five thousand men, plus women and children, had gathered to hear Jesus preach. Testing His disciples, Jesus asked them to feed the hungry crowd.

Read or listen to **Luke 9:10–17**.

What did Jesus teach the disciples through this miracle?

(See also Matthew 14:13–21; Mark 6:30–44; John 6:1–15.)

90

The living water that Jesus spoke of is faith, given by the Holy Spirit. See **John 7:37–39**.

Many Samaritans came to believe in Jesus as the Savior. Jesus interacted with the Samaritan woman, breaking Jewish custom, out of love for her and the Samaritan people. Jesus was continually teaching His disciples that God wanted to include Gentiles in His kingdom.

Through this miracle, Jesus showed the disciples that He is the Christ. They can trust Him to do the seemingly impossible. Jesus provided more than enough—they picked up twelve baskets of leftovers, one for each disciple.

MIRACLES OF JESUS

What is a miracle? It is an extraordinary event that can't be explained in human terms. A miracle shows God at work.

About thirty-five miracles are recorded in the four Gospels.

Why did Jesus perform miracles?

They show He is the Son of God, the promised Messiah. *(Matthew 14:22–33)*

They show His authority and power over heaven and earth. *(John 11:1–45)*

They show His compassion in caring for people's needs. *(John 6:5–13)*

They show He came to fulfill Old Testament prophecy. *(Isaiah 35:5–6)*

Does God still perform miracles today?

JESUS WALKS ON WATER

Jesus' disciples were in a boat in the middle of the night, and the wind was blowing hard against them. Suddenly, they saw something—they thought it was a ghost! But it was Jesus, walking on the water toward them. He said to them, "Take heart; it is I. Don't be afraid." In faith, Peter said, "Lord, if it is You, command me to come to You on the water." Jesus said, "Come."

Read or listen to **Matthew 14:22–33**.

What happened to Peter, and why? How are we sometimes like Peter?

What did the disciples do as a result of this miracle? How does this compare to their reaction at an earlier time? See **Matthew 8:27**.

(See also Mark 6:45–52; John 6:15–21.)

PETER CONFESSES CHRIST

Jesus asked His disciples, "Who do people say that the Son of Man is?" How did the disciples answer Jesus? How do people today answer that question?

Read or listen to **Matthew 16:13–18**.

What did Peter confess? What was Jesus' reply?

(See also Mark 8:27–29; Luke 9:18–20.)

91

God performed many miracles, as recorded in the Bible. God has the power to work miracles, though He most often cares for us through natural means. Either way, we know that God cares for us and we can trust in His care.

At first, Peter stepped onto the water in faith. When he stopped looking at Jesus, the object of his faith, he started to sink. Jesus reached out, saved him, and stopped the wind. In times of trouble, we may forget the object of our faith. But God is faithful. He will never leave us.

At an earlier time when Jesus stopped a storm, the disciples wondered what sort of man He was. Now, they worship Jesus as the Son of God.

Some thought Jesus was John the Baptist, Elijah, or another prophet come back to life.

Today some people talk about Jesus as a good man, while others don't believe He even existed.

Peter confessed, "You are the Christ, the Son of the living God." Jesus answered that God the Father had revealed that truth to Peter. Peter's confession of faith is the foundation on which the Christian Church is built.

Similar to the previous lesson, these pages cover quite a bit of content and have a lot of print on them. See previous lessons for ideas about how to cover this content in smaller groups and ways to help students keep from being overwhelmed or distracted by so much print.

Some calming words from you, their leader, can also help with student anxiety when they see so much print on a page, especially for students who aren't particularly comfortable with academics.

Jesus taught the people with compassion about the kingdom of God.

Jesus showed love and acceptance to the Samaritan woman—someone most Jews would never even approach.

Jesus fed the hungry crowd spiritually and also physically with bread and fish.

Jesus performed many miracles of healing.

Jesus' greatest act of service was to go obediently to the cross to suffer and die for our sins.

CONNECTIONS

JESUS, SERVANT

Jesus came to serve. His whole life on this earth was one of service to others, bringing hope and healing, fulfilling needs, offering forgiveness, and finally laying down His life for us. Look back at this lesson and pick out one way you see Jesus being a Servant to others. What was His greatest act of service?

TIMELESS TRUTH CONNECTION

God has redeemed me to be His own. Jesus' disciples had a hard time changing their attitude from one of being served to one of service to others. They often argued about who was the greatest among them. Two of them even had the nerve to ask to be at Jesus' right and left hand in His kingdom! (They didn't understand what the kingdom of God really was yet.) Jesus laid it out for them when He said this:

> *You know that those who are considered rulers of the Gentiles lord it over them, and their great ones exercise authority over them. But it shall not be so among you. But whoever would be great among you must be your servant, and whoever would be first among you must be slave of all. For even the Son of Man came not to be served but to serve, and to give His life as a ransom for many. (Mark 10:42–45)*

How does Jesus' servant attitude toward you change your attitude about serving others? Think about it and write below what you might do differently in your life, living as a redeemed child of God.

CHRIST CONNECTION

Jesus is an active, compassionate Servant who ministered to the physical and spiritual needs of the people when He walked this earth. His greatest act of service was to go obediently to the cross to suffer and die for our sins. Jesus still serves His people today as He intercedes for us and gives us His body and blood for the forgiveness of our sins in the Sacrament of the Altar.

92

Option: Have learners work in pairs or small groups as they review the lesson. Then let the pairs share with the rest of the group.

Option: Give learners a half-sheet of paper with **Mark 10:42–45** on it, and let them write their response on it. Encourage them to stick it in their backpack or locker to remind them how Jesus' love for us helps us to love others.

For students who struggle with writing, have them tell you their response and have you write it for them.

CHECKS FOR UNDERSTANDING

Before your learners leave, consider ways you can give them feedback for next week.

- **Paired Discussion:** Have learners turn to a partner and share one thing they didn't know before this lesson. Listen in on several conversations.
- **Learning Log:** Ask learners to choose one section from the Sermon on the Mount and describe (by writing in their Learning Log or verbally telling you) what Jesus was teaching in that section. How does His teaching on that affect their life?

JESUS' LATER MINISTRY

TIMELESS TRUTH

God has redeemed me to be His own.

LESSON FOCUS

The learner will be able to give examples demonstrating that Jesus is both true God and true man and will explain why this truth is important for our salvation.

Some human characteristics include having a body, needing to eat and sleep, having relationships with others, and being able to think, speak, invent, and love.

If some students struggle with the concept of being human, reword the question. Perhaps ask them to think about what they can do that an animal can't do, or that an object can't do, giving examples of animals and objects that are familiar to your students.

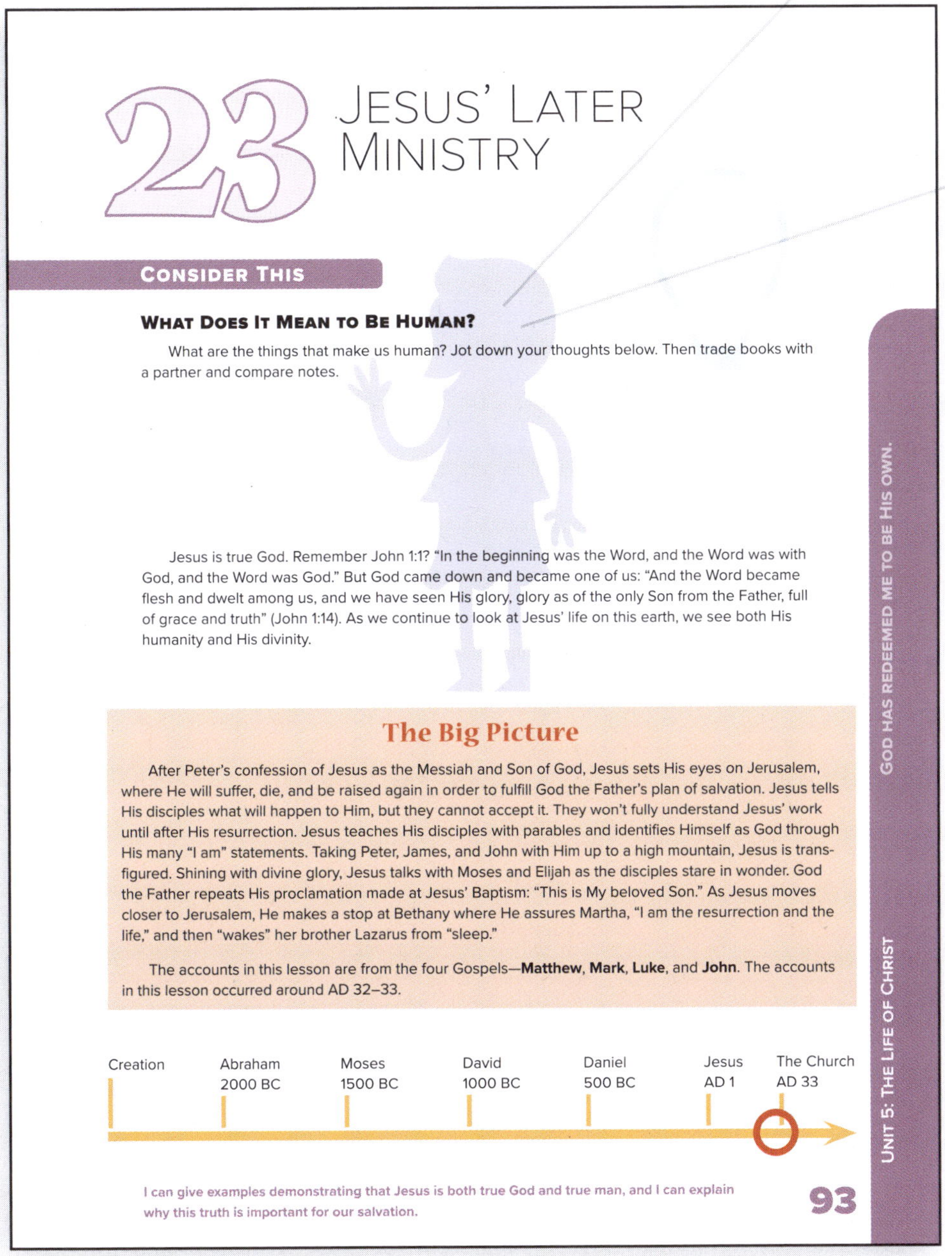

23 JESUS' LATER MINISTRY

CONSIDER THIS

WHAT DOES IT MEAN TO BE HUMAN?

What are the things that make us human? Jot down your thoughts below. Then trade books with a partner and compare notes.

Jesus is true God. Remember John 1:1? "In the beginning was the Word, and the Word was with God, and the Word was God." But God came down and became one of us: "And the Word became flesh and dwelt among us, and we have seen His glory, glory as of the only Son from the Father, full of grace and truth" (John 1:14). As we continue to look at Jesus' life on this earth, we see both His humanity and His divinity.

The Big Picture

After Peter's confession of Jesus as the Messiah and Son of God, Jesus sets His eyes on Jerusalem, where He will suffer, die, and be raised again in order to fulfill God the Father's plan of salvation. Jesus tells His disciples what will happen to Him, but they cannot accept it. They won't fully understand Jesus' work until after His resurrection. Jesus teaches His disciples with parables and identifies Himself as God through His many "I am" statements. Taking Peter, James, and John with Him up to a high mountain, Jesus is transfigured. Shining with divine glory, Jesus talks with Moses and Elijah as the disciples stare in wonder. God the Father repeats His proclamation made at Jesus' Baptism: "This is My beloved Son." As Jesus moves closer to Jerusalem, He makes a stop at Bethany where He assures Martha, "I am the resurrection and the life," and then "wakes" her brother Lazarus from "sleep."

The accounts in this lesson are from the four Gospels—**Matthew**, **Mark**, **Luke**, and **John**. The accounts in this lesson occurred around AD 32–33.

I can give examples demonstrating that Jesus is both true God and true man, and I can explain why this truth is important for our salvation.

UNIT 5: THE LIFE OF CHRIST — GOD HAS REDEEMED ME TO BE HIS OWN.

93

Peter did not understand a suffering Messiah. That was not the way Jews thought of the Messiah. He tried to talk Jesus out of suffering and dying. But Jesus knew He needed to go to the cross for our salvation. He would not let Satan keep Him from fulfilling God's plan.

Moses and Elijah represented the Old Testament Scriptures, the Law and the Prophets. Jesus would soon fulfill the Old Testament prophecies in His suffering and death.

The transfiguration was another confirmation for the disciples that Jesus is truly the Messiah.

At Jesus' Baptism, God the Father said similar words: "This is My beloved Son, with whom I am well pleased" (Matthew 3:17).

The father said, "Let us eat and celebrate. For this my son was dead, and is alive again; he was lost, and is found."

God is not a mean Father who only loves His children if they obey the rules. If that were the case, none of us would be loved by God. Instead, God loved us even when we were far from Him. He comes to us and offers us Jesus' righteousness. He invites us to join Him in His heavenly banquet.

Digging Deeper

Jesus Foretells His Death and Resurrection

Jesus began to tell His disciples that He would suffer many things, be killed, and rise on the third day.

Read or listen to **Matthew 16:21–23**.

What did Peter have to say about this? How did Jesus respond to him? How are we sometimes like Peter?

(See also Mark 8:31–9:1; Luke 9:21–27.)

The Prodigal Son

Jesus told the parable of the prodigal son to teach people about our sinfulness and God's unconditional love and forgiveness.

The younger son demanded his inheritance, left home, and wasted all the money on food and entertainment. Penniless, he ended up feeding pigs and longing to eat their scraps. He decided to head home and plead to become one of the servants. But his father saw him from far off and ran to embrace him. All was forgiven—he welcomed him home as a son, not a servant. The older brother was angry, since he had stayed home and followed the rules.

Read or listen to **Luke 15:11–32**.

What does the father say? How does that help you understand the heart of God, our Father?

Did You Know?

A parable is an earthly story with a heavenly or spiritual meaning. Parables compare two things side by side in order to teach a truth. Jesus used parables to teach people about Himself and the kingdom of heaven. Parables invite us to search the Scriptures and think deeply about what Jesus is teaching us through these stories.

See "Parables of Our Lord" in *The Lutheran Study Bible* for a list of Jesus' parables.

The Transfiguration

Jesus took His "inner circle" of disciples, Peter, James, and John, to a high mountain. There, Jesus was transfigured, completely changed in appearance, as His body became dazzling white. The disciples were terrified. Moses and Elijah appeared and talked with Jesus. Then a cloud overshadowed them and the disciples heard a voice say, "This is My beloved Son; listen to Him."

Read or listen to **Mark 9:2–13**.

What did Jesus' transfiguration show the disciples?

Do the words of the voice sound familiar? In which other account did you hear them?

(See also Matthew 17:1–8; Luke 9:28–36.)

The Good Samaritan

Jesus told the parable of the Good Samaritan in response to a Jewish teacher who asked what he needed to do to get into heaven.

Read or listen to **Luke 10:25–29**.

Describe the conversation between the lawyer and Jesus. What was the lawyer trying to do?

Now read or listen to Jesus' parable in **Luke 10:30–37**.

What do you think surprised the lawyer in this story?

What is Jesus teaching through this parable?

94

The lawyer first tested Jesus by asking Him about the Law. Then he tried to find a way to justify his limited keeping of the Law.

Jews and Samaritans were enemies. In this parable, a Samaritan helped a Jew while fellow Jews (Jewish leaders, no less) refused to show love to their brother.

Jesus taught that we are to love and do good to all people. However, we realize that we cannot fulfill this Law completely. Jesus became the Good Samaritan for us, laying down His life for us.

These are small spaces for writing. Students could also use a notebook to write answers for discussion, or you could record answers on the board for the entire class.

In the Old Testament, the name for God is Yahweh, which came from God Himself when He told Moses, "I AM WHO I AM" (Exodus 3:14). Jesus identified Himself as God in His many "I am" statements.

John 8:58 records Jesus saying, "Truly, truly, I say to you, before Abraham was, I am." What is Jesus declaring by this statement?

Look up some of the following "I am" statements of Jesus. What is Jesus saying about Himself in these statements?

John 6:35 (context: John 6:22–59)—"I am the bread of life."

John 8:12 (context: John 8:12–30)—"I am the light of the world."

John 10:11, 16 (context: John 10)—"I am the good shepherd."

John 11:25 (context: John 11:17–27)—"I am the resurrection and the life."

Jesus also spoke other "I am" statements that are recorded in the Gospel of John. Christ spoke these statements to lead others to faith in Him as the promised Messiah, the Savior of the world.

Jesus Raises Lazarus

In the account of Jesus raising Lazarus from the dead, we see both Jesus' human emotion and also His divine glory.

Jesus was good friends with sisters Mary and Martha and their brother Lazarus. When news came to Him that Lazarus was very sick, we would expect Jesus to go immediately to heal him. But Jesus waited three days. Finally, He told His disciples that they would go to Judea. When they arrived, they found that Lazarus had been dead four days.

Read **John 11:21–27**.

What message of hope does Jesus give Martha? How is this a hope for us as well?

Read **John 11:28–44**.

Describe how Jesus' miracle showed both His compassion and His power.

95

Jesus is declaring His eternal preexistence. John began his Gospel, "In the beginning was the Word, and the Word was with God, and the Word was God. He was in the beginning with God" (John 1:1–2).

Bread of life: Jesus connects His life with the manna God provided the Israelites in the wilderness. The manna kept them alive, though they eventually died. Jesus also came from heaven, but He gives eternal life.

Light of the world: Jesus shows that He is the fulfillment of the messianic prophecies about light, such as Isaiah 42:6 and 49:6. Jesus the Messiah delivers us from spiritual darkness.

The Good Shepherd: Psalm 23 speaks of God as the "shepherd" of His "sheep," His people. Jesus protects His sheep and will lay down His life for them. He also speaks of "sheep that are not of this fold," thereby including the Gentiles.

The resurrection and the life: This is Jesus' last "I am" statement in John. Lazarus had died. Jesus told Martha with these words that He has power over death. Everlasting life can be found in no one but Jesus.

Jesus tells Martha, "I am the resurrection and the life. Whoever believes in Me, though he die, yet shall he live, and everyone who lives and believes in Me shall never die" (John 11:25). Jesus assures her that everyone who believes in Him will live eternally, even though they die physically. This promise is for all believers of all time.

Jesus weeps in sympathy for the sorrow of His friends. Death brings the pain of separation for all people. Jesus shows His power over death by bringing Lazarus back from the dead. Jesus is truly the resurrection and the life.

Guide learners in this activity by asking questions such as these: What do you see in Jesus' life that shows He is fully human? (He was born, grew up, ate and drank, felt emotion, etc.) What do you see in Jesus' ministry that shows that He is true God? (He turned water to wine, calmed the storm, multiplied food to feed over five thousand people, etc.)

Let students use a notebook for writing if these spaces are troublesome for them. Remind students that you are not concerned about spelling, complete sentences, or proper grammar.

CONNECTIONS

JESUS CHRIST: TRUE GOD AND TRUE MAN

Jesus Christ is true God who came down from heaven and became true man. Look back at the past three lessons and find examples from Scripture that show Jesus as true God and write them on the left. Then find examples that show Jesus is true man and write them on the right.

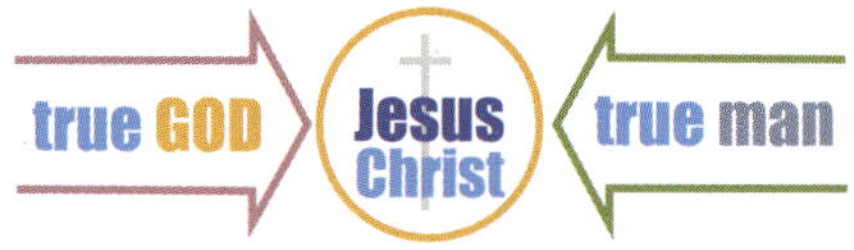

TIMELESS TRUTH CONNECTION

God has redeemed me to be His own. Read the following verse. Then, in your own words, describe what Jesus has done for you.

Have this mind among yourselves, which is yours in Christ Jesus, who, though He was in the form of God, did not count equality with God a thing to be grasped, but emptied Himself, by taking the form of a servant, being born in the likeness of men. And being found in human form, He humbled Himself by becoming obedient to the point of death, even death on a cross. Therefore God has highly exalted Him and bestowed on Him the name that is above every name, so that at the name of Jesus every knee should bow, in heaven and on earth and under the earth, and every tongue confess that Jesus Christ is Lord, to the glory of God the Father. (Philippians 2:5–11)

CHRIST CONNECTION

Jesus Christ, true God, Creator with God from the beginning, became man to fulfill the Law on our behalf; to die, paying the punishment for our sin; and to rise from the dead so that one day we will also rise to eternal life with Him.

96

CHECKS FOR UNDERSTANDING

Before your learners leave, consider ways you can give them feedback for next week.

- **Exit Ticket:** Ask learners to write a question or comment they have about the lesson on a sheet of paper to leave with you. Review the questions so that you can address them in your next class.
- **Learning Log:** Ask learners to explain why it is important for our salvation that Jesus Christ is true God and true man.

Jesus' Passion

Timeless Truth for Lesson

God has redeemed me to be His own.

Lesson Focus

The learner will be able to describe the events of Jesus' Passion and connect them to the different messianic promises in the Old Testament.

24 Jesus' Passion

Consider This

Christ's Passion for Us

What comes to mind when you hear the word *passion*? Brainstorm different ways the word is used below.

The week or so leading up to the crucifixion of Jesus is often called the Passion. Though we use the word in a lot of different ways, it can best be defined as "strong emotions." As Jesus went to the cross, He experienced suffering for us. Let's take a look at these important events and what they mean for us.

The Big Picture

A lot happens in the last week before Jesus' crucifixion. On the Sunday before, the day when God's people would select the Passover lamb, Jesus enters Jerusalem for the last time. On the way, crowds of people sing, shout, and wave palm branches, hailing Jesus as the powerful King and Messiah who will reestablish the greatness of God's people once more. Jesus' kingdom, however, will come about in a different way than expected. He teaches for a week, all the while the religious leaders hatch a plot to ambush Him and sentence Him to death. The night before He is crucified, Jesus celebrates the Passover meal with His disciples, revealing that the meal was always meant to point to Him and what He would do. He says that the bread and wine taken are His true body and blood and institutes the Sacrament of the Altar for all believers. After this, He takes His disciples out to pray, and while He prays to the Father, He is betrayed by the disciple Judas, arrested, and taken to the high priest's house. After a hasty trial by the religious leaders, He is accused of the high crime of blasphemy. Jesus is then sent to the Roman governor Pilate, who finds no reason to execute Jesus. After a hasty trip to King Herod, Jesus is sent back to Pilate, who, under the pressure of the religious leaders, sentences Jesus to death even though Pilate knows Jesus is an innocent man. Jesus is about to die for the sins of the world.

This section is contained in the books of **Matthew**, **Mark**, **Luke**, and **John**. The narrative occurred near the time of Passover around AD 33.

Creation | Abraham 2000 BC | Moses 1500 BC | David 1000 BC | Daniel 500 BC | Jesus AD 1 | The Church AD 33

I can describe the events of Jesus' Passion and connect them to the different messianic promises in the Old Testament.

Unit 5: The Life of Christ — God has redeemed me to be His own.

97

Take care about the mood with this question. The word *passion* may bring up some giggles, especially among youth. That said, we encourage you to talk about this word in a straightforward manner instead of ignoring it. The fact remains that in the Christian Church we do talk about Passion Week and the Passion of Christ. Use this as an opportunity to talk about what the word really means and what it means for us as God's people.

There is a lot of reading in this lesson. Consider skimming or reading over "The Big Picture" here rather than going in depth about the specific events.

Option: If you have an ongoing timeline in your space, consider thinking about how you will present this and the next two lessons. These all happen in a very short amount of time, but make up the critical center of the narrative of Salvation. Be creative and have fun.

The organization of this activity is a little different, as the narrative flows with the journey of Jesus through Jerusalem. Encourage your learners to trace their way through the different locations and times to help them get the context of Jesus' Passion.

Go in numerical order, not positional order on the page. The events are positioned on the page to correspond with where they occur on the map.

Option: There's not enough space in this lesson to talk in depth about the Sacrament of the Altar. That said, to help supplement this part of the lesson, consider pausing to look up the four sections under "The Sacrament of the Altar" in *Luther's Small Catechism with Explanation* (2017 edition) to answer any questions that may arise about the nature of this Sacrament.

Digging Deeper

Passion Week

The last week of Jesus' life, which Christians around the world remember as Passion Week, is really important to understanding the narrative of salvation. In it, we start to see how Jesus fulfills all of God's promises from the Old Testament and also how He sets up our lives as New Testament people today!

For this lesson, we'll track some of the events in this last week of Jesus' life before His crucifixion by using a map of Jerusalem at the time. For this activity, follow the numbers on the map, starting with 1. Read and reflect on that event, then trace a line on the map to the next number, following the path Jesus and the disciples may have taken during this time.

2. The Lord's Supper

By Thursday, a lot had happened. Jesus had cleared the temple of moneychangers and spent a lot of time teaching. But by Thursday evening, Jesus had gone back to the Upper Room and was going to celebrate the Passover feast with His disciples. Read or listen to **Luke 22:1–3**. How was Satan at work here to bring about the death of Jesus? How was this similar to how Satan worked elsewhere in the Bible?

Read or listen to **Luke 22:7–23**. Jesus was celebrating the Passover. Refresh your understanding of this important meal by flipping back to Lesson 9. How did Jesus add to the meal?

What does that tell you about what He came to do?

How do Christians still practice this today? What gifts does God give us in the Sacrament of the Altar?

At the end of the meal, Jesus had an interaction with Peter. Read or listen to **Luke 22:31–34.** Do you think you would have said what Peter said here? Why or why not?

4. Peter Denies Jesus and Judas Hangs Himself

Read or listen to **Luke 22:54–62**. Peter denied he knew Jesus because he feared losing his life. How do you think Peter felt after Jesus' prophecy came true?

Read or listen to **Matthew 27:3–5**. Judas, the disciple who had betrayed Jesus to the authorities, committed suicide. Why do you think his reaction was different from Peter's here?

98

Jesus conducts the Passover meal as normal, but at the end consecrates the bread and wine and passes it to His disciples. This tells us that He came to fulfill the promises of the Old Testament, that He is the sacrifice, and that He has come to give His body and blood for the world. He continues to pour out these gifts to us, His true body and blood in the Sacrament of the Altar, to give us forgiveness, life, and salvation.

Peter felt terrible, betraying his Master and Friend, Jesus. This is a demonstration for us not only of how we fail Jesus but also of His power to forgive us even when we betray His trust and sin against Him.

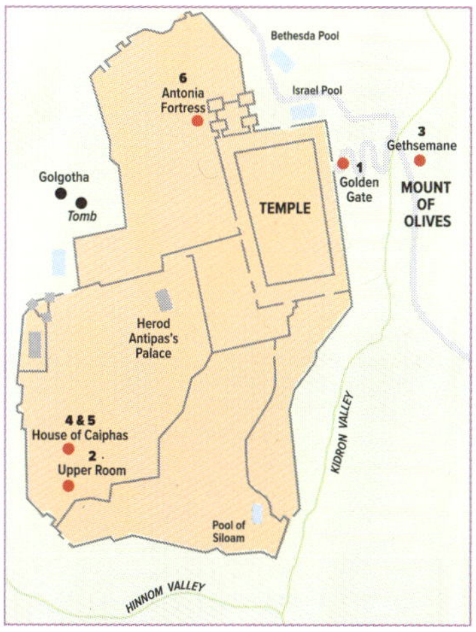

1. Jesus Enters Jerusalem

After Jesus raised Lazarus from the dead, He entered into Jerusalem for the last time (on Sunday, the first day of the week). Read or listen to **Luke 19:28–40**. In a few words or sketches, what would this scene have looked like?

Talk about what you think the people were looking for in Jesus. How did Jesus meet and not meet their expectations?

3. The Garden of Gethsemane

After the meal, Jesus went out to the Mount of Olives to pray. Read or listen to **Luke 22:39–53**. What do you suppose is the "cup" that Jesus asked the Father to take from Him?

Discuss how Jesus shows His love for you and the whole world here.

5. Jesus before the Council

Jesus was held in a sort of prison at the high priest's house all night (while being mocked and beaten). Some time the next morning (Friday), after the leaders had already decided to sentence Jesus, they brought Him out. Read or listen to **Luke 22:63–71**.

What do they accuse Jesus of? Why does Jesus' response enrage them?

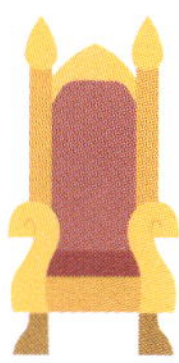

6. Jesus before Pontius Pilate

Though the Jewish council sentenced Jesus to die, they didn't have the authority to do this. The Roman governor, a man named Pontius Pilate, was the only one who had the authority. Read or listen to **Luke 23:1–25**. What did Pilate do to try to avoid sentencing Jesus to death? Why did Pilate do it, in the end, even if he didn't find Jesus guilty?

Note: In the Creed, we mention Pontius Pilate by name. When we confess this, in church or on our own, we are not just naming the one who sentenced Jesus to death. We are confessing before the world that Jesus did indeed live and die in history and that this is not a made-up story. It is true!

99

Option: If your students need to be active, let them act this out in small groups rather than write or sketch it on paper.

The "cup" that Jesus mentions here, as He does throughout the Gospels, is His suffering. When it's time to drink the cup, it's time to endure suffering. This shows His love for creation, enduring so much, even though He knows it will be the most difficult road anybody has ever taken, suffering the punishment of sins for all people of all times.

Jesus' response, that He is the Son of Man, hearkens back to the prophecy in Daniel 7, where the Son of Man descends in power and glory to judge the world. The leaders knew that Jesus was calling Himself this figure, and thus they sentenced Him to die for blasphemy.

This is a long section of text, so if you're short on time, consider just reading over parts of it quickly. The point, ultimately, is that the political leaders could find no real reason to sentence Jesus to death, as He was completely innocent. Pilate still gave in to the pressure of the people and killed Jesus rather than lose popular support.

This section may be too abstract for some learners, especially when trying to compare the Isaiah prophecy to events in Jesus' Passion. If so, consider helping your learners along by showing them how Jesus was betrayed by His friends, rejected by the world, took ridicule humbly, and suffered for us. If you have time, encourage your learners to look up **Isaiah 53** and see how all these events about Jesus' Passion and death were part of God's plan of salvation from the beginning. He endured all these things for us out of love for us.

Connections

Timeless Truth Connection

God has redeemed me to be His own. In today's readings, we see that Jesus endured so much in the last week of His life. Write or sketch in the space below different things Jesus had to endure on His way to the cross.

Old Testament Connection

Jesus fulfilled the prophecies of the Old Testament. Seven hundred years before Jesus, Isaiah (remember from Lessons 16 and 17) wrote some powerful prophecies looking to Jesus' Passion. Look over these sections from Isaiah 53 below, then draw arrows between what you wrote or drew on the left and what Isaiah said Jesus would endure for you on the right. How many fulfillments can you find?

Who has believed what he has heard from us?
And to whom has the arm of the LORD been revealed?
For He grew up before Him like a young plant,
and like a root out of dry ground;
He had no form or majesty that we should look at Him,
and no beauty that we should desire Him.
He was despised and rejected by men,
a man of sorrows and acquainted with grief;
and as one from whom men hide their faces
He was despised, and we esteemed Him not.

Surely He has borne our griefs
and carried our sorrows;
yet we esteemed Him stricken,
smitten by God, and afflicted.

He was oppressed, and He was afflicted,
yet He opened not His mouth;
like a lamb that is led to the slaughter,
and like a sheep that before its shearers is silent,
so He opened not His mouth.
By oppression and judgment He was taken away;
and as for His generation, who considered
that He was cut off out of the land of the living,
stricken for the transgression of My people?

For students who struggle with reading, this Isaiah passage will be a challenge. That doesn't mean you shouldn't do it. It just means that you will need to have supports in place to help your students navigate it. This might include reading the sections together, providing simple illustrations, or providing a larger print, highlighted version of the Isaiah text.

Christ Connection

As He endured so much suffering and betrayal, Jesus took our sins upon Himself and carried them to the cross. There, He took the punishment for the sins of the human race to make us His own.

100

Checks for Understanding

Before your learners leave, consider ways you can give them feedback for next week.

- **Exit Ticket:** Have each learner summarize on a piece of paper, in his or her own words, what happened to Jesus during Passion Week and why that matters for people today. Have learners leave this summary with you so you can review it for next time and see what they learned.
- **Learning Log:** Have each learner write down a key point they learned in this lesson about the connection between the Lord's Supper and the Passover, and the blessings we continually receive in it in the Church today.

JESUS' CRUCIFIXION

TIMELESS TRUTH FOR LESSON

God has redeemed me to be His own.

LESSON FOCUS

The learner will be able to summarize the events of Jesus' crucifixion and express what that means for his or her life as God's redeemed child.

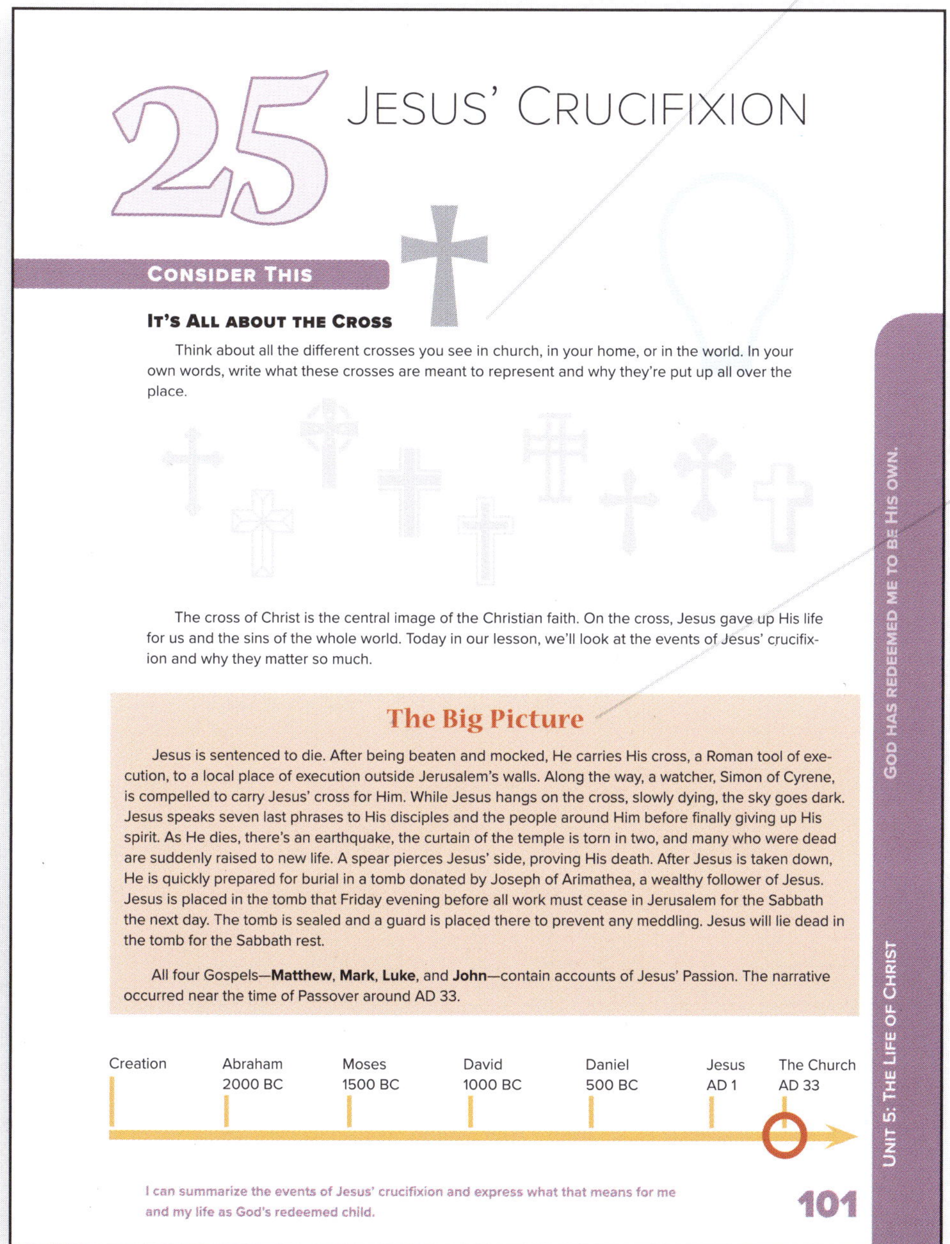

25 JESUS' CRUCIFIXION

CONSIDER THIS

IT'S ALL ABOUT THE CROSS

Think about all the different crosses you see in church, in your home, or in the world. In your own words, write what these crosses are meant to represent and why they're put up all over the place.

The cross of Christ is the central image of the Christian faith. On the cross, Jesus gave up His life for us and the sins of the whole world. Today in our lesson, we'll look at the events of Jesus' crucifixion and why they matter so much.

The Big Picture

Jesus is sentenced to die. After being beaten and mocked, He carries His cross, a Roman tool of execution, to a local place of execution outside Jerusalem's walls. Along the way, a watcher, Simon of Cyrene, is compelled to carry Jesus' cross for Him. While Jesus hangs on the cross, slowly dying, the sky goes dark. Jesus speaks seven last phrases to His disciples and the people around Him before finally giving up His spirit. As He dies, there's an earthquake, the curtain of the temple is torn in two, and many who were dead are suddenly raised to new life. A spear pierces Jesus' side, proving His death. After Jesus is taken down, He is quickly prepared for burial in a tomb donated by Joseph of Arimathea, a wealthy follower of Jesus. Jesus is placed in the tomb that Friday evening before all work must cease in Jerusalem for the Sabbath the next day. The tomb is sealed and a guard is placed there to prevent any meddling. Jesus will lie dead in the tomb for the Sabbath rest.

All four Gospels—**Matthew**, **Mark**, **Luke**, and **John**—contain accounts of Jesus' Passion. The narrative occurred near the time of Passover around AD 33.

I can summarize the events of Jesus' crucifixion and express what that means for me and my life as God's redeemed child.

UNIT 5: THE LIFE OF CHRIST — GOD HAS REDEEMED ME TO BE HIS OWN.

101

Option: Take a short field trip to the sanctuary and look around the space for all the different crosses. Talk about what each one may mean and why it was placed there. It may be a appropriate to stay in the sanctuary for this lesson due to the nature of the topic.

If you have access to a digital device, locate photos of historic crosses from around the world to show your students.

As always, this is a sizable block of text. Read the text and, if you have time, have your learners underline or highlight one word or phrase that sticks out to them about this summary. Then they can share with a partner why it sticks out to them.

Option: If you have a developing timeline, consider adding the lesson number and name, dates, and books of the Bible at this time.

These two pages cover some intense content. To save time and increase student focus, mark a Bible with sticky notes at the Scripture passages listed. Help students highlight their own Bibles at these important passages.

Keep a careful eye on students for signs that the intensity of this lesson is overwhelming to them. Work on these sections together as needed.

As the soldiers beat Jesus, they mocked Him as a pretender king. The truth is that Jesus is their King, as He is the King of kings. This only leads back to the truth that Jesus humbled Himself in coming to earth.

Jesus suffered so much in His Passion that He wasn't physically able to carry the heavy load of the cross. He gave His everything for us and never gave up or gave in. That's how much He sacrificed for the sins of the whole world.

Digging Deeper

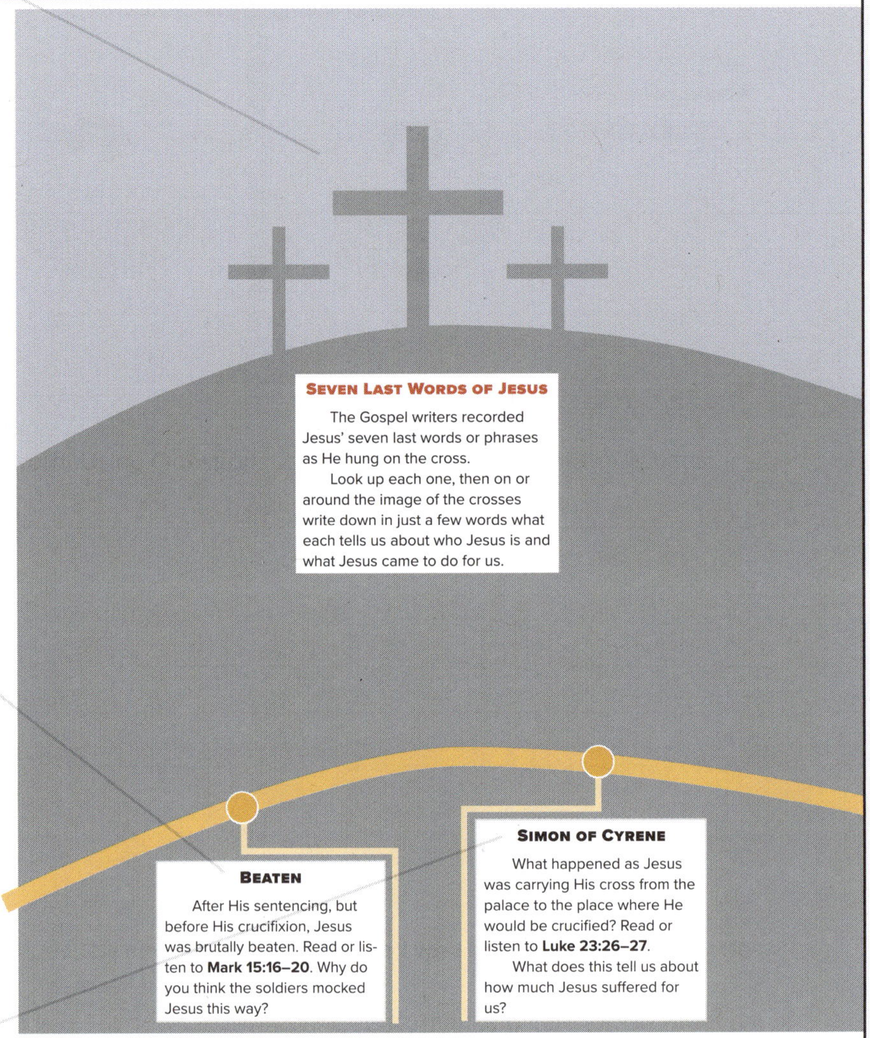

Seven Last Words of Jesus

The Gospel writers recorded Jesus' seven last words or phrases as He hung on the cross.

Look up each one, then on or around the image of the crosses write down in just a few words what each tells us about who Jesus is and what Jesus came to do for us.

Beaten

After His sentencing, but before His crucifixion, Jesus was brutally beaten. Read or listen to **Mark 15:16–20**. Why do you think the soldiers mocked Jesus this way?

Simon of Cyrene

What happened as Jesus was carrying His cross from the palace to the place where He would be crucified? Read or listen to **Luke 23:26–27**.

What does this tell us about how much Jesus suffered for us?

102

Options: For the section on the seven last words of Jesus, consider making this a different kind of activity. Divide up the seven words equally among the learners (or pairs of learners) and have each learner present his or her findings to the rest of the group. Alternatively, you could ask each learner to spread out around the space and spend a set amount of time independently reading through and meditating on the last words of Jesus. Switch this up, and show how the different words of Jesus reveal both His divinity and humanity, as well as His vast love and sacrifice for His creation.

1 **FORGIVE** Luke 23:32–38

2 **PARADISE** Luke 23:39–43

3 **MOTHER** John 19:26–27

4 **FORSAKEN** Matthew 27:46–49

5 **THIRST** John 19:28–29

6 **FINISHED** John 19:30

7 **SPIRIT** Luke 23:46

Amazing Events!

At the time of Jesus' death that Friday morning, after suffering the punishment of all people's sins for all time, finishing the mission to forgive mankind their sins, Jesus gave up His spirit and died. Right after that, some amazing things happened. Read or listen to **Matthew 27:51–54**.

What does the supernatural tearing of the temple curtain—which separated the Holy Place, where only the high priest could go, from the rest of the temple—show us about what Jesus' death accomplished?

What do you think all the people being resurrected at this time shows us about Jesus' mission?

Buried

After Jesus' death, He was buried in a donated tomb. Read or listen to **Matthew 27:57–66**. Why do you suppose they put guards around the tomb?

103

The supernatural events include the earthquake, the dead coming back to life, and the curtain of the temple being torn in two. Consider flipping back to Lesson 14 for a rough map of the interior of the temple. These signs all point to Jesus' power and mission. He came to open the way between God and man by His death (the curtain) and to bring mankind the promise of new life (the resurrection). The earthquake and darkness reveal not only His power as Lord of creation but also the injustice of His execution for the sins of the whole world.

The text says they put guards around the tomb because Jesus had prophesied that He would come back from the dead. The local religious leaders didn't want to give Jesus' followers the opportunity to steal the body. Jesus would not let these guards stop Him, however.

The word *redeem* may be very foreign or abstract for some of your students. Talk through this section together.

Examples of this include things like getting grounded and having to work off your punishment, or getting in trouble in school and having to do chores during recess. Focus on the ideas of justice and needing to pay off debts by working for it.

For this final prayer/reflection time, consider your learners. If they are responsible, give them some space and time to independently pray. If they are less so, keep a watchful eye, or alternatively read through the Bible verses out loud together and talk about how they connect to the crucifixion. Make this less about just factual knowledge and more about consideration of what Christ has done for us.

CONNECTIONS

BOUGHT BACK

As we make connections, let's dig into what the word *redeem* means. The word *redeem* means "to buy something back"—something that was once yours but you lost or sold away and is not yours anymore.

Think about having to "redeem" yourself after you've done something wrong or bad. Have you ever gotten into trouble at home or at school and had to work your way out as a punishment? Think of one time, and write it below.

TIMELESS TRUTH CONNECTION

God has redeemed me to be His own. In the cross of Christ, we see God acting out all His promises to redeem us. The crucifixion of Christ is the center of the Bible, and the center of God's plan of salvation, for a reason. The whole narrative of salvation leads to this point. God made man perfect, man disobeyed God, and because of that, mankind had to suffer the consequences for our disobedience: earthly brokenness, death, and eternal hell. *Nothing* we can do as humans can be good enough to redeem ourselves back from these consequences.

CHRIST CONNECTION

The narrative of the Bible is all about God's plan to redeem us, or to buy us back, from the consequences of our punishment. In fact, Jesus redeems us by offering up His life as a substitute. He makes us right, or justifies us, with the Father as a gift of love for you. He is the hero of the Bible, and He's the hero of your life story too.

But now the righteousness of God has been manifested apart from the law, although the Law and the Prophets bear witness to it—the righteousness of God through faith in Jesus Christ for all who believe. For there is no distinction: for all have sinned and fall short of the glory of God, and are justified by His grace as a gift, through the redemption that is in Christ Jesus. (Romans 3:21–24)

For while we were still weak, at the right time Christ died for the ungodly. For one will scarcely die for a righteous person—though perhaps for a good person one would dare even to die—but God shows His love for us in that while we were still sinners, Christ died for us. Since, therefore, we have now been justified by His blood, much more shall we be saved by Him from the wrath of God. (Romans 5:6–9)

THINK ABOUT IT . . .

Read the above passages, and spend a few minutes in silent prayer considering what Jesus endured to forgive you your sins and thanking Him for your salvation.

104

CHECKS FOR UNDERSTANDING

Before your learners leave, consider ways you can give them feedback for next week.

- **Closing Prayer:** Consider just watching your learners as they conclude in the final prayer activity to see how seriously they're taking the lesson. Alternatively, encourage them to write down a prayer and leave it with you to read later.
- **Learning Log:** Have your learners write down one thing from the lesson that helps them understand what it means that Jesus has redeemed them from sin, death, and the power of the devil.

Jesus' Resurrection and Ascension

Timeless Truth for Lesson

God has redeemed me to be His own.

Lesson Focus

The learner will be able to paraphrase the events of the resurrection and connect Jesus' resurrection to his or her resurrection hope as God's redeemed child.

Option: Consider making this first reflection more active, dividing up your learners into groups where they each have to silently act out what they would do in a world without sickness or death. The other groups would have to try to guess what they were acting out. Then conclude with a reflection period talking about why they chose to act out what they did.

26 Jesus' Resurrection and Ascension

Consider This

What a Wonderful World!

What do you suppose it would be like to live in a world where nobody gets sick or hurt or dies? What would that world be like? Describe or sketch your thoughts below.

As Christians, we have an amazing hope and promise. Jesus died to forgive us our sins. He then came back to new life to promise us a new future. We will one day be raised like Him and have a new earth, where we will live in perfect relationship with Him and each other. Let's investigate His resurrection together.

The Big Picture

After the Sabbath rest on Saturday, something amazing and unexpected happens. As the climax of God's plan of salvation so far, Jesus is resurrected. He has buried the sins of the world in His death and has now come to new life in a perfected body. Women come to the tomb only to find it empty. They go and tell the disciples, who also race to the tomb to see the sight. After they leave, Jesus appears to Mary, revealing Himself to her as the first person to witness His resurrection. Later that day, Jesus visits some of His followers on the road, then appears to His disciples, breathing on them the Holy Spirit and giving them authority to forgive sins in His name. After a week of visiting people, Jesus returns to the disciples, this time revealing Himself to Thomas, who was not there the first time, and Thomas declares Jesus to be both Lord and God. Later, Jesus reinstates Peter as a disciple and tells him to feed His sheep. After forty days, Jesus goes back to the Mount of Olives and ascends into heaven, telling His disciples to wait in Jerusalem for the coming Holy Spirit.

This lesson once again comes from the books of **Matthew**, **Mark**, **Luke**, and **John**. The narrative occurred after the time of Passover around AD 33.

Creation | Abraham 2000 BC | Moses 1500 BC | David 1000 BC | Daniel 500 BC | Jesus AD 1 | The Church AD 33

I can paraphrase the events of the resurrection and connect Jesus' resurrection to my resurrection hope as God's redeemed child.

Unit 5: The Life of Christ — God has redeemed me to be His own.

105

As always, this is a sizable block of text. Read the text and, if you have time, have your learners underline or highlight one word or phrase that sticks out to them about this summary. Then they can share with a partner why it sticks out to them.

Option: If you have a developing timeline on a wall in your space, consider adding the lesson number and name, dates, and books of the Bible at this time.

Take time with your learners to really dig into how this might have looked and felt like for the first disciples. Luke and John go into such great detail here. When Jesus talks to Mary, He is on the move, knowing that by His death and resurrection He has fulfilled God's promises and is letting as many people know about it as He can before His ascension into heaven.

Jesus Himself, in His resurrected body, reveals how all of Scripture pointed to the Gospel promise that He had just fulfilled. He is spreading the Good News in fellowship with His followers.

Jesus reveals Himself to the disciples, and immediately tells them to not fear. Instead, He breathes the Holy Spirit on them and commands them to go and forgive sins in His name, giving them the Office of the Keys. Jesus is clear that, now that His mission is done, it's time to multiply the Law-and-Gospel work through the Church. This work continues to this day.

Digging Deeper

Sunday Morning

On Good Friday, Jesus died on the cross to take the punishment for the sins of the world. During the Sabbath, or Saturday, the Jews could not work. On Sunday morning, the first day of the week, some of the women who had quickly prepared Jesus' body for burial returned to the tomb, intending to finish the preparation. Read or listen to **Luke 24:1–12**. In your own words, summarize what happened below.

But the surprises weren't finished! Read or listen to **John 20:11–18**. Imagine you're Mary. What would it have been like to experience Jesus' new life?

Discuss: Why do you think Jesus, newly raised from the dead in a perfect, deathless body, would say what He said to Mary?

Jesus Appears to His Disciples

That same evening, Jesus appeared to the disciples (not including Thomas). Read or listen to **John 20:19–23**. They must have been surprised! Jesus was back in a perfected body, and He could just appear. Jesus wasted no time. What does He tell them to do? How does this continue to extend His work on earth?

Jesus on the Move

Right away Jesus went to work, moving about the countryside revealing that He had been raised from the dead to fulfill all of God's promises. One such encounter is recorded in **Luke 24:13–35**. Read or listen to the passage, then consider this question: What did Jesus say about His role in God's plan of salvation here?

106

The Scripture passages on these pages could be stumbling blocks for struggling readers. Remind students how to use a Bible app to listen to passages or to listen and read at the same time.

Jesus Forgives Peter

Remember Peter? He denied that he knew Jesus on the night Jesus was betrayed, even though he said he would die rather than leave Jesus. Well, after Jesus' resurrection, He showed up to the disciples while they were fishing. He caused a miraculous catch of fish and made them breakfast! Then Jesus spoke with Peter. Read or listen to **John 21:15–17**. What did Jesus tell Peter? What does that mean for us?

Jesus Appears to Thomas

One disciple of Jesus, Thomas, was missing when Jesus appeared to them the first time. Thomas refused to believe his friends when they told him Jesus was alive again. Read or listen to what happened one week later in **John 20:24–29**.

What is so special about Thomas' confession and Jesus' response?

Jesus Ascends into Heaven

After forty days of visiting His followers, Jesus went to the Mount of Olives to say some parting words before ascending (or returning) to heaven. Read or listen to the events and the words of Jesus in **Luke 24:44–52** and **Matthew 28:16–20**. Then consider the question at the bottom of the page.

Why Did Jesus Return to Heaven?

This is a big question. If Jesus did all this for us, why would He be so eager to leave? Look at all the readings and questions you've gone over on this page so far, and jot down in the space above any reasons you see for Jesus ascending. We'll look more into this on the next page.

107

Thomas's confession shows not only that the disciples saw Jesus as God but also that Jesus accepted their worship as God. There is no doubt in this confession that Jesus is both Lord and God.

Jesus forgave and reinstated Peter as a disciple. He commanded Peter to go and feed His sheep. This continues to this day in the church as God uses pastors to distribute the Means of Grace and as God uses all believers to proclaim His Word to this lost and broken world.

Jesus' ascension into heaven did not mean He was leaving His people. Instead, Jesus went to the right hand of the throne of God to rule over His Church and distribute His gifts through the Holy Spirit. It is easy for learners to miss this point, so really get them thinking about the actual words and commands of Jesus at His ascension.

Consider covering this material in ways that have been successful for students in previous lessons—perhaps using pairs or small groups of students, acting out sections of the Scriptures, or using digital devices.

Though there's a lot of content to cover here, it's important for your learners to make the connection between Jesus' death and resurrection and our death and resurrection in Christ. If you feel comfortable, summarize these important truths in your own words. Often the meaning of the resurrection—that is, the promise of new life in the new creation—is lost on younger learners. Death is a difficult topic. For Christians, death is not the end, and neither is a spiritual life in heaven. Instead, the ultimate hope is that those whom God has called through His Means of Grace will one day rise again to a perfect creation. Christ led the way, and through our Baptism we will follow from death to life.

If your learners are tired or you're short on time, consider skipping this activity in class and making it something to reflect on at home.

CONNECTIONS

THERE . . . AND HERE!

The truth remains that when Jesus ascended, He didn't leave us. In fact, He ascended so that He could be with us always here on earth. Jesus reigns over the whole Church now by grace from heaven, and yet He works in and through us in the world by the Holy Spirit through the Word and Sacraments. He is very much alive and active in His mission.

Think of it this way. Jesus' Passion, death, and resurrection all came about so that Jesus could win the victory over sin, death, and the devil for His people. As we receive the gifts of God's Word—that is, forgiveness, life, and salvation—Jesus shares His victory with us! The primary way Jesus shares victory with us is through Baptism. Read or listen as someone reads the passage from Romans below. Underline any mention of death, being buried, dying, or being dead. Then circle any mention of being raised, life, living, being alive, or the resurrection. Go!

> *Do you not know that all of us who have been baptized into Christ Jesus were baptized into His death? We were buried therefore with Him by baptism into death, in order that, just as Christ was raised from the dead by the glory of the Father, we too might walk in newness of life.*
>
> *For if we have been united with Him in a death like His, we shall certainly be united with Him in a resurrection like His. We know that our old self was crucified with Him in order that the body of sin might be brought to nothing, so that we would no longer be enslaved to sin. For one who has died has been set free from sin. Now if we have died with Christ, we believe that we will also live with Him. We know that Christ, being raised from the dead, will never die again; death no longer has dominion over Him. For the death He died He died to sin, once for all, but the life He lives He lives to God. So you also must consider yourselves dead to sin and alive to God in Christ Jesus. (Romans 6:3–11)*

TIMELESS TRUTH CONNECTION

God has redeemed me to be His own. Over this lesson, we've considered that statement. Let's unpack it as we look at the Christ Connection.

CHRIST CONNECTION

Our lives are connected to Christ in Baptism. One day, unless Jesus comes back first, we will all die. Because of His death on the cross, our sins are forgiven and buried forever with Him. Because of His resurrection, our bodies will be one day raised like His. This is what our faith is all about! Jesus has done this for us. Take a moment and, in the space around the crosses, write a little prayer thanking Jesus for the gift of forgiveness. In the space around the empty tomb, write a little prayer thanking Jesus for the gift of eternal life.

108

CHECKS FOR UNDERSTANDING

Before your learners leave, consider ways you can give them feedback for next week.

- **Summary:** Pass out note cards and have each learner write a two- or three-sentence summary of God's narrative of salvation in this lesson. Have them leave this summary with you so you can review it for next time and see what they learned.
- **Learning Log:** Have your learners write down one thing from the lesson that helps them connect Jesus' death and resurrection to our death and resurrection through Him.

Unit 6: The Church

Essential Questions

What is the Church?

What has God called His Church to be and to do?

How do all the narratives of Scripture reveal how God has worked to fulfill His promises to me in Christ?

Focus Statements

27. The learner will be able to summarize the events of the first Pentecost and connect them to the life of the Church today.
28. The learner will be able to explain how God's Word spread from the Jews to the entire world and will reflect on how God uses him or her to proclaim His Word to the people in his or her life.
29. The learner will be able to explore the Epistles in the New Testament and consider how God still speaks through them for His Church today.
30. The learner will be able to summarize the narrative of salvation from Scripture and joyfully describe how it will conclude.

Assessment Options

1. **Preassessment Options**

   Before you begin, have each learner spend a few minutes writing down answers to the questions below.

   For some students, writing is a stumbling block to sharing their real understanding. You may have some students who can express themselves more clearly in other ways. Allow those students to tell you their answers to these questions. Another option would be to have them dictate their answers to parents before class.

   - What do you know about how the first Christians lived?
   - What do you know about the Holy Spirit?
   - What do you know about the Epistles in the New Testament?
   - What do you know about the Book of Revelation and how the world will end?

   After they have written these down, either collect the answers to read and leave feedback or quickly go over them together as a class.

2. **Formative Assessment Options**

   Formative assessments are ways to monitor student learning. Choose from the following:

   a. Weekly Summaries: As you go through the lessons in this unit, there's a lot of information. One of the checks for understanding common to the lessons in this unit is a two- or three-sentence summary of the events of the lesson. Since this is the last unit, any chance to review everything that has come before would be helpful for tying the entire course together.

   b. Learning Log: After each class, the students write in their Learning Log (or tell you) one important thing they learned in that class.

   c. Reflection Tools: These may include sermon notes, memory work, and self-reflections. As you move through the unit and your learners do these formative assessments, consider asking questions like these: How has doing memory work helped in your understanding of Scripture? What have you learned about sermons from taking sermon notes? How have you grown as a learner through this course?

3. **Summative Assessment Options**

   Summative assessments evaluate student learning at the end of an instructional unit: Choose from the following assessment methods:

   a. Learning Portfolio: Have students complete a variety of formative assessments over the course of this unit. At the end of the unit, have learners compile at least one of each type of formative assessment, along with completed lesson notes and other samples you require. If they've completed these tasks to your satisfaction over the course of the unit, you can use their work as a great summative assessment. *Note:* At the beginning of the unit, make a list of samples you will collect so there are no surprises at the end.

   b. Portfolio Presentation: As this is the final unit, you may want to consider collecting everything that your learners have put together over this course in one place, including notes and reflections. As a summative assessment, you could have your learners present what they did in the course to their parents or guardians, either in a parent-teacher-style conference or as an end-of-the-course large-group get-together.

   c. Written Responses: Check for understanding by asking learners to write a short-answer paper with three to ten questions. This could be done inside or outside of class, and the length of the answers will vary. Here are some sample questions based on this unit:

      - What happened at Pentecost? Why does that matter?
      - How did the Gospel message spread from that first Pentecost to other nations in the Book of Acts?
      - What kinds of epistles are there? What is their main message?
      - Why is Revelation important?
      - In your own words, what is the overall message of the narrative of salvation?

Teaching Tips

1. As mentioned in other places, consider building a visual timeline in your learning space, each week adding important events and people, as well as the books of the Bible mentioned in the narratives. There is a lot of information to be covered here, and a visual organizer can be a great way to keep learners on the same page.
2. This unit is shorter than some and takes the narrative of salvation a little slower than other units. That said, especially with the section on the Epistles, there is a lot of text. As you choose what you're going to do for the unit, keep in mind that this section of the New Testament is used a lot in the church readings, so any connection you can make between the topics and events in the narrative and what is being talked about in the worship service readings will extend the learning.
3. Due to lack of space in the material, there are few visuals to accompany the narratives. As a supplement, you may want to look online or in Bible story books for visuals for different narratives as they arise in your readings.
4. There are more reading activities and less active sections in this unit. That said, it doesn't have to be boring. Encourage your learners to move around your space, pair up with a partner to reflect, or work in small groups as you read and discuss. Be creative in your examination of the text together.

Color Key for Teacher Notes

Tan = Specific additional assessments

Blue = Extra activities or questions

Green = Educational tips and directions for specific activities

Gold = Explanations of theological concepts or background for the teacher

PENTECOST AND THE EARLY CHURCH

TIMELESS TRUTH

God has redeemed me to be His own.

LESSON FOCUS

The learner will be able to summarize the events of the first Pentecost and connect them to the life of the Church today.

Though this is a fun subject to talk about, be careful with your learners. It is easy for them to either intentionally or unintentionally poke fun at people and nationalities that are different from them. Watch your words and their words, and if it comes to it, remind them that God chooses people from all over the world. In fact, most Christians don't live in North America. You might even do some research prior to class to find out how many Christians are in different countries around the world. They are our brothers and sisters in Christ.

27 PENTECOST AND THE EARLY CHURCH

CONSIDER THIS

A SYMPHONY OF LANGUAGES

Have you ever visited a busy market or shopping center or an event with lots of people speaking different languages all around you? If so, what was it like? If not, what do you imagine it might be like? Write notes in the speech bubbles.

The Big Picture

Ten days after Jesus' ascension, during the Feast of Pentecost, the Holy Spirit descends on 120 men and women who are followers of Jesus, just as Jesus had promised. The disciples speak in different languages, proclaiming the Good News of Christ to the people from around the world who are visiting Jerusalem. Peter gives an amazing sermon, and three thousand people are baptized that day. The first believers gather together in their homes and worship and preach in the temple. One day, God uses Peter and John to heal a lame man in the temple, and the disciples must give an account of Jesus' power in front of the very men who had sentenced Jesus to death less than two months before! Peter and John are released, and through much adversity and suffering, all the apostles and believers continue to preach. The Church grows so quickly that the disciples must appoint some helpers, or deacons, to serve the needs of the people. One of these deacons, Stephen, is cornered by the religious leaders. After giving a testimony of Christ, Stephen is brutally killed, yet not before Stephen sees Jesus and asks for forgiveness for them. One of the men who oversees this killing is Saul, who, after Stephen dies, travels around throwing Christians into prison. Another one of the deacons, Philip, travels around the country proclaiming Christ, and on one occasion, he is able to share the Gospel with an Ethiopian leader, who is then baptized on his way back to Ethiopia. The Gospel is now spreading throughout Judea and even to the end of the earth.

This section is contained in the **Book of Acts** and is written by Luke. The narrative occurred roughly around AD 33 and the years following.

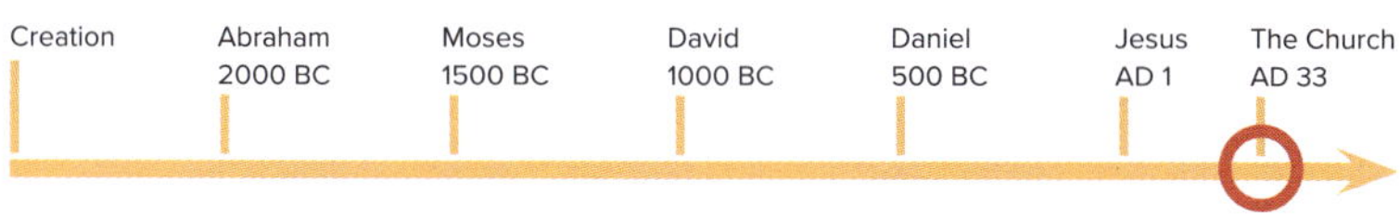

I can summarize the events of the first Pentecost and connect them to the life of the Church today. 109

GOD HAS REDEEMED ME TO BE HIS OWN.

UNIT 6: THE CHURCH

As always, this is a sizable block of text. Read the text and, if you have time, have your learners underline or highlight one word or phrase that sticks out to them about this summary. Then they can share with a partner why it sticks out to them.

Option: If some learners struggle to identify key words on their own, guide your students to highlight or circle the words that you identify as key and talk about why you had the students circle or highlight those words.

Option: If you have a developing timeline on a wall in your space, consider adding the lesson number and name, dates, and books of the Bible at this time.

There is no definitive answer to this question. However, Pentecost represented a harvest of God's good earth, so for the early Christians the event happening on that day represented God's bringing in of the nations into His family through the Gospel.

Jesus told the disciples to wait in Jerusalem for the Holy Spirit and that, when they did receive the Holy Spirit, they would be called to witness the Gospel to the very ends of the earth.

The qualifications included being a witness to the life and ministry of Christ. The disciples would continue to bear witness to the truth of Christ throughout their ministries.

The early disciples prayed together, gathered around the Word together, sang together, shared what they had, and ate and drank together. In the Divine Service, we do these things today, including gathering around the body and blood of Christ in the Sacrament of the Altar. We also gather around the Word in our households and groups in our congregations.

Digging Deeper

Pentecost?

Pentecost was a celebration that Jews observed fifty days after the Passover. They gave a grain offering of thanksgiving for the harvest. It was a big day of thanks for God's gifts. Many Jewish people were in Jerusalem from all over the Roman world, and since it was not too long after the Passover, some of them would have stayed in Jerusalem the whole time and seen Jesus' Passion unfold.

Why do you think God chose this day to send the Holy Spirit to really empower His people to share the Gospel?

A Big Day

Finally, the day that Jesus had promised happened to the disciples in Jerusalem.

Read **Acts 2:1–4**. Do some quick reporting of the scene. What happened?

Read **Acts 2:5–13**. Who was there?

Read **Acts 2:14–36**. Why did Peter give His sermon?

Read **Acts 2:37–41**. How did the people respond?

Note: That day, three thousand people heard the Word of the Lord and were baptized. This gift was for both adults and children. God has always used His Word to create faith and save people. He is the one who worked to bring people to repentance and faith. He used Word and Sacrament (Baptism) to do this. God gave a special measure of the Holy Spirit to the Church. He continues to give us the same Holy Spirit as a gift today through His Word and Sacrament.

One Last Command

Before Jesus ascended into heaven, He gave the disciples one last command. Read **Acts 1:4–11**. What did Jesus tell them to do? What did He say their job would be?

Life for Early Christians

What was life for the early Christians like? Read or listen to **Acts 2:42–47**. In the space below, sketch some reflections.

Discuss how this is like the church today.

A New Disciple

While they were waiting in Jerusalem, the disciples picked a new disciple who would replace Judas. Read or listen to **Acts 1:21–26**. In Peter's speech, what was the qualification for being a disciple? What were the disciples' purposes?

110

The Holy Spirit rushed upon the praying believers, granting them the ability to communicate the Gospel in the languages of all the people from around the world who gathered there. The sermon Peter gave was to communicate Law and Gospel so that the people there would repent and be baptized for the forgiveness of their sins. God used Peter's message to do just that, and three thousand were baptized that day.

Philip the Deacon

After Stephen was stoned to death, it would have been easy for the early Christians to hide. Many, however, still preached the good news. One was another deacon, Philip. Read about one of his encounters in **Acts 8:26–40**. In your own words, summarize how God empowered Philip to witness Jesus.

God's desire is that none should perish but that all would come to saving faith. We can demonstrate this by not only sharing the Gospel with the world, but as we do so show mercy to those in need.

A Healing at the Temple

After Pentecost, the disciples still worshiped each day in the temple. One time, on their way, something happened. Read **Acts 3:1–10**. What can you learn from this about God's heart and what He calls us to do?

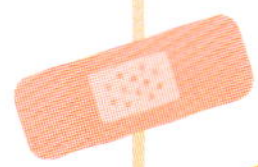

If your learners have been sitting a lot, consider breaking them up into small groups and asking them to figure out how they would act out the scene here. Have fun with it! The point is that the Holy Spirit used the Word of God to create faith and spread the Gospel then, and He continues to do so even today.

Stephen

Through the work of the Holy Spirit, the Church continued to grow, and it grew so quickly that it wasn't long before the disciples needed help to make sure everyone, especially the needy, was cared for. They prayerfully appointed seven deacons, or men who served to assist them. One of these men was Stephen.

Read **Acts 6:8–15**. How did the religious leaders plan to trap Stephen?

After this, Stephen gave a long message to those who were seeking to kill him. He outlined the narrative of salvation for them, ending with Jesus. He finished the speech with a final statement. Read the statement and what happened afterward in **Acts 7:51–8:3**. What happened? How did Stephen follow Jesus' example?

Note: Saul is important. His story continues later.

111

The people trapped Stephen by spreading lies about his message. Stephen followed Jesus' example by not only pulling no punches in his proclamation of the truth but by also giving up His life. Jesus showed Himself to Stephen right before his death, and like Jesus, Stephen asked the Father to forgive those who killed him.

Remember that this student book is not for grading—it's for guiding discussion and learning. Students do not always have to write complete sentences or spell correctly. Use the questions to guide discussion. Students can also doodle or draw responses if that suits their learning style better.

The Word was spoken not just by Peter and the apostles but also by the early believers, both publicly and in their homes. Many who heard the Word believed and were baptized (including the Ethiopian eunuch). Those who believed and were baptized then went on to gather around the Lord's Supper together in the early house churches, receiving the gifts of forgiveness, life, and salvation there as well.

CONNECTIONS

COME, HOLY SPIRIT!

The Holy Spirit came to the Church in a special way to work through the early Christians to call more people to faith, life, and salvation. Look back over the different Scripture passages in this lesson. Identify, in as many ways as you can, how the Holy Spirit delivered God's gifts of forgiveness, life, and salvation through the Means of Grace—Baptism and the Lord's Supper—or through the written and spoken Word to people. Write these ways in the spaces around the images of the Word and Sacraments below.

TIMELESS TRUTH CONNECTION

God has redeemed me to be His own. This was a really big deal for God's people in the Early Church, but guess what? It's a big deal to us today as well. The same Holy Spirit who came to them in a special way at Pentecost has come to us as well. In the Third Article of the Apostles Creed we confess,

I believe in the Holy Spirit, the holy Christian church, the communion of saints, the forgiveness of sins, the resurrection of the body, and the life everlasting. Amen.

The Explanation of the Third Article of the Creed continues:

I believe that I cannot by my own reason or strength believe in Jesus Christ, my Lord, or come to Him; but the Holy Spirit has called me by the Gospel, enlightened me with His gifts, sanctified and kept me in the true faith. In the same way He calls, gathers, enlightens, and sanctifies the whole Christian church on earth, and keeps it with Jesus Christ in the one true faith. In this Christian church He daily and richly forgives all my sins and the sins of all believers.

Option: As you read this section out loud, encourage your learners to underline or circle in the text from the catechism whatever they can find that connects to their readings from Pentecost and the Early Church. See what they can come up with.

CHRIST CONNECTION

Jesus has called you by the Gospel. Go back to the symbols above, and write down how Jesus delivers His gifts to the Church today through the Means of Grace.

Jesus ascended into heaven but did not leave us alone. Now He freely and continually delivers and multiplies His gifts to His Church through the Holy Spirit working in the Means of Grace.

THINK ABOUT IT . . .

What is something new that you've learned today about how the Holy Spirit works?

112

Making connections between the people of the Bible and people today is an abstract thought process. For students who are not yet abstract thinkers, you may need to provide more concrete guidance to help them make these connections.

CHECKS FOR UNDERSTANDING

Before your learners leave, consider ways you can give them feedback for next week.

- **Paired Discussion:** Have learners turn to a partner and share one thing they didn't know before this lesson. Listen in on several conversations.
- **Learning Log:** Have learners write down one thing from the lesson that connects the life of the Early Church and the early Christians to the life of God's people today in our community and in our worship.

PETER, PAUL, AND THE MISSIONARIES

TIMELESS TRUTH

God has redeemed me to be His own.

LESSON FOCUS

The learner will be able to explain how God's Word spread from the Jews to the entire world and will reflect on how God uses him or her to proclaim His Word to the people in his or her life.

28 PETER, PAUL, AND THE MISSIONARIES

CONSIDER THIS

OUT INTO THE WORLD

What's the hardest part about making new friends? Why is that? Jot down your thoughts below.

In this lesson, we will see how God works to bring many people to faith. The early Christians now have to go into the world, meet new people, and tell them the saving message of Christ so that more may hear and believe. This, however, was not going to be easy. Let's take a look.

The Big Picture

After the events of Pentecost and the first few years of the Church, the Holy Spirit continues to empower His people to preach the Gospel to all nations. Jesus confronts the Pharisee Saul, dramatically calling him to faith. From now on, Saul will go by Paul, and he will be one of the most important apostles in the Bible. At the same time, Jesus comes to Peter in a vision and calls Peter to proclaim the news to the non-Jewish Gentile Romans. After this, even amid great persecution with the disciple James being killed, God empowers missionaries to carry the Gospel message to the Jews and non-Jews spread throughout the Roman Empire. Paul and his team embark on three missionary journeys, traveling to different cities and nations. On each journey, they are confronted with opposition and even violence, yet the Holy Spirit still works to spread the Good News of Jesus. Amid this, the Church in Jerusalem makes great efforts to support and encourage these missionaries to carry the Good News of Jesus to Jerusalem, Judea, Samaria, and even the end of the earth. God is at work in the world.

This section is contained in the **Book of Acts**. The narrative occurred roughly between AD 33–55.

Creation	Abraham	Moses	David	Daniel	Jesus	The Church
	2000 BC	1500 BC	1000 BC	500 BC	AD 1	AD 33

I can explain how God's Word spread from the Jews to the entire world and reflect on how God uses me to proclaim His Word to the people in my life.

GOD HAS REDEEMED ME TO BE HIS OWN.

UNIT 6: THE CHURCH

113

This question is a little personal, so it may be good, especially if you have a shy group, to brainstorm this opening question together in class. What makes it so hard to make new friends, and why? Write the learners' answers on the board or on a big piece of paper up in front of the class. If you have time, consider what it might feel like to be a missionary, sharing Jesus with people you may or may not know. How would you overcome your fears to do this?

This may include some familiar narratives to your learners. If so, consider this. As you or a volunteer from the group reads the narrative of this section, ask learners to find one new detail they didn't already know. Then as you go through the lesson, challenge learners to find the text and dig deeper into this new learning.

Option: If you have a developing timeline on a wall in your space, consider adding the lesson number and name, dates, and books of the Bible at this time.

Option: To answer this question, divide your group into four clusters, and give each group one unit to look over (units 2–4). Each group has a couple of minutes to find as many times as they can when God's people felt hopeless and how God answered them in that section of the narrative of God's salvation. Each group will quickly report their recalling of events to the whole group.

This narrative shows how God can work to create and sustain faith. Saul was unworthy, yet God called him. Ananias was scared, but God still used him. God used both of them for His work, and Saul went on to be very effective and bold in preaching, not only because of his conversion experience, but also because of his background and education as a prominent Pharisee.

The angel's appearing and Jesus' vision both show how God desired to bring the Gentiles to faith. Though there had been Gentile believers before, never before had there been such a missionary push. Peter likely had never entered a Roman's house before, and the Holy Spirit's appearance only cemented what this event represented for the Church.

Digging Deeper

It's All Smooth Sailing Now, Right?

One might think that after Jesus' ascension into heaven and the coming of the Holy Spirit in a special way at Pentecost, everything would have been easy from that point for the Early Church. But things were far from simple. The Gospel message was still being heard mostly by people in Jerusalem and Judea, Stephen had been killed (and more people were threatening to kill Christians), and a Jewish man named Saul was going about the country throwing Christians, both men and women, into prison for their faith. It would seem like a difficult time for God's people.

Think back to other Bible narratives you've studied where God's people felt like everything was hopeless. Brainstorm these times together. How did God answer in each of these?

Saul

Saul was still going around, thinking he was doing what God wanted by locking up Christians. God was about to set him straight. Read or listen to **Acts 9:1–9**. Imagine you're Saul. What do you think it would feel like to hear and experience this? Why?

After this, Jesus talked to a man named Ananias in a vision. Read or listen to **Acts 9:10–18**. Imagine you're Ananias. What do you think it would feel like to hear, experience, and see what God was doing with Saul? Why?

Read or listen to **Acts 9:19–22**. After Jesus came to Saul and Saul was baptized, he became a great witness for Jesus.

Discuss what made Saul (soon to be called Paul) such an effective missionary.

Peter's Vision

At the same time, Jesus came to Peter in Jerusalem in a vision with instructions. Read or listen to **Acts 10:1–16**. What do you suppose the angel appearing to the centurion and Jesus appearing to Peter have in common? Why?

Once Peter arrived in the Roman soldier's house, what happened? Read or listen to **Acts 10:34–48**.

Why do you think this was such a big deal? Talk about it.

James and Peter

Right after Jesus called Paul, and Peter brought the Gospel message to the Gentiles, something shocking happened in Jerusalem. Read **Acts 12:1–5**. If you were a member of the church at that time, what would have been your reaction?

God, however, had other plans for Peter. Read or listen to **Acts 12:6–18**. What is one detail about this episode that sticks out to you? Why? What does it tell you about how God is able to keep His promises?

114

Now in addition to Stephen, Jesus' disciple James had been killed for the faith. Peter was in prison awaiting execution for spreading the Gospel. Peter's rescue demonstrates how Jesus' promise that the Gospel would indeed go out to the nations came to pass. Peter would eventually be killed for the faith, but not until later after the mission work was well under way.

Paul's Missionary Journeys

With all the direction God was giving to the Early Church to go to the nations, and with the growing number of believers outside of Judea and Samaria, the Church sent Paul, along with a team of people including (at various times) Barnabas, John Mark (who wrote the Book of Mark), Silas, Timothy (the books in the Bible were written to him), and Luke (who wrote the books of Luke and Acts). Paul went on three different journeys, some taking years while he stayed at different churches helping to pastor the believers there. Below is a chart that shows each missionary journey. There's a map that shows their paths in Lesson 29. For each journey, there is one narrative. Read the narrative, sketch what happened, and then write down what the narrative shows you about what their missionary journeys were like.

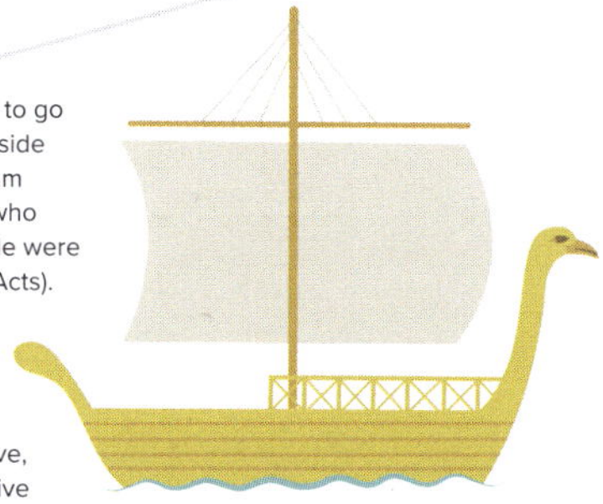

First Missionary Journey (Acts 13–14)	Second Missionary Journey (Acts 15:36–18:22)	Third Missionary Journey (Acts 18:23–21:40)
Read or listen to **Acts 13:4–12**. Sketch what happened.	Read or listen to **Acts 16:11–15**. Sketch what happened.	Read or listen to **Acts 20:7–12**. Sketch what happened.
What does this tell you about what their journeys were like?	What does this tell you about what their journeys were like?	What does this tell you about what their journeys were like?

115

On their missionary journeys, the team encountered all sorts of false prophets and people possessed by demons. Satan was at work trying to stop them, but God protected them on their way and countered the lies of Satan.

The team also had great cause to celebrate as the Holy Spirit worked in the lives of those who heard the Word. God used His Word to give faith to Lydia, and she and her whole household were baptized. These sorts of encounters were not uncommon on their journeys.

As the team went out, they also performed miracles. In this case, a young man fell asleep and fell out of a window, died, and was resurrected through Paul. The miracles served to help spread the Word of God on their way.

For these longer Scripture readings, help students learn how to use a Bible app to listen while they follow along in their Bibles. Some students will do better with only listening, because to try to listen and process visual information at the same time is overwhelming.

Examples include parents, pastors, teachers, godparents, grandparents, and friends.

Option: Encourage your learners to take this more seriously this week. Give learners note cards, and have them write down names and Bible verses for the people they chose so they can take those names with them this week. Encourage your learners that, even if they don't feel bold in sharing the Gospel with unbelievers, they can always just ask their friends in need if they have anything they could pray for this week. That in itself can be a great witness of the faith.

Connections

Sharing God's Word

Why are you reading this right now? Who are the people God has put in your life who have passed on God's Word to you so that the Holy Spirit has given YOU faith? Write down a list of names here:

Part of living the Christian life as God's redeemed child is to bear witness to the Gospel by sharing God's Word in the world around you. You may not be a missionary like Paul or a preacher like Peter (though you may be one day), but God still uses you. You are God's child no less than they are! Think about people in your life that need to hear the hope of Jesus or could be comforted by His Word right now. Think about people in your household, in your church, or out in the world (like in an activity or at school). Next to each image below, write down one or two names of people who would really be blessed with God's Word right now. Go!

Now, next to each, think of a Bible verse that might help them. How will you share these verses with these people? How will you share the hope of Christ with them this week?

Timeless Truth Connection

God has redeemed you to be His own. Jesus died for you to forgive your sins. He rose again for you so that you will rise one day with Him. He has connected Himself to you in your Baptism, and He continues to forgive your sins through Absolution. He feeds His Church with His true body and blood in Communion. It's all Him!

Christ Connection

Jesus loves you, and He wants all to know Him and come to faith in Him. You are Christ's missionary to those around you right now.

Jesus loves you and desires for all to know Him and come to saving faith. He has called you by His Word and Sacrament and now can use even you as a messenger of His Word to the world around you.

Think About It . . .

Do you know of any professional missionaries? What is one question you'd ask him or her if you had a chance?

116

Checks for Understanding

Before your learners leave, consider ways you can give them feedback for next week.

- **Summary:** Pass out note cards and have each learner write a two- or three-sentence summary of God's narrative of salvation in this lesson. Have them leave this summary with you so you can review it for next time and see what they learned.
- **Exit Ticket:** Have learners write down their answer to the question "What have I learned today about how God works in bringing faith to people?" and leave it with you on their way out.

The Place of the Epistles

Timeless Truth

God's Word is living and active in my life.

Lesson Focus

The learner will be able to explore the Epistles in the New Testament and consider how God still speaks through them for His Church today.

Have fun with this! Your learners likely aren't used to thinking about not being able to instantly communicate with people. Encourage them to really think hard about what life would be like without mass communication, and what it must have been like to receive a hand-delivered letter from someone during this time.

29 The Place of the Epistles

Consider This

A Letter from a Friend

Imagine a world without telephones, texting, or the internet (hard to do, right?). Imagine that the only way you could receive messages from anyone at any time was through letters and these had to be hand delivered by special messengers (no postal service). How would you react if you got one of these letters from your best friend, whom you haven't seen or communicated with in months or years? Write or sketch what you would do below.

In today's lesson, we'll look at these letters, the Epistles, that Paul and early Christians wrote to the first churches to see how the Holy Spirit encouraged them through God's Word.

If you need to, go back to Lesson 3 in the first unit to talk about what it means for a book to be part of the canon. Just because these epistles were distributed and collected in a different way from other books in the Bible does not mean that the early Christians didn't consider them God's Word. This might be a good time to review how we got the Bible.

The Big Picture

After the third missionary journey, Paul goes to Jerusalem. There he is arrested and is on trial for his life. Since he is a Roman citizen, he can appeal, and he eventually goes to Rome to appeal his case before the Roman emperor. Around this time, both before and during his imprisonment, Paul writes letters (epistles) to different congregations he helped start or visited, or to different individuals. These letters are read by their audiences, but also copied and distributed to other Christians and congregations. These Pauline Epistles, from early on, form part of the canon of New Testament Scripture. At the same time, other authors who were either witnesses of Christ or near witnesses write letters as well, and the ones that are copied and adopted by the early Christians, the General Epistles, form another part of the canon of New Testament Scripture.

This section is contained in the **Book of Acts**; the Pauline Epistles of **Romans**, **1 Corinthians**, **2 Corinthians**, **Galatians**, **Ephesians**, **Philippians**, **Colossians**, **1 Thessalonians**, **2 Thessalonians**, **1 Timothy**, **2 Timothy**, **Titus**, and **Philemon**; and the General Epistles of **Hebrews**, **James**, **1 Peter**, **2 Peter**, **1 John**, **2 John**, **3 John**, and **Jude**. The narrative occurred roughly between AD 50–68.

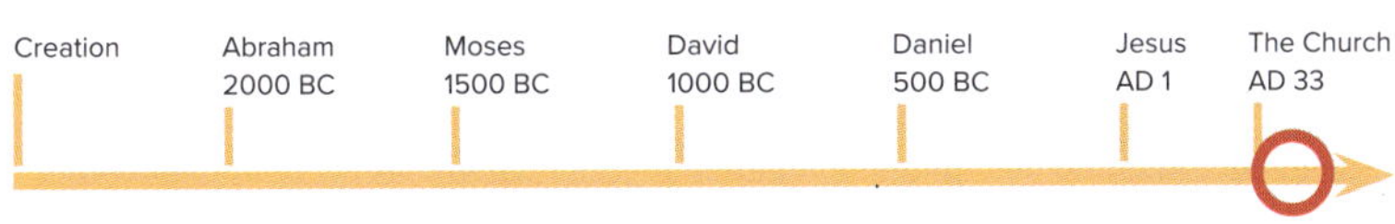

I can explore the Epistles in the New Testament and consider how God still speaks through them for His Church today.

117

God's Word is living and active in my life.

Unit 6: The Church

Option: If you have a developing timeline on a wall in your space, consider adding the lesson number and name, dates, and books of the Bible to it now.

This lesson is a little different from the others. There is no timeline of events. Instead, there are the names of the different letters, or epistles, in the New Testament. Remind your learners that they won't be expected to read all of these in class, but instead will have the opportunity to choose a few and summarize what they tell us on the next page. This isn't to say that you shouldn't encourage your learners to read or highlight these passages in their own Bibles, as they are pretty important to helping us understand our life together in Christ. For a more complete look at this section, consider dividing all the Bible books equally among your learners, giving each learner a little time, and then having each one present his or her Bible verses for the rest of the class so that the entire group gets a better idea of the messages from these Bible books.

Digging Deeper

The Epistles

In total, there are twenty-one New Testament books that are Epistles, or letters, of Paul and others. Before and during his final journey to Rome, Paul wrote the letters to the churches in the cities of their titles (in purple) and letters to young pastors Timothy and Titus and to a man named Philemon (in green). Besides Paul, the apostles Peter and John wrote letters to Christian churches. James and Jude, the brothers of Jesus, wrote their letters to Christians, and the Book of Hebrews (unknown author) was written to Jewish Christians. These books, the General Epistles, are in blue.

Pick three or four of these letters, read the key verses, and summarize what they tell you about who Jesus is and what Jesus has done for us on the next page. If it's a purple letter, use the map to identify the city or the region to which the letter was written.

Share what you read and wrote with a partner.

Romans (AD 55)

Picture of Jesus: Christ, our righteousness

Key Verses: **Romans 1:16–17**

1 and 2 Corinthians (AD 55)

Picture of Jesus: Christ, our glorious Lord, our comfort in life and death

Key Verses: **1 Corinthians 15:50–58**

Jude (AD 68)

Picture of Jesus: Our keeper

Key Verses: **Jude 20–23**

1, 2, and 3 John (Late First Century)

Picture of Jesus: Our eternal advocate

Key Verses: **1 John 1:8–9**

1 and 2 Peter (AD 67 and 68)

Picture of Jesus: Our soon-coming Savior

Key Verses: **1 Peter 3:18–22**

James (around AD 50)

Picture of Jesus: The Lord of glory

Key Verses: **James 1:16–17**

118

If you have students with special learning needs in your class, have them prep for this activity by doing some of their work at home before they come to class. Another option is to work in pairs or trios rather than independently.

Some students struggle to know where to begin in an independent activity like this. You may need to do some coaching to help students know what steps to take and what to do next after they get started.

EPHESIANS (AD 60)

Picture of Jesus: Christ, the Head of the Church

Key Verses: **Ephesians 2:8–10**

PHILIPPIANS (AD 60)

Picture of Jesus: Christ, our joy

Key Verses: **Philippians 3:7–11**

GALATIANS (AD 51–53)

Picture of Jesus: Christ, our freedom fighter

Key Verses: **Galatians 2:19–20**

COLOSSIANS (AD 60)

Picture of Jesus: The true God, our eternal hope

Key Verses: **Colossians 1:11–14**

1 AND 2 THESSALONIANS (AD 51 AND 52)

Picture of Jesus: Our returning Savior"

Key Verses: **1 Thessalonians 4:13–18**

1 AND 2 TIMOTHY (AD 65 AND 68)

Picture of Jesus: Our Savior and faithful witness

Key Verses: **1 Timothy 2:5–6**

TITUS (AD 68)

Picture of Jesus: Our great God and Savior

Key Verses: **Titus 3:4–7**

HEBREWS (BEFORE AD 70)

Picture of Jesus: The final, perfect sacrifice for our sin

Key Verses: **Hebrews 9:13–14**

PHILEMON (AD 60)

Picture of Jesus: Our Lord and Master

Key Verses: **Philemon 17–18**

119

Option: To make this more active, consider writing the different names of the different books around your learning space, maybe on note cards taped to the walls. Have your learners get up and walk around the space, either individually or in pairs, looking at the different books, reading the key themes, and recording their observations on the next page. This could last as long as you like before you gather them together to debrief their experiences. Encourage them to pick a phrase or verse that really stuck out to them and explain why to the rest of the group.

Encourage your learners to really challenge themselves to pay attention to God's Word this week. They can do this by reading the Bible but also by listening to it. Encourage them to pick up a devotional book or use a devotional resource and try to get some intentional Bible reading in this week if they aren't already in the habit.

Connections

God's Word for You!

In the scroll below, write down your observations about the key verses from the previous pages. What have you learned about who Jesus is and what Jesus does for you?

Timeless Truth Connection

God's Word is living and active in my life. The early Christians were under a lot of pressure. As we've read, not only were they often unpopular, but they also were oppressed by the government and sometimes even killed by the community and the government for preaching Christ! Yet the Holy Spirit speaking through these letters gave the early Christians encouragement and hope. God's Word speaks His Law and Gospel into our lives today.

Pick one of the Bible passages that you looked up that really connected with you. Now share that same verse with a partner, and explain why that passage spoke to you right now. Do this a couple of times. Write down three of these verses from your conversations on a note card or piece of paper. Where can you put them this week so that you will be reminded of God's faithfulness to you in Christ?

Christ Connection

The world is filled with lies and falsehoods. God's Word, however, is living and active to speak God's truth.

Jesus is not only our great King who sits at the right hand of the throne of the Father, but He is also living and active in our lives by the Holy Spirit through the Word and Sacrament.

Think about It . . .

How will you listen to God's Word this week?

120

If copying three Bible verses is too much for students who struggle with copying or fine-motor skills, provide several verses already printed out on note cards or cardstock. Give students the opportunity to illustrate these verses to show their meaning. Look up resources online to help students understand how to illustrate their verses to give them meaning.

Checks for Understanding

Before your learners leave, consider ways you can give them feedback for next week.

- **Summary:** Pass out note cards and have each learner write a two- or three-sentence summary of God's narrative of salvation in this lesson. Have them leave this summary with you so you can review it for next time and see what they learned.
- **Learning Log:** Have learners write down one thing from the lesson that helps them understand how God's Word is living and active in their lives.

Revelation and Conclusion

Timeless Truth

God's Word is living and active in my life.

Lesson Focus

The learner will be able to summarize the narrative of salvation from Scripture and joyfully describe how it will conclude.

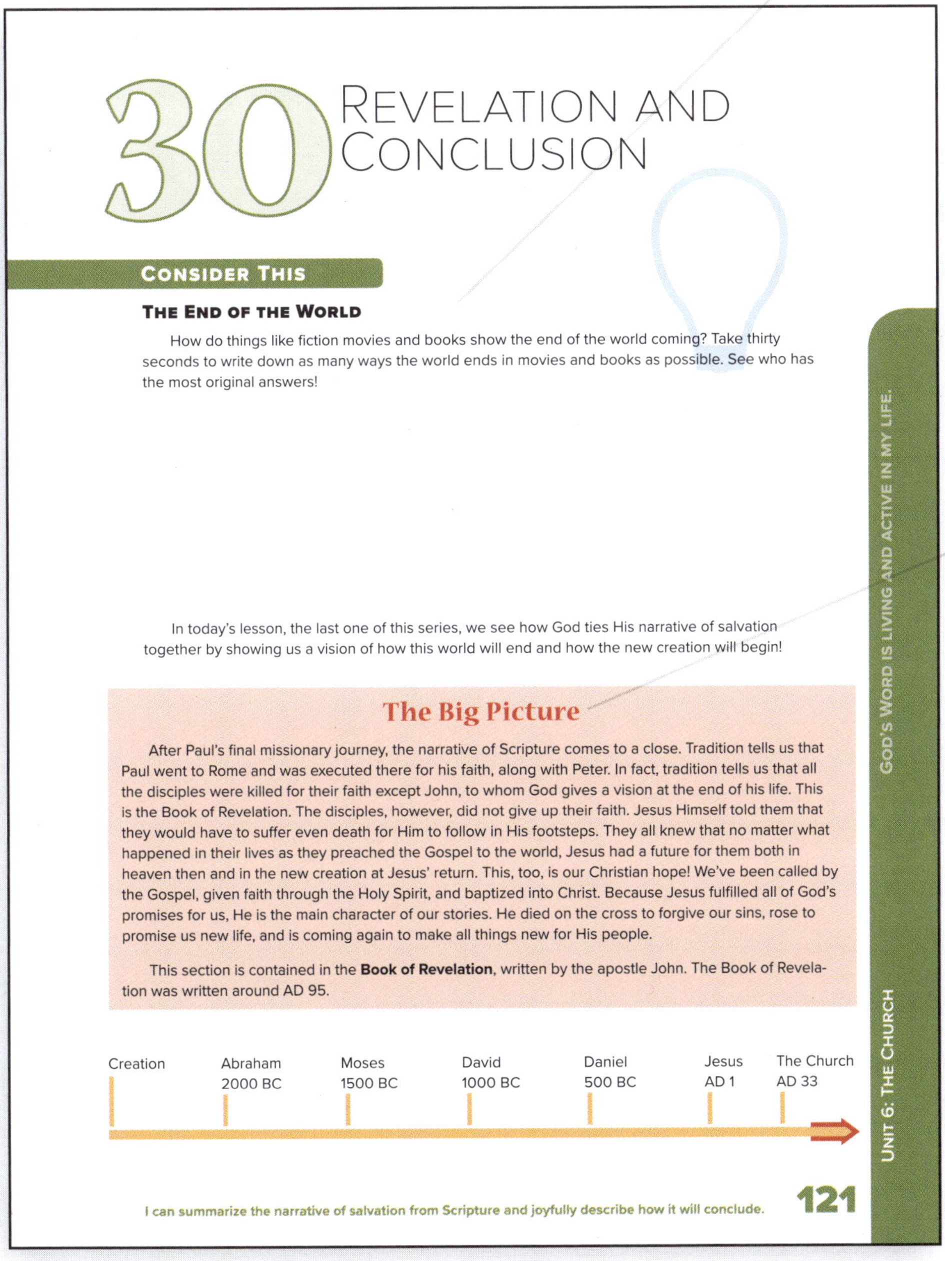

30 Revelation and Conclusion

Consider This

The End of the World

How do things like fiction movies and books show the end of the world coming? Take thirty seconds to write down as many ways the world ends in movies and books as possible. See who has the most original answers!

In today's lesson, the last one of this series, we see how God ties His narrative of salvation together by showing us a vision of how this world will end and how the new creation will begin!

The Big Picture

After Paul's final missionary journey, the narrative of Scripture comes to a close. Tradition tells us that Paul went to Rome and was executed there for his faith, along with Peter. In fact, tradition tells us that all the disciples were killed for their faith except John, to whom God gives a vision at the end of his life. This is the Book of Revelation. The disciples, however, did not give up their faith. Jesus Himself told them that they would have to suffer even death for Him to follow in His footsteps. They all knew that no matter what happened in their lives as they preached the Gospel to the world, Jesus had a future for them both in heaven then and in the new creation at Jesus' return. This, too, is our Christian hope! We've been called by the Gospel, given faith through the Holy Spirit, and baptized into Christ. Because Jesus fulfilled all of God's promises for us, He is the main character of our stories. He died on the cross to forgive our sins, rose to promise us new life, and is coming again to make all things new for His people.

This section is contained in the **Book of Revelation**, written by the apostle John. The Book of Revelation was written around AD 95.

I can summarize the narrative of salvation from Scripture and joyfully describe how it will conclude. 121

Unit 6: The Church — God's Word is living and active in my life.

The topic of this lesson is pretty heavy. You will be talking about the end of the world, judgment, heaven and hell, and the point of God's narrative of salvation. Keep a close eye on what your learners are doing for this opening activity to help gauge their attitudes toward this topic. While heaven may seem comforting to us, some young people find the idea of eternity overwhelming and frightening, even knowing that Jesus will be there. Be sensitive to your students' reaction to this topic.

As always, this is a sizable block of text. Read the text and, if you have time, have your learners underline or highlight one word or phrase that sticks out to them about this summary. Then they can share with a partner why it sticks out to them.

Option: If you have a developing timeline in your space, consider adding the lesson number and name, dates, and books of the Bible to it now.

Option: To make this more active and collaborative, divide your class into small teams. Give each team some markers and a large piece of paper. Have them draw out the timeline on the piece of paper and give them a set time to read the Gospel promises and sketch out their own timeline leading to Christ. At the end of the set time, have each group present what they made and why to the rest of the class. Then compare what the different groups did and drew and why.

Digging Deeper

Setting up the Ending to the Narrative of Salvation

Revelation is the last book of the New Testament and the last book of the Bible. In it, we catch many glimpses of what has already happened in the past and get a picture of how the very end of the narrative of salvation will come to pass. Before we jump to the end, we need to take a good look at what has come before. This is the narrative of salvation and God's promises.

Look over the timeline below, and read each of the Old Testament Bible verses at critical sections. Each one is a promise of the Messiah, the One who would save the world from sin, death, and the devil. Read and review each promise. Then in the space below find a creative way to represent the promise of the Messiah. It could be a sketch, a written statement, or a combination of those. Or together with your leader come up with your own idea. Record or represent some key words or ideas for each one of the promises of the Savior that helps describe who He is or what He does. When you're done, share it with someone in your class or present it to your whole class. Have fun with this!

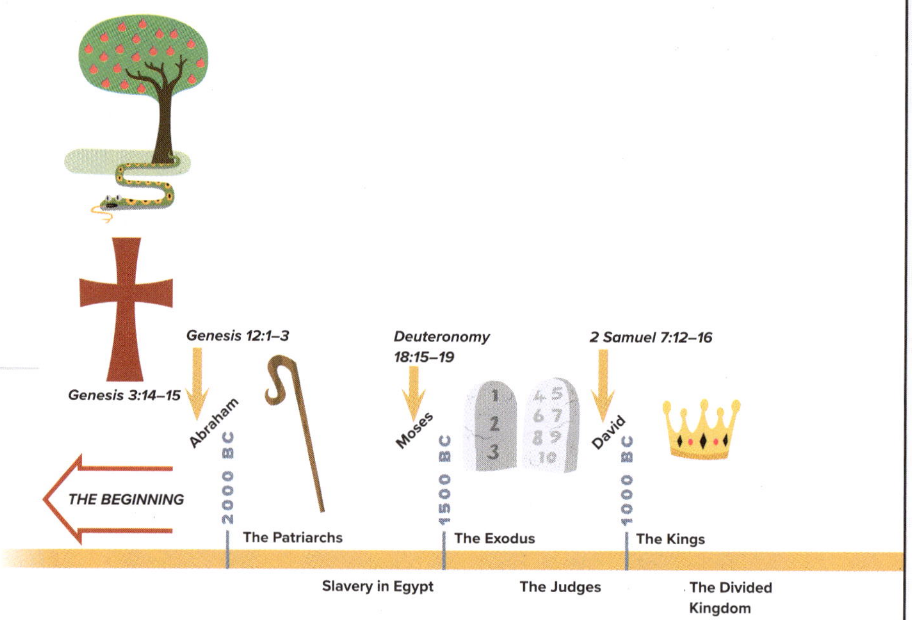

122

If this seems repetitive to your learners, assure them that this is review. Nothing should be new to them. Instead, this is meant to help them wrap their heads around the vast amount of what they've learned and remind them of how the narrative of salvation points us to Christ.

Some students love the creative expression of an open-ended activity like this and get right to work. Others find it overwhelming and scary when activities do not have clear-cut steps to accomplish. Without any idea where to start or how to organize their ideas, they may not start at all. This causes them to look noncompliant when they really need some guided coaching on what to do. The story of salvation is an epic story to represent. Help your students break things down into smaller chunks. This is not a class session for you to sit back and do nothing while your students work. This is a time for you to guide and coach them through this review.

What's the Deal with Revelation?

Revelation is unique in the New Testament as it is the only book of pure prophecy (it looks a lot like Ezekiel or Daniel in the Old Testament), and it's the last book of the Bible. In it, Jesus came to His old friend John the disciple one last time in a vision. By this time, Jerusalem had been destroyed by the Romans, the other disciples had been killed for their faith, and John was a very old man likely living out his last days. Read **Revelation 1:9–19**. According to Jesus, what is the purpose of this vision?

There is a lot of confusion about all the visions that happen immediately after Jesus' letters to the seven churches. Quickly page through **Revelation 4–20**. What's one thing that sticks out to you?

People try to read a lot into this, but Lutheran Bible scholars agree that Revelation 4–20 shows three visions of the same thing in different ways. Each one shows how Jesus on the cross fulfilled God's promises and how Satan, in this time before Jesus comes again, attacks and threatens God's people. He cannot win the war, and Jesus is the victorious King, but Satan can still make things difficult for God's people. The spectacular ending of Revelation, however, is on the next page.

When else in the narrative of salvation have God's people needed comfort from God in their suffering?

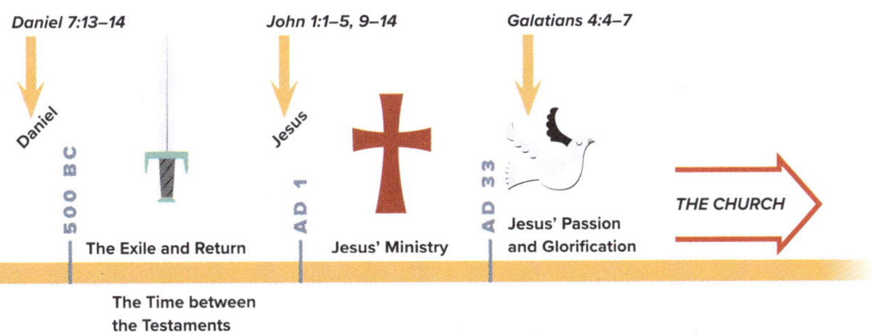

123

Revelation can be a very controversial book in that it is often misinterpreted. For the sake of this lesson, we focus on the central message of the Book of Revelation: that Jesus is coming back to make all things new for His people in waiting. Take a moment with your learners and investigate some details of the visions as you page through. Remind them that ultimately these visions are to give God's people comfort as they await the return of Christ.

These Bible passages contain a lot of reading. Mark a Bible prior to class with sticky notes to guide students to these verses. Or encourage students to use a Bible app to listen to the Scripture. Or do both. By this time in the course, you know what your students need and how they will handle this reading task.

In the Garden of Eden, God made all things good. He told man and woman to be fruitful and multiply, to fill the earth and have dominion over it. This perfection, and communion with God was lost at the fall.

CONNECTIONS

ENDING AT THE BEGINNING

As we've seen, the Bible is an amazing library of sixty-six books written over a period of some 1,500 years by dozens of authors. Even with all this, it tells one narrative: God's plan of salvation. What is that salvation? It's a restored creation. God created all things good. Look back or think back to Lesson 4. Around the image of the tree, write down some words that describe what that first creation was like for God's human creatures.

But we also know that mankind fell into sin. We disobeyed God and lost that perfection. Because of this, sin came into the world and with it death. Draw an *X* over the tree.

But God promised to send a Messiah who would restore His creation. The narrative of salvation is really about God's people waiting for God to fulfill that promise. The people kept rebelling, resisting, and being unfaithful to God. God was always faithful to them. Jesus came to restore all things.

Remind your learners that, though we may not understand everything about this vision, we get the message that the new creation will be a return to perfection for God's people. We will live with Him forever in a new earth. This is our joy and future hope as Christians, and this is what we pray for when we pray, "Come, Lord Jesus." Encourage your learners in this.

THE NEW CREATION!

When we die, our spirit is separated from our body. In heaven, our spiritual selves will be happy with the Lord, but we will be awaiting the final day when Jesus returns and restores our spirits to our perfected and remade bodies and we will live on a new earth forever.

Read what this new creation will be like in **Revelation 21:1–8, 22–27**. Then read **Revelation 22:1–5**. In the space below, write or sketch what that new creation will be like, with the new, restored tree of life.

Jesus has done it all for you. This future is your free gift by the forgiveness of His grace. Read **Revelation 22:16–21** for Jesus' final words to us in the Bible.

Option: As a final reflection, challenge learners to come up with one way that they can continue to be faithful in receiving the gifts of God's Word in their daily lives after the class is done. Have them write this challenge down in their notebooks or on a piece of paper to share with their parents (or write it for them as they dictate to you). Conclude by praying together for the strength and wisdom to continue learning God's Word for life.

THINK ABOUT IT . . .

How will you continue to receive the gifts of God's Word for life?

124

CHECKS FOR UNDERSTANDING

Before your learners leave, consider ways you can give them feedback.

- **Mini Quiz:** Quiz your learners on a scratch piece of paper with some simple questions from the different lessons, including facts about the Bible, the names of the patriarchs, the names of important kings from the Northern and Southern Kingdoms, and so forth. Try to keep it light and fun for recall purposes.
- **Final Reflection:** Use the optional final reflection at the bottom of the "Connections" page as a way to see how excited the learners are about continuing to read and understand God's Word after the class is finished.